JASON BEACON

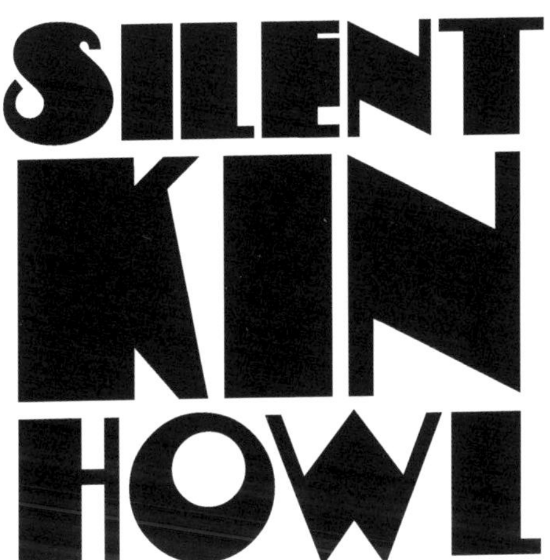

GUERILLA

LONDON

Cover Graphic and Book Layout:
D E S I G N   T H I N

Extra Joker

courtesy of

K I D A L

Typeset:

Kerfuffle, Optima

ISBN:

978 - 1 - 907248 - 25 - 2

1. Michel de Montaigne - Essays. 2. Travel - Adventure. 3. Philosophy - Sociology. 4. Excalibur - Fiction. 5. Nature - Non-Fiction. 6. Science - Non-Fiction. 7. Spirituality - Non-Fiction.
I.Title

For my Treasures and my Kin; for Kidal and all the Troubadours; first and last, always, for Ustoz.

Begin Transmission:

A Swallow was flying south for the winter when she decided to change course. Veering off from the main flight, she headed north and soon found herself battling into an icy wind. The sky grew dark and ever colder. Below her, the earth turned bare and before long everything was white with snow. Exhausted, unable to flap her wings any more, the Swallow folded her delicate body and crashed down into a snowdrift.

A rumble and the ominous crunch of snow brought her around. When she opened her eyes, the Swallow was perturbed to see an enormous wall of dirty white hair descending towards her head. Another rumble followed. Before the Swallow could blink, the creature in charge of this hairy apparition opened its bowels and buried her in an avalanche of excrement.

Satisfied, the Polar Bear shook itself down and continued on its way.

The Swallow now found herself in unknown territory, both in substance and smell. However, the warmth from the bear's faeces soon revitalised her frozen body. Pushing her sleek form through the filth, she managed to poke her head out into the air and survey her position.

The land was white and empty in all directions for as far as she could see.

Not knowing what else to do, but not wanting to leave the warmth of her pungent shelter, the Swallow called out. Her shrill song echoed through the wasteland about her until, finally, she spied a movement in the distance. Camouflaged against the whiteness, a figure on four legs approached. It was smaller than the bear, and moved cautiously, stealthily, sniffing the air as it came. Something in its gait was familiar to the Swallow, and made her remember the sunny meadows and shadowed woodlands where she had summered. In moments, a whiskered face was before her. The creature gently lifted her from the pile of bear poo. Its warm tongue proceeded to clean her all over. Relieved, the Swallow looked up into her saviour's warm, hazel eyes. They appeared to smile. Then, in a flash, the creature opened its jaws and ate her.

Satisfied, the Arctic Fox licked its lips and continued on its way.

o

We may divine several morals from this tale. First, the person who puts you in the shit is not necessarily your enemy. Likewise, the one who gets you out of the shit isn't necessarily your friend. Thirdly, above all, when you're in the shit, don't shout about it.

Another cautionary note, familiar to any fan of the original *Top Gun* movie, could be put thus: never leave your wingman. If you *do* decide to part with the group, be aware of the potential consequences. Connected to this rule of thumb, for me the greatest mystery of this pithy fable comes as ever in the form of the old question: *why?*

Why did the Swallow change course in the first place?

THE
TOWER

Montaigne's Ghost

We can be knowledgeable with other men's knowledge, but we cannot be wise with other men's wisdom.

- Michel de Montaigne

There once was a man who lived in a tower. One day, when he was in his late thirties, the man said to himself *Je m'en fous de ce bordel!* (he was French) which means roughly "I'm done with this mess!" and that's when he did it. He just shut himself up in a tower. For ten years. In fact, until his kidney stones got the better of him, he rarely came out. When eventually he did come out, he got on his horse and rode over a thousand miles to Italy. Once there, he had a hot bath. Nipped down to Rome to call on the Pope. Got made a citizen of Rome. Then rode home.

Gotta love the French. They don't do things by halves. They just do it. Or not at all.

Whilst immersed in the intimate solipsism of his fortress, the man read and he wrote. There was a library in this tower, and it contained around fifteen hundred books. From these books, and from the vaults of his memories and the contemplations of his soul, he distilled during that decade pretty much everything he thought and felt about life on this planet into what later was collected into three volumes of essays. The man then did a little business, attended to family issues and dabbled in a spot of national diplomacy and king-making. Then he died.

"We do not know where death awaits us: so let us wait for it everywhere," he once wrote. "To practice death is to practice freedom. A man who has learned how to die has unlearned how to be a slave."

The man's body disappeared. A little over four hundred years later, some people rediscovered what might be the remnants of it. As a historical curiosity, perhaps that means something. What is undoubtedly more meaningful is the body the man left in full view of anyone who cared to look for centuries after: the body of his contemplations. As well as mere mortals, this collection of essays has reached, been absorbed by and influenced some of the world's most celebrated thinkers, scientists, artists and statespersons from the Enlightenment to the present day. From his modest garret – in effect a poorly heated third-floor bedsit with crude amenities, restricted access and lamentable plumbing – this reclusive little Frenchman really made some waves. Which is an apt idiom on which to launch our journey, dear Kin. For what Michel de Montaigne accomplished in life was to become a pioneering broadcaster – a Renaissance social media influencer of substance, if you will – whose transmission continues to create ripples in space and time. The time being now.

The space being that which you, dear Kin, at least for now, occupy.

It all started in the tower.

It may appear that the world's a bit screwed up. Does it, Kin? Or is it just you and me? As I write, the planet's climate is warming, politics are polarising, the human population is exploding, the world economy is tanking and a global pandemic we presently don't fully understand is about to ruin Christmas. To top it all, my $800 cell phone absolutely refuses to charge unless I stand there and nurse it like some bad father, jamming the lead into the socket and cursing this evil techno baby to drink its Gaia-killing juice.

Je m'en fous de ce bordel!

How do you feel about it all, Kin? What do you think we should do?

We could adopt the stance of the Resigned Philosopher: "Ah well – the world has ever been thus." Indeed, it has looked worse on occasion. Montaigne himself, nominated unwittingly as Mayor of Bordeaux late in life, fled from a plague that killed a third of the city while his home country tore itself to pieces over religious differences in a series of bloody wars and massacres. We haven't passed our fellow humans out on the road and witnessed them digging their own graves. Yet.

But that wasn't global. It wasn't the entire biosphere. It was one species, numbering a little over half a billion, going through an obligatory rough patch in its slowly ascending life spiral. Most of the planet's land mass was still wild and covered in trees. The wetter parts were cool and clean and full of fish. When we petition our touchscreen deities today, and reliable scientific experts appear like prophets to tell us we face catastrophe before the end of the century to the point of a Sixth Extinction in the age of our grandchildren, well – ruminate all you like: that stuff beyond our skin is going to get us sooner or later. Looks like it may well be the former. Given the situation, unless you're the type whose idea of family fun Friday is a Jonestown cocktail followed by a snuff movie, perhaps aloofness is not the most effective attitude to embrace.

Breathe...

From my tower, I see forests and fields and sky. I see our neighbours' homesteads – some have been there nearly a thousand years; some more. Looking closer, I see the vegetable garden and the orchard, a semi-ordered island cornucopia in a bursting sea of green. My wife tends it, while above swallows race and wheel. Below the window, children buzz as bees play. An early autumn sun abides. I breathe, and set myself to task.

These fragments I have shored against my ruins.

If we're here simply to observe, we may as well hack off our limbs and bite off our tongues right now. Live a sort of "YouTube till death with comments off" existence. If, on the other hand, we wish to participate in life, we need more than just habitual locomotion and our rambling mouths to make things any better. We need our minds and our hearts, and we need them in their rightful spaces. Only this can open the possibility of conscious evolution for our species. Anything else will be history repeating.

But what do I know? What do any of us?

I don't have an answer, Kin. I'm not here, speaking to you now wherever you are, to propose a way. There are as many of those as there are people on the planet, and who's to tell another theirs is better or worse, blessed or cursed? What I *do* have, tucked away in my own Armageddon Survival Toolkit, is a practice. It's a practice that came out of a story, and maybe through that practice I might get a shot at – what? Redemption? Sounds grandiose, doesn't it, Kin? When all's said and done, though, no one else is going to save us from ourselves. I've done a lot of searching – maybe you have, too – but I don't claim any credit for finding this practice, because really it found me. Maybe by sharing it with you, something could change. Maybe not. After all this time, one thing I know is that *not* sharing it isn't doing anyone any good, myself included. Could the act of sharing be enough? We'll see. Ultimately, there's only this choice: carry on in the same vein and watch our ship go down, or pick ourselves up and actively be involved in our own transformation, and by extension that of humankind.

No pressure.

This story started with a choice, just as did the story of our poor frozen Swallow back at the start, as did the story of our universe. As did your arriving here. Before the choice, there is no story, only a state. Once there is a choice to be made, there is conflict – the "either/or" – without which stories cannot exist. There it is, Kin, the price of your story: conflict. From the Latin, it means "to strike together", and when you do that you get friction, and pain, you get suffering – repercussions. Separation. Movement. Change. You have to take both, or you get nothing.

Example? Imagine: Luke Skywalker, hanging out on the farm, fixing droids. For two and half hours. Frodo – just chilling in the Shire. For three epically long movies. Miguel, staring at his grandmother, Coco, sitting mutely in her chair until she just...dies. Without ever singing Remember Me again for the very last time. Okay, stop now: you're going to make me cry.

By accepting the appearance of suffering, the presence of conflict, we catalyse our story and we go somewhere in life. It's rarely where we envisage it might take us, but at least we consciously make that journey. In doing so, we also willingly enter the Duality Trap.

You may have heard about the Duality Trap. It has many names and metaphors to describe it in many languages and traditions, but in essence it's this: the way we people are set up on this planet, we perceive everything only in relation to its opposite. Positive and negative. Night and day. Light and dark. Love and hate. Young and old. Fast and slow. Hot and cold. Hot and ugly. Male and female. Agony and ecstasy. Left and right. Here and there. Smart and stupid. Sickness and health. Good and evil – now that's a real peach. Apple, whatever, I wasn't there. The reason it's a trap is because it beguiles our senses and by extension our minds into believing it's true. It isn't. But we believe it so much, it becomes our reality.

Our reality isn't true, and neither is this statement. First bumper sticker. Use it freely, there's no copyright on truth.

Reality as we perceive it is our present theatre, however, and when we choose a story over state, we accept the stage as we find it and pitch on in. "This experience called Life," you enlightened human, Kin, "is just a play," you tell yourself, and occasionally others. (Especially if you're hitting on them.) You've read the conditions and you'll accept the odds, because YOU are going to have a Goddamm STORY in this tiny little moment you have here. Others may survive, but you are going to LIVE. That's when you choose. And so you slip – in the words of St Leonard of Cohen – into the masterpiece.

If I've lost you already, Kin, come back. I love you, and I'd like you to stay with me. There's so much to share, you see? Kurt Vonnegut said, "We are here on Earth to fart around, and don't let anybody tell you different." If you're into chasing rabbits down holes, we can have some fun together, but it isn't essential. I'll admit, having spent years of this life on subterranean adventures (metaphorical, obviously), this book intends to avoid too much mental burrowing. It's all been done before and, besides, we now have the internet for that. Let's fart around together.

Why am I writing this? What does this peculiar love letter hope to achieve?

Truth is, Kin, and sad as it may sound, we're not all going to make it. Not to the end of our natural lives, nor to the life we so desperately want to live: the one where we've got it all, or we are it; where we're enough, and secure, and rich, and loved, and sexy; the one we dream about minute after minute, day after hour, month after week, decade after – GAME OVER. Truth is, not all of us will even make it to the end of this book together. Talk about low ambitions.

Could you be one of the few? Could you, Kin? I so hope it's you.

This book is a few things: a story, a transmission, and a howl. Undoubtedly, it's some kind of mid-life therapy for me, but if it worked for Montaigne, I'll sign up. "I write to keep from going mad from the contradictions I find among mankind," said he, "and to work some of those contradictions out for myself." If you make it to the end, I'll tell you how it went. So far, all is groovy.

More importantly: it's firstly a story because that's how we humans connect. Through harnessing the processes of recall and imagination, we bring ourselves closer together in the present. Another bright spark, alive at time of writing, said: "Humans think in stories, and we try to make sense of the world by telling stories." If you want to know more about the past, present and future of our species, I don't hesitate in recommending the books of Yuval Noah Harari. He doesn't know about my story, though that's through no oversight on his part. If you want to discover more about this glaring omission in Harari's planetary overview, read on.

As humans, we connect and work stuff out through the creation of stories – emotional, mental, and actual. We literally "enact" them. Usually unconsciously, but that's the nub of being human: we get the choice. This book, and the practice I'm going to share, may help you choose yours. If not, it may at least give you some entertainment and distraction from your own. Our stories can be heavy at times – can't they, Kin? Sometimes we read to know we're not alone.

This is also a transmission.

I said earlier that Michel de Montaigne was a pioneering broadcaster. That was no whimsical anachronism. In Montaigne's day, printing was the new technology, the vehicle for the wider dissemination of information, while the written word carried the substance. Despite our many advancements, this ancient piece of tech still has its function in our world. Witness now. What Montaigne undertook from his tower in the idyllic French countryside was not dissimilar from what media companies do today from radio towers and masts all over the world. Transmitting – "sending across" (from the Latin again) – information.

Ask a programmer or geneticist, or perhaps even a democrat (small "d") and they may well tell you that information is the currency of the system in which they specialise. It is the basis of any system: physical, biological, psychological or other. It is the stuff that makes up the code that creates – in-forms – the systems we recognise as entities or processes. From an amoeba to a mountain range, a firing synapse to a whole civilisation, information is the building blocks of the enterprise, and transmission is the act that keeps the whole show vital. Without transmission, without a flow, new receptors to engage, information is impotent. Lifeless. Seed spilled upon barren soil. The end of the evolutionary road.

Montaigne knew this. He could have shut himself up in his tower, thought "What do I know?" and then drunk himself to death. Living as he did on an estate that produced – and still produces – wine, I'm sure he considered the notion. Given the state of the world, who wouldn't? But that was not what he did. Instead, he thought "What do I know?" and followed the question, that weaving, teasing, philosophical will-o'-the-wisp, for ten long, almost solitary years. He wrote down his findings. Why? For himself, partly, of that there is no doubt. "I am myself the matter of my book," he declares to the reader in his introduction: "You would be unreasonable to spend your leisure on so frivolous and vain a subject." Note to the present YouTube generation...

Writing was Montaigne's passion, therapy, and calling. You might say it was his sole devotion. Or his soul devotion. Probably, there weren't many open salsa evenings in downtown Castillon-la-Bataille back in the day, besides. Owning a tower may seem cool to most people, but once you've walked up and down it a few times, the novelty quickly wears off. Alone in your citadel, before long, the voices set in. As he himself expressed, he transmitted his thoughts to paper to stop them building up, churning around and sending him crazy. There is no doubt, however, engagingly modest as he could be, that he also hoped his musings might pass into the minds of other humans and there be of some interest, solace and perhaps, even, use.

And so they were. Not just to Shakespeare, and Bacon, to Byron and Emerson, Virginia Woolf, Aldous Huxley, Eliot, and of course pretty much every French writer that ever followed. Thousands, if not millions of his fellow humans have, in the time since he began transmitting, benefitted, either directly or indirectly, from the stuff that brewed up, condensed in and dissipated out of the brief cloud of being that was Michel Eyquem de Montaigne. Moreover, a little over four centuries after those quiet, solitary and often uncomfortable hours at his desk, that information was transmitted to me.

It would be inaccurate to say that it was Montaigne who sparked my life's quest and the present task: to transmit something of interest, solace and use to you, dear Kin. There are so many influences, and influencers, in any one life that if we listed them all there would be more text than you'll find on Shakira's Facebook page. It was another, altogether more shadowy character than Seigneur M. who finally put the fire under my butt and got me on my way, but we'll come to him in due course. Nonetheless, meeting Michel was like that moment when you bump into someone at a mediocre wedding and realise here is a person you can really talk to, listen to, and lower your guard with amidst all the social white noise. Later, you go home feeling surprisingly warm and connected with the world. Apart from the synchronicity of ideas, and despite the inconsequential difference of four hundred years between our lifetimes, we had so much in common.

When Montaigne and I first met, I was living in Italy overseeing a renovation project and launching a publishing empire. The empire kind of got crushed by some rebels called Amazon; the renovation still stands, on a hillside above a small spa town in Tuscany called Bagni di Lucca. The same spa Montaigne visited in the early 1580s in a bid to relieve the affliction to his kidneys. And there I was, reading his words, looking out of my 'tower' and the unchanging river below – "click": we were connected. I soon discovered further coincidences.

As a young man, Montaigne studied law. Not so much out of a desire to become an attorney, more to please his father. Snap. Or to appease his father, perhaps – it appeared, on further investigation, that Michel had been quite the wild young thing and he needed to balance his ship. He admits to having burned himself with lust, and "...suffered all the furies that the poets say come upon all those who let themselves go after women without restraint and without judgment." Um, okay: ditto.

Montaigne was known to be a great horseman; I have a thing for horsepower. I know, uncanny, right? And get this: while out riding one day, he had an accident that very nearly cost him his life and gave him a vision of the other side. Well, this is where the hand holding the book starts shaking. Just over a year before reading that information, I had been involved in a car accident that very nearly cost me my life and gave me a vision of the other side. In the space of an Italian summer's afternoon, we'd gone from being strangers to confidants to soul buddies across time. Such is the power of reading.

And now I sit here, in my tower. Typing to you. Conveniently, it's taken me about ten years to get this far. I haven't been confined in this space all that time, far from it. As we shall see, however, dear Kin, towers are not always made of earth and stone.

Do I over-identify with this hero, this prototype humanist, the first "modern man" as some put it? Not really. I see myself, as does my wife, I'm sure, far more as the creature in the attic than some philosopher in his castle. But Michel does haunt me, in a non-invasive fashion. What do his visitations reveal, this benign phantom, once so presently here, now only an echo of something at the heart of us all? What unfinished business could he have that he now extols me to take up my keypad, access the millions of texts available at my fingertips, and pour from my marrow for anyone to see? Perhaps, the only dictate worth obeying: "Kin – know thyself."

Knowledge. Self-knowledge. The destination of information.

And the destination of knowledge?

Que sais-je? – what do I know?

Listen, but I can't tell you; draw nearer, though in truth you were never away: the Howl, Kin. I'm going to show you the Howl.

Only The Lonely

Shall I say, I have gone at dusk through narrow streets
And watched the smoke that rises from the pipes
Of lonely men in shirt-sleeves, leaning out of windows?

- T.S. Eliot

What will it take for us to set our lands in order? Well, we all like to give the little guy a chance, so let's begin with Frodo.

In Tolkien/Jackson's *The Lord of the Rings* trilogy, the hobbits live a bucolic existence in The Shire. They bicker and argue and plot against each other in the way of most creatures who don't realise how good they have it, but all in all life is pretty cosy and, of course, predictable. Then Gandalf shows up. Now, the last time the wizard came a-calling, Frodo's uncle, Bilbo, was whisked off with a bunch of other small people on quite a #roadtrip. The experience affected the old boy, and his being known as something of an eccentric among his fellow Shire-dwellers is partly why his nephew Frodo never feels fully part of the clan. The shadows our families cast, eh? Gandalf knows, of course, the wider picture, which at that moment is impossible for the hobbits in their comfy bubble to see, ie: darkness has awakened and if left unchecked will soon overcome the whole of Middle-earth. He also suspects the significance of the ring that Bilbo stole from Gollum, telling Frodo to "Keep it secret – keep it safe" until he returns. When he does return, always full of good news Gandalf tells Frodo the ring must be destroyed in a faraway volcano if the imminent destruction of Middle-earth and the enslavement of all its races is to be averted.

For Luke Skywalker, the journey begins when a buffering video of a revolutionary hairstyle influencer accidentally gets projected out of a self-propelling wheelie bin. In myth-honoured fashion, he refuses this first call. Returning later to find his home destroyed and his uncle and aunt incinerated convinces him there is something more important at stake than going to the academy or managing another harvest.

Miguel needs a guitar to enter the annual music competition since his borderline psychopath granny has smashed his own. Believing Ernesto de la Cruz to be his famous great-great-grandfather, he steals the deceased icon's guitar that hangs in his crypt, and in doing so crosses into the land of the dead.

Katniss stands up to take her sister's place in the Hunger Games.

The Narrator returns home to find his gorgeous Ikea-lined apartment destroyed, leading to the creation of Fight Club.

Anna's sister loses her cool, turns her kingdom into a permanent freezer and does a runner. Anna hails a reindeer.

Hostile aliens/robots/mutants/the NSA attempt to take over Earth. It makes Will Smith angry and – well, we know the rest.

What do these scenarios from well-known English language stories all have in common? Two things: one, they represent the hero's call to action. It is the moment the central character – the as-yet unknown, either to themselves or others, future "hero" – faces the unavoidable choice: a new direction has opened in my world – which way do I now proceed?

Two: in all the above, the kind of choice on offer is one that 99.9% of us will never have to face.

Where are you reading this, Kin? Time is short, so let's not overplay the literary "cat & mouse" device in the name of high grade creative writing. Suffice to say, my guess is that wherever you are now, it's fairly comfortable. You could think of ways to improve your environment, sure: a temperature adjustment, a more luxurious seat; newer mattress, tastier latte, people nearby who know and understand you better, etc etc, we're never fully satisfied. But you're okay. Even if you're reading this in prison, hey, at least your meals are paid for. You probably aren't in searing physical pain. I doubt you've just lost your entire family to war or a natural disaster. Even if you're terminally ill, there's a good chance you're going to make it till tomorrow. If there isn't, may I suggest you close this book and do something fun and meaningful with the remaining hours?

Sauron is never going to come looking for us. Our genetic father is not the galactic equivalent of Heinrich Himmler. You are not going to play a concert in the land of the dead. You will never shoot an arrow as well as Katniss Everdeen, however much you spend on archery lessons; you won't get stuck in a magical winter, move in with your imaginary alter ego or be as downright cool as Will Smith.

We're never going to be asked to be that hero who saves the world. These stories are fantasies, fictions, fables far removed from our own daily existence. We engage with and enjoy them because for a moment they drag us out of our habitual, boring routines and give us a license to dream. For a couple of hours, we escape. Then we switch off, come back, worry about next week's mundane tasks and bills, check out an object of desire on social media, and go to sleep.

Or do we? Are you asleep, Kin? Is that the rhythm of your life? Or are you one of the waking ones? Maybe, in a surprising development, the call is closer than we believe.

It is no accident that, just like those stories above to which we will never belong, this book adheres to the template of The Hero's Journey. If you already know about it, great. If not, or for a refresher, there are hundreds of books and thousands of net pages about what is also known as the 'monomyth', popularised by Joseph Campbell in his 1949 book *The Hero with a Thousand Faces*.

Who is the hero of this book you are now reading?

We are, Kin. You and me.

It turns out, you don't need to be caught in an impending catastrophe to be a hero. If we open our eyes and look with polished hearts, the everyday world we live in is already terrifying enough and reason enough to act. If it seems boring and dull and predictable to us, that's because we live in isolation. We've cut ourselves off from it and buried our souls beneath our masks in return for fantasies, trinkets, comfort – at the least, for less hassle, for convenience. For 'normality'.

"You are locked into your suffering and your pleasures are the seal." Ah, that sweet saint, Leonard of Cohen...

And do you know what? *That very monotony is our call*. That perceived ordinariness. Because this world isn't ordinary. It isn't mundane. It isn't about money, and getting by, and just getting ahead of the other guy, or keeping up with the Jones clan. The call is: do you truly want that to become you? Because here's the thing: getting stuck in the shit is not your destination. So what is?

Breathe...

Which brings us to the lonely men.

Those of you with literary inclinations no doubt have spotted the various tidbits lifted from the writings of TS Eliot, strewn with apparent pretentious abandon about the text. Since early adolescence, dear old

Thomas Stearns has been one of my favourite poets. I include these seasoned morsels not to reflect my own aspirations but to acknowledge a debt of thanks and to continue the transmission of what I have found to be wholesome information. The same goes for all the other musings I've pilfered, including those of our earlier hero, Michel M., who said "I quote others only in order the better to express myself." By the way, while we're at it, it wasn't CS Lewis who said "We read to know we are not alone" – it was screenwriter and novelist William Nicholson. Check it online. But we digress. Let's thank our mentors and depart this rabbit hole before we tumble in. Maybe we can accept some truths as self-evident no matter who expressed them.

Eliot was writing during and between two world wars when the pre-eminent civilisation into which he had been born – so-called Western Civilisation – was looking a little worse for wear. The strained environment, melded with Eliot's mind, gave rise to such works as *The Wasteland, The Four Quartets* and (cited above) the earlier poem *Prufrock,* among many others. As with Montaigne, there's pretty much the totality of the human condition covered in Eliot's writing. What I found and still find exhilarating is how the poetry can conjure imagery, if we allow it, in our own internal screening room so vivid that it never leaves. Like Tamo's shadow, the imprint remains, unseen by all but those who enter the cave.

In any case, this image of the lonely men, hanging out of their windows at sundown for a cheeky puff, profoundly affected me. Within a society that was much more stiff and formal than our own, with strongly implied if not explicit boundaries between gender, class and race, the workers (unlike the affluent, they live close together on "narrow streets") whose labour upholds the system, find a momentary respite. They have removed their jackets. The jacket is a symbol of their conformity to a hierarchy over which, as individuals, they believe they have little influence, and the men shun the company of their families indoors, which after a hard day's toil is but further work. They smoke. In the day, of course, little was understood about the dangers of tobacco to the human system. Like religion, drink and football, it is a substance they have been introduced to and to which they willingly have become attached or addicted, because it occupies their minds and soothes their nerves. A golden moment, then, or so it would appear. The smoke, the waning daylight – the solitary interlude. Yet Eliot sees they are lonely. Prisoners, scenting a brief taste of freedom, from the respective windows of their everyday towers.

What are they lonely for? Perhaps we can guess. Just over a century on, apart from the substance of choice (TV, Smart Phone, Internet, takeout, pick a drug – prescription or otherwise) has much really changed?

You could argue I suppose that these days we're more informed. Thanks to Freud and Jung & Co. we understand more about how we operate subconsciously, what pulls our triggers, how to deal with ourselves and others, both personally and on a wider social level. We've evolved as societies, too. More equality between genders, and races and creeds. Sure, there's still rich and poor, but class division is less of a thing these days. Anyone with the right grit and aptitude can make it, right? A better standard of living across the board. Better medicine, even if access to it is still problematic in places. Improved education around the world, assisted by new technologies: radio, television and video, the World Wide Web. Which overlaps with the field of Communication and Information (that word again) Technology.

Are we less lonely?

You tell me, Kin. Tell me true. Am I less lonely than those pipe-smoking men, or the young poet who observed them that evening, back in c.1910? Ask yourself. Were I less lonely than them, would I be writing to you now?

"The Love Song of J. Carlyon Beacon?" Hah! Moving on.

They weren't "grand" heroes, these men. They lived ordinary lives in an everyday world that leads to loneliness. We get lonely in life when someone or something is missing. Whether they articulated it or not, what they were suffering from was the fallout from separation. But separation from what?

Then they were called to war. Many of them would die. Their children would die in the subsequent war that followed soon after. Some of them heroically. The ordinary world was ripped apart, not by aliens or Siths or orcs or CGI, but by the separation in each of us that when magnified creates the divisions we see in the world outside. By the lonely people who become angry people, and arrogant people, and smug people, and greedy people. And desperate people. The system cracked, then made them go to war to save it. Was there a choice?

So this is the nub, the point of this chapter: being a hero doesn't mean becoming a box office phenomenon. Or a sports star, a fashion model, a billionaire entrepreneur, a business mogul or the President of the USA. If recent examples are anything to go by – wait, too much judgement. Duality Trap at work, we're not going there. You get the picture. The point is, most of us never get that call to be The One.

However.

Each of us is the hero of our own story. Define the word "hero" as you will. Just don't get lost in the idea of it being some fantasy character. The hero is simply the main character in the extremely brief tale that is your life, over whom you as the author exercise some control. It's the "you" that I'm speaking to. Here is your choice:

You can do something now in response to your sense of separation from the ordinary world. At heart, you know that's just a reflection: that fundamentally it's a sense of separation from your true self. It isn't natural to feel this way. Maybe you have lots of friends, or colleagues, or family, or lovers, or employees; maybe a lot of the time you feel connected. But in those moments of sincerity when you look at your soul in the mirror without prejudice, you know you're a fake. An imposter. The ego you're posing as doesn't reflect the truth of what you feel inside. Big deal, say you. That's just the way it is and, besides, you can handle it. Just look at how many friends I have on Facebook. And indeed that may be so. Just so long as everything stays the same in the nice little life simulation you're building yourself. Which leads us to option number two:

Nothing stays the same. You're only prolonging the inevitable. And here's the big spoiler: the longer each individual puts off answering the call to become their true self, the sooner the world outside is going to force us into a cliffhanger. When it comes, as it always does, our call won't present us with a life decision in the fuzzy realms of Pixar and Lucasfilm. It's going to be a car crash. The kind where live or die is not our decision to make. Just like those lonely men. They carried on, stealing precious pieces of doomed liberty, smoking their pipes, because they thought there was no choice to make. But that was simply because they didn't see what was coming. At which point, it was too late.

"I have seen the future, baby, it is murder..."

I don't want to get you down, Kin. Come on, relax. Have a drink, or breathe, or whatever you do to find your zen. I said earlier we're never going to be asked to be that hero who saves the world – we don't need an impending catastrophe to spur us into stepping up. Right? I meant it. Trust me, it's late and I'd rather be watching Ozarks on Netflix to wind down right now, this typing gig isn't always the soft option. When it comes to being honest, though, to the best of my ability I feel I owe it to you. Owe it to all of us. At the same time, like everything down here, it seems, those statements are sort of true, and they sort of aren't. Here we go.

The ordinary world is about to turn mad. I don't know when you're reading this, but believe me: however crazy things seem right now, it's going to get more so. Do you know how to tell when things are at their darkest? Simple: you won't be reading this. Or anything else, for that matter. If you're reading this now, whenever that is, things will get worse. The flip side is, if you're reading this, you can ensure things will also get better. Don't say there's no sweet justice down here in our backstreet cosmic candy store. It's just that it's hidden under the counter. You have to ask for it, and then you have to pay. Luckily you don't need money. A little effort will do.

If we don't step up now, in this present environment which is relatively conducive to positive personal and collective evolution, we're missing the golden ticket. We all know we're living on credit we can't repay – financially, ecologically, emotionally. We kid ourselves the world will just keep giving, that it's someone else's job to deal with our shit down the line, that we can win on our own. That's when the trap closes and takes us down. Like the Balrog's fiery whip that reaches out of the chasm and catches Gandalf around the knees. Just when we think we've defeated the demon, it's always holding another trick. Some call it karma. I call it Killing the Wizard.

Are you lonely? Do you feel separated, divided, alone? Do you have doubts, depression, anxiety, recurring or seemingly ineradicable fears? Do you get angry too quickly? Are you too sad or tired or ashamed to speak your truth? Over-attached to something, or someone? Addicted, even? Does it all seem hopeless – even pointless? Is something simply...missing? Or, perhaps, you're well in your groove. On your way somewhere, at least. You're dealing with your shit, you've got your life under control: you've got vision. You know what you have to do, right? You're a winner. It's the other pelicans that bring everything down.

In either case, welcome to our ordinary world. This is where the heroes (you and me, Kin ;) find ourselves at the outset of our story together. It's the world we tell ourselves is normal though, in actual fact, it's a long way from that. In the age of pointless acronyms in which I write, F.U.B.A.R (that's with a capital "Fucked", incidentally) puts it aptly. All of which leads to:

THIS IS YOUR CALL

The threshold is waiting. Are you game, Kin? Come on, no pills or anything, I promise. Just a good old-fashioned buddy adventure. We've some fairly awesome mentors looking out for us, just around the page. With the drawing of this Love, it's all possible. It is, in truth, inevitable.

In Search of the Fisher Kin

In life, never do as others do. Either do nothing – just go to school – or do something nobody else does.

- Beelzebub's Tales to his Grandson

Hello Kin. I'm glad you're here. Writing can be lonely. Just knowing you're reading this, somewhere, somewhen, makes this tower a bit less echoey, if you know what I mean? Not quite as haunted. Michel's fine, sure, he doesn't mean any malice, and St Leonard croons sweetly from the other side, we still have the music, it picks old Thomas Stearns out of the doldrums. But it's hard to create any real warmth with the departed, rest their souls. It's heartening to contact the living. Thanks for answering the call.

Have you noticed how some stories refuse to die? Take Batman, for instance. Now, don't get me wrong: I've always been a fan of the caped crusader. Without getting into too much analysis, I find something deeply enthralling about the hero who wears his psychological shadow – and his underwear – on the outside. Faces his innermost fear and turns it to his advantage. Not to mention all those gadgets. Yet beyond all that, Bruce Wayne is never settled. He's always fighting with something in himself, externally represented by his playboy life by day and his raiding the fancy dress closet at night. Try as he might, he cannot be master of both worlds.

I'm not the only one fascinated by this creation. Otherwise, how do we explain the presence of so many versions? The figure of Batman is familiar to cultures the world over, as recognisable as McDonalds or Coca-Cola. Seemingly around forever (he first swooped into our consciousness in 1939) he accompanied my generation's road to adulthood. Between being a teenager, in awe of Jack Nicolson (and in love with Kim Basinger), to becoming a father a couple of decades later when Christian Bale's character finally hung up the Kevlar, there were seven major Hollywood Batman movies. Seven! Not to mention the spin-offs and series and every other money-siphoning tool in the screen industry's golden garage. I don't begrudge the creators their paychecks. Well, except when they make a fine actor like George Clooney look ridiculous. He's over it now. As we know, being advanced social animals we use stories not only to function/disfunction practically (the story of money, of nation, of marriage, of pandemics etc) but to understand ourselves better – to shine a probing searchlight into the depths of this existential mystery called humanity. Which is why, notwithstanding Oscar Wilde's wry assertion, useless artists get paid.

I also like Batman because his outward persona, billionaire Bruce, lives in a fortress-like mansion, while his essential being, a.k.a. The Dark Knight, hangs out in a secret cave. This will be of interest, solace and use later on.

If the Batman story is still doing the rounds as it heads towards its centenary, it's only a toddler compared to others. Sticking with gothic fiction for a moment, the original vampire, Dracula, has been baring his fangs at us since 1897, while Mary Shelley's Frankenstein has been retold countless times for twice as long. Want more mainstream storytelling? How about Shakespeare? Histories, comedies, tragedies and love poems, here is a catalogue that has stood the test of time. Avon's finest folk-pleasers are heading for the half-millennium, now, though in truth that's selling the stories' longevity short. Without taking anything from possibly the greatest writer to ever live, at least in the English-speaking world, the tales he presented to us are themselves by and large much older. That's not to say crafty William stole them. People were much less worried about copyright in those days and saw stories rather as public property. By the time The Bard got his quill on it, the story of King Lear, for instance, had been declaimed, performed, gabbled and written about since the founding of Rome. It wasn't considered as belonging to any one artist; what mattered was how it was transmitted for the age in question. In modern speak, and given his ongoing popularity, one could assert old Bill nailed it.

Peering even further past, we have in our 'Tales of the Ancients' collection such masterpieces as The Odyssey and the Iliad (a.k.a. Troy, thank you Brad 2004) dating from around three thousand years ago; The Vedas of ancient India c. three and a half; The Epic of Gilgamesh – generally acknowledged as the oldest surviving work of great literature, from ancient Sumer around four thousand years gone by; and some of the early Bible stories, which date from...a long, long time ago. Oh, and some relatively recently discovered papyri from the Egyptian desert, probably the world's oldest to survive till now, from over 4.5k years back. Unfortunately, these are more of an inventory for materials, shipping and labourers' wages than a story. However, considering that they possibly deal with the building of the Great Pyramid at Giza, as a foreman's journal they are at the very least of considerable historical interest. And no, alien contractors are not listed among the invoices.

What does this tell us? How does it help us on our own hero's journey?

For one, it confirms the earlier notion that stories are nothing without conflict. Without the clash of two opposing forces, we humans don't stay interested for long. Certainly not for millennia. Why, even ancient Egyptian Inspector Merer's apparent Groundhog Day diary of moving massive stones about by boat has got something in the subtext. My reading of hieratic isn't the best, but although Merer is too smart to ever state it explicitly, with a wait of four and a half thousand years for the invention of a delete button ahead of him, I swear you can hear him thinking it: "The Pharaoh is a wanker; the Pharaoh is..."

We had better be prepared for conflict on our quest. That's lesson one. So far, it's been fairly plain sailing. Or plain reading, rather. Given you're still here, I trust there's *something* in this transmission to engage your attention as we journey together into the darkest recesses of your soul. Just kidding. Possibly. Maybe there have been some words and ideas you may not have immediately appreciated. A hash-up of citations, interspersed with emotively-hued assertions, that so far does not generate confidence for a concerted logical progression of argument, perhaps? Get you, Kin – get you. Quite possibly, you just don't automatically warm to this narrator's tone of voice.

Hang in there, Kin. If there's one other thing we must remember from those heroes of old, it's that they never believe there's a master plan bigger than themselves. Until it bites them on the butt. Howl.

What we can take from these perennial tales is this: true reflections never go out of fashion. Clothes and cultures and settings may change (you can find Shakespeare staged anywhere between ancient Egypt and a future galaxy), languages and details get chopped around, but the essence of the human condition barely wavers. Boiled down, whatever we're going through, someone's been there before. It's the great paradox: basically, the solitary hero treads the same path every other hero has ever trodden whilst feeling they're the only one to do so. So it is with us, Kin. I and thou – we're the heroes now.

With that, let's get inspired, and meet some role models. We'll start with the breathing in.

Inspiration. "Breathe" or "blow into." From – how did you guess? That's right. That old Latin lingo again.

The last thing an Empire loses is its language. Witness Greece, Rome, Persia, Ottoman, Soviet and the Brits, to name a few. When an Empire dies, its previous subjects and enemies arrive in hoards to feed off its juicy bloated corpse. They dine wholly, voraciously, not only off its former chattels but also off its customs, its technologies and its intellectual and artistic culture. Like the physical food we eat, the language is ingested, absorbed and then reformed to integrate more economically into its new host. A new age, and new ways – but though it blends and transforms, that informational linguistic code is still there, embedded in the evolving construct. As DNA tracing has shown, all we really are in the present is a compilation mash-up album of Homo Erectus' Greatest Hits. And we know how we feel about those hits in hindsight, right?

Why the fascination with all these Latin roots? In fact, the actual roots are themselves often pre-Roman: the Romans borrowed from the Greeks, who purloined from the Phoenicians, who filched from the Canaanites, who...we get the picture. The reason being, the language of the everyday world that we take for granted is full of clues as to meaning. We use this language, as we're doing now, be it the original English or a translation thereof, because we learned it so as to communicate in the present day, in our current lives, to survive and interact with our kin which, ramped up on a global scale, equals the world's present cultures. These roots, of these sounds we make daily and the glyphs we read when checking our Twitter feed or ordering stuff on Amazon, are often thousands of years old. Just like the stories they were coded together into – "in-formed" – way back when, in order to express and transmit various experiences, knowledge or truths.

As ever, nothing stands still. Meanings can change over time. A word that meant something to our ancestors may still be in use in our time but have different nuances or even a completely different significance to the one it did then. Check out terrible, awful, pretty, bully, nice, hussy, clue, gay. Et cetera. (That hasn't changed, btw.)

According to various dictionaries, inspiration means: "the process of being mentally stimulated to do or feel something, especially to do something creative." On a less figurative level, it also means "the drawing of air into the lungs." Indeed, these meanings remain by and large unaltered since Caesar & Co. were spreading the Latin love via @bloodandpillage all across Europe. In Medieval times, however, the word carried a widely accepted implication of divine interference. That is, if you felt inspired, it wasn't because your brain hooked onto a bright idea or you were performing mathematical thought experiments in the bathtub: it was because GOD or one of his minions was speaking to you. An interesting notion that we'll put on the back burner for later.

I must be one of the last gen who, just like old Michel M., learned my Latin pre-Google translate. A "proper classical education" it was called, usually to the tune of a snotty British accent as sported by the villain of some second-rate American heist movie. (NB: villain didn't always mean "bad guy.") I must confess, I've forgotten most of it now. Don't use it/lose it and all that. Sic friatur crustulum. In any case, the years spent declining and conjugating and covertly flicking ink across the exercise book of Samuel Duffett must have "inspired" something in this mixed up mind, because it got me fascinated with languages. Where they came from, how we use them, and where they're going. Not in some reserved, academic sense either, but for their essential purpose: to communicate, connect and accurately convey meaning between kin and kin.

Which brings us to education. And, hopefully, the relevance to our story.

I had this classical education, you see? Imagine Hogwarts, take away the magic and delicious food, and you're there. "Never begin a sentence with 'and'..." Still sends a shiver up my spine. And we're off again.

Education: nature or nurture; private or public; privilege or basic human right; secular or religious; to lead out or to shovel in? Remember, Kin, in the hero's initial ordinary world, he or she is fully caught, stuck in and probably not even trying to escape from, the Duality Trap. Their only chance of seeing it and of getting out is to first: receive the call, and second: to learn how to get past the threshold and into the special world that lies beyond. For that, they need a mentor. What the mentor gives them is: an education.

Of course, the education they get to become the hero and save the world (okay, hold it steady on the fantasy) is usually almost completely at odds with the education they received to be in the position where they needed the call in the first place. Why? Because in most cases, they'd already become a slave, willing or not, to the system they find themselves in. Their education had put them in that state.

Which is most likely the same thing as happened to you and me.

Let's look – I promise this'll be the last time – at the root of the word "education." Do you know where it comes from? We use it, hear about it on a daily basis. It forms one of the pillars of what we deem, possibly under mild delusion, a "civilised" society: politicians are constantly pledging more money to improve it; teachers – along with nurses – must have among the highest value to lowest income ratios in any of our so-called egalitarian systems. Right? And to some degree, disregarding the periodic inability to resist initiating sentences with a conjunction, we've all been through it. You went to school. Someone taught you to read. You taught yourself? You can be *my* teacher.

So what does it mean?

There are two versions. We get the verb "educate" and its derivative noun from either the Latin "educare" – to bring up, rear or train; or from "educere" – to lead out, bring up or rear. Subtle at times, isn't it, this old Duality Trap? In the first, the pupil is having something put or programmed into them; in the second, something is being led out of them, or they themselves are being led out of something. While the two versions may appear similar in form, the results are sure to be anything but.

This is not going to be a discussion of which is wrong or right. You can have both or neither as easily as either/or and it's a long old argument. We're not here for that, Kin, and we've tarried enough already. There's knights and grails and dragons waiting and you've got to choose your own avatar, besides. Before I hand over to my learned colleague and beautiful soul, Muriel Spark, I just want to say this: beware of anyone who attempts to assume a higher moral ground on the basis of their "education." A person or society deemed by themselves to be educated is often but a menace to another.

> "The word 'education' comes from the root e from *ex*, out, and *duco*, I lead. It means a leading out. To me education is a leading out of what is already there in the pupil's soul. To Miss Mackay it is a putting in of something that is not there, and that is not what I call education, I call it intrusion, from the Latin root prefix in meaning in and the stem *trudo*, I thrust."
>
> – from *The Prime of Miss Jean Brodie*

Rabbit hole, I know, Kin. Accepted. But it's important to convey this: how do we know what we know? Why do we know it, for what or whose purpose? If you don't know what you're made of, how are you going to survive; how are you going to triumph over the conflict that's coming to your world? Most pertinent of all: how are you free to choose?

Don't think it over too much. It just makes things messier. Let's take a step back, breathe/inspire and...

Perceval.

That's another story that refuses to die. At least, it refuses to die in me. This is what we're talking about, Kin: creating a story for ourselves that lasts a lifetime.

Family Sundays at the Beacon household used to fall under the "cliché" section in the archives of British Culture. They can be located in the "home counties" sub-section towards the end of the second millennium CE. Mum would roast an animal, Dad would tinker with antique mechanical appliances and make jokes to annoy Mum while amusing mainly himself, and the rest of the family and any smart/casual visitors would chat politely over an aperitif with the obligatory witty remarks and innuendo demanded by this once proud and menacing culture. After lunch, if head, stomach and weather permitted, we'd often fall into the yard outside and join in fiddling about with one of Dad's old wrecks or, as he would reference them, superbly engineered classic cars. The petrol obsession for your narrator started here.

If the combination of dead beastie, banana flambé and excess alcohol had put its recipients into a flatlined state of consciousness and locomotion, a younger member of the tribe would be dispatched to the sitting room, there to hook up the almost square television with a state of the art VHS recorder. Eventually, the adults would shamble in, chocolates would be passed around, and the video (chosen by the high command) would begin its grainy cycle. Even here, there was no escaping the "classical education". Famous Westerns, insufferable (for a child) musicals, black & white war movies; Bond, McQueen, Clint, Faye Dunaway (Dad's choice), The Italian Job (version 1.0, we were happy with that) – we drank it all down, eyes and mental gullets open, with a Quality Street chaser. Then, one Sunday, it changed.

My father was always a "man of the people," at least to his own mind. His family came from trade – my grandfather was a silversmith – so it was no surprise when one dreary Sunday lunchtime, the local carpenter arrived with his wife. Over the decades, Dad had gone from being an angry young medical student with a healthy disdain for the upper class, to a well-heeled country gentleman (the label is opaque) with a penchant for all the things said upper class once viewed as essential to one's lifestyle. Paintings, rare books, fine porcelain, Persian carpets, handmade furniture, old crystal, quality booze, vintage motors, silver cutlery, and so on. Not to mention, of course, a wife from a "good family". In fairness, this wasn't snobbery on the old man's part, or a simple tale of becoming the very thing against which we first rebelled. Being a silversmith's apprentice as a lad, he had visited the country's most lavish hotels and sumptuous private residences. From an early age, and high-class ladies aside, he had therefore been exposed to all the artistry and beauty these objects contain and project and had fallen under their spell. He could not possess them himself, however, so later, once his medical practice began to take off, he couldn't not. Along with the company stash left over from his own father, that meant a lot of silver spoons.

The carpenter was well-known to us kids and greatly liked. He was often at the house, fixing and improving cabinets, hanging doors on garages, drinking tea and at one point designing an entire panelled library. He had recently finished said project, not as grand as it may sound but in ambiance an almost sacred space, a bibliophile's veritable wet dream, and hence was here for lunch. I figured understandably it was part of the folks' wish to say thank you for his efforts.

There was a secret bookcase in this library. It wasn't so much hidden, it was just that it had solid doors and was kept locked. At first, I assumed it must contain the obligatory Kama Sutra and maybe some mildly pornographic literature, though I knew at heart that wasn't really my parents' guilty pleasure. That being so, and seeing as children know without needing to be told that all adults have at least one vice they wish they could conceal, what *was*? What was hidden in the secret bookcase?

The clue came in the Sunday movie.

"Now, this may be a bit advanced in places," said my father. Lighting his obligatory cigar (Havana, naturally), he gave me a look and then nodded towards my brothers. I was in my early teens at the time, making them about five and seven respectively. That meant I was on duty in the event of inappropriate levels of sex and violence. I didn't suspect it, but I was going to be busy. I took the chunky video cassette and looked at the label. *Excalibur,* it read. Thanks to my posh schooling, in tandem with Walt Disney, I thought I knew all there was to know about the legend of King Arthur and the Knights of the Round Table. I put the tape in and pressed play. Dad was whispering something to our guests. Mum was telling him to be quiet. Then the Wagner started.

It's one of my Proust moments. When I hear the opening strains of Siegfried's Death and Funeral March, I return body and mind to that curtained room on a drizzly English afternoon sometime in the late 1980s. Looking at John Boorman's film now, then already several years old, it's easy to be dismissive. The script can be clunky, the effects unconvincing (you can almost see the bubbles from the Lady of the Lake's Aqua-Lung but hey, it was 1981) and in spite of what is in hindsight an all-star royalty cast, the acting is decidedly iffy in places. But all of that can and should be forgiven for the SUBSTANCE. Launching out of the decade that sealed our fate as a one-way spiralling consumer species, the era in which capitalism finally won its Pyrrhic conquest over the planet, here were themes and values and symbolism to open and challenge and rupture us to our core. These knights were loyal to the death, yet inwardly torn in all directions; fierce and brave and true, yet vulnerable and uncertain and alone. They built a fellowship to which they gave their souls, unwillingly at first, becoming overly proud of their achievements, and ultimately they gave their lives with the deep realisation it could not possibly endure. They vowed to protect everything they loved, though they knew their individual mortal failings would spell destruction of the only things they cared for. They were human, and heroic, and fallible, and the armour was pretty cool, and limbs were severed ("I did two of those last week," observed my father the surgeon from his Monte Cristo fog in the corner) and Merlin wasn't a stereotype, and the music vibrated the floorboards, and there were breasts, and forsooth moreover bottoms, and an eternal sword of power, and a revelation about the Holy Grail (ahhhhh!) and there was Camelot. In attempting neither to be overly romantic, nor overly factual, it felt true. And we met Perceval properly for the first time.

The trouble with King Arthur, at least as most of us are taught is, well: it's all about Arthur. Him and his childhood; him and his mentor; him and his sword; him and his castle; him and his disastrous love triangle; him and his heroic death, saving...not much, it turns out. We get to know the other knights bit by bit over time, though mostly as caricatures. Gawain is bold and cocky and loves the ladies; Lancelot is the ultimate warrior and doing well for a first generation immigrant, but running off with the boss's wife will be his undoing; Kay is loyal and true but narrow of vision and, well, just a bit thick. They're presented as the necessary ensemble to give the King a broader platform from which to shine. There is and always has been an exception, however. In *Excalibur*, Boorman outs him. If the first half of the film is about Arthur and the creation of Camelot, the second part belongs to Perceval.

If you've seen it, you know where it's coming from. Profoundly moving and insightful – awful '80s mythic mish-mash – bit of both or something other? It's your call. If you haven't, I won't spoil it for you, but there are worse ways to write off 141 minutes of your life. What happened in the sitting room back in circa 1989, as Perceval called out to Arthur's departing body and Avalon's mists dispersed beneath a dying blood-red sun, was that the lights came up to reveal the floor strewn with a chaos of Lego pieces and half-chewed chocolates and none of the adults cared. Dad and Mike, the carpenter, were engaged in heavy parley while Mum and Mike's wife, Hilary, raised their eyebrows at one another, no doubt returning to an England where sex, violence and the meaning of existence were not the regular menu for conversation on a Sunday social visit. Then everyone went downstairs to the bookcase.

I'd glimpsed inside before once or twice when Dad had gone in to find something, usually on a Wednesday morning before going to work. Now, I was more than curious. He took the key from its hiding place (noted) and opened Mike's beautiful handiwork wide. "Now where is...?" Dad began – the eternal opener from a man with too many secretaries and scrub nurses in his life. While he searched the crammed shelves, I was scanning. As I'd suspected, no porn or illicit taboos, like bound leather tomes of Satanic ritual or such voodoo. Nothing that was on my GCSE reading list, either. Typically, for something "organised" by my father, it appeared a total hotchpotch. Authors like "Ouspensky" and "Nicoll" and "Bennett" sat alongside vaguely familiar names like "Hesse", "Pirsig", "Richard Bach" and "Somerset Maugham". Plus a very thick tome that took my attention, for its title as much as for its girth: "All and Everything – Beelzebub's Tales to his Grandson." Its creator was one "G.I.Gurdjieff."

"Ah, here it is!" exclaimed Dad triumphantly. He retrieved a fragile-looking book, bound in faded leather and with gilt edging to the pages. "The original version of Excalibur," he proclaimed. It was a 19th Century edition of Malory's Arthurian compendium, "Le Morte D'Arthur."

Further tea was offered to Mike and Hilary, further brandy and cigars for Dad; further 'Oh do shut up!'s proceeded, quite justifiably, from Mum. I stayed on and listened while the brothers destroyed another plastic space station. What I discovered fascinated me, and disturbed me in equal measure.

The contents of the bookcase were what my parents loosely referred to as their "most valuable spiritual guides". Not in monetary terms, necessarily; in the pre-internet age, it was more about accessibility, with their net worth meaning what was written within them. The Arthurian tales, they opined amongst themselves as smoke once more billowed about our heads, were part of the body of collective myths that humanity employs to decipher the soul's journey, both individually and as a perennially advancing species here on the planet. More revelatory for your narrator, who was starting to feel like that guy who after an indulgent lunch and a medieval slasher movie is about to discover his family is part of a dark conspiracy to take over the world, was to realise that this humble carpenter of ours was more than your everyday tea-drinking chippy. In fact, he and his wife were far more plugged into whatever secret society it was they all evidently belonged to than his bourgeois employer.

Though they included me in the conversation, I felt the opposite. An outsider. I spoke the same language, but I didn't understand the contexts. Yet something from the film, fresh in my senses, my memory and moreover in my core, was keeping me connected. I couldn't vocalise it, certainly not to join the adult chat that was littered with alien notions like octaves and food diagrams and the laws of three and seven, but it felt important. Fundamental. Vital, even, for living. Why then, I contemplated later on, when Mike had finally left with a warm smile and a twinkle in his eye, am I being educated as I am? My parents are not only allowing me to study in a system they don't actually condone: they're paying for it to happen! I felt excited – and I felt torn. Conflict. I didn't know it then – bullshit: that's a pat writer's device. I *did* know it. That afternoon, in the secret bookcase in middle-England, I'd met the first real mentor who would change my life.

Hello, Kin. I'm sorry. If I take a look through your eyes it all seems very self-indulgent on my part. The thing is, writing is just like life: you set off thinking you know where you're headed, then one day you wake up, look at the page you're on and say "How the hell did I get here?" I'll let you in on a secret: this isn't the first book I've written. Seeing as we're heroes together in the present story, I just want you to know who you're travelling with. Helps us develop trust, you see? There is a method to all these reminiscences. Would you believe, it's taken me three weeks and about a dozen years to write this far? Seriously! How long has it taken you to read? Talk about the law of diminishing returns, my oh my. But see, I'm doing my bit to carry as much of the load as I can. Of course, you're free to leave now and continue on your own. That's the benefit of controlling your own hero. You can go whenever, wherever you want. That's what I did. I met Gurdjieff, listened to some people talk about him for a couple of hours, then forgot about him for ten years. So it goes. It took a while for me to realise that, really, the Universe doesn't mind if we take our time. It isn't ours for the taking.

While everyone is dazzled by Arthur, the real quest is being undertaken by Perceval. You know the quest in question, right? (*Questa, quaerere* – no more Latin, I know, I promised.) That's it, the MacDaddy, the BIG ONE: that elusive Holy Grail.

To save you the suspense, given that you've probably realised by now that the book you are reading isn't a regular mystery thriller, Perceval finds the Grail. In the film, he overcomes some personal demons, kicks off his rusty armour while drowning in a river (symbols, symbols) and stands naked but for a fluffy white towel before the throne of Truth. Represented by a supernatural shape-shifting silhouette of Perceval's Lord and King, Arthur.

"Have you found the secret that I have lost?" asks the king.

"You and the land are one," replies Perceval.

That's it. Job done. Arthur drinks from the cup and his spirit is restored. He forgives and apologises to Guinevere, who's been hiding out with Excalibur in a nunnery for about twenty years, before the Knights ride out with their King for a final epic confrontation, with further amputations thrown in for good measure.

You and the land are one.

We could stop there. As we consider our presence on this planet at present, is there anything more important we need remember than this? I doubt it. If centuries-old legends or visionary filmmakers don't persuade you, ask a man who is both: David Attenborough. The trouble is, even though we *know* it, we don't act on it. Not enough, we don't. Individually – collectively. Either that's because we're incapable of acting – or we don't know it in the fullest sense.

I guess we don't stop there.

As you may have inferred, I'm a fan of *Excalibur*. I must have watched it a dozen or more times over the years. It's a compass, of sorts. More than just entertainment or mental morphine, it's a tool for checking occasionally to remember and to confirm I'm on the right course. Interest, solace and use. I even had the opportunity to meet its creator on a couple of occasions. An Irish friend's parents were neighbours of the Boorman family, and the great man used to wander over every now and then for a coffee and a chat. I guess lonely men are everywhere. Being much younger and slightly in awe of this famous director, I didn't do much of the talking. There was one question I wish I'd asked him, though: where was the Fisher King?

Arthur's story is incomplete without the Grail Quest. The Grail Quest is incomplete without Perceval. Perceval's story is incomplete without the Fisher King. The Fisher King is incomplete full stop.

There are so many early versions and continuation versions of Perceval's tale that it is difficult, perhaps impossible, to establish such a concept as "the original". A 2-minute modern-day trailer might go something like this:

A BOY living in the Dark Ages is raised alone by his MOTHER in the forest. He doesn't know who his father is. (Good device, eh? Not the last time we'll see that, I'll wager.) One day, he catches sight of a KNIGHT in shining armour on horseback. Their paths cross just long enough for the KNIGHT (bearded, swarthy, aloof, and terribly good-looking) to deliver an epic line, like: "Once you've seen Camelot, boy, you'll forget about your dreams." Wow. We are close on the BOY's eyes as the KNIGHT disappears through the autumn leaves.

The BOY tells his MOTHER he wants to be a knight. Mum cries, for mothers know and bear too much: "You're too innocent, Perceval," she wails, revealing his name for the audience's benefit, "the world is a murderous place!" And so he soon discovers it to be. Leaving the forest (nature/purity/contentment/Eden) he arrives at the city (humankind/ distortion/greed/ Bedlam) and finally Camelot = overarching symbol of justice and power and unity over the Land. Only – surprise, surprise, PERCEVAL – Camelot is not as perfect as it first appears. There are dark whispers in the corridors. There is temptation everywhere. We catch a glimpse of LANCELOT leaving the Queen's Chamber whilst adjusting his armoured codpiece. "Not a word, boy," the King's finest breathes ominously to our hero: "Camelot's future will depend on your silence."

Then a montage: shit turns bad. KNIGHTS shout, swear and attack each other. ARTHUR yields to anger and uses his legendary sword to do rather silly and ignoble things. He loses his power. His BASTARD SON challenges the throne. Deserted by most of his supporters, he beseeches the few loyal men that remain to help him on a mission. PERCEVAL, till now a lowly squire and not realising the full implications of his actions but trusting his heart, steps up. ARTHUR makes him a knight. "Go," says the King, with his Lee Strasbourg-perfected thousand yard stare: "find the chalice that restores all life (never call it "The Grail") and bring it to me."

PERCEVAL nods resolutely.

A drum beats once – twice – three times as we cut between: images of BIG SCARY WARRIORS; a creepy-looking castle; a banquet hall with a staircase leading down into a cave, where at last is revealed in silent awe (obligatory this one) the opening eye of a dragon.

Cut to: a bloodied PERCEVAL from a later scene is asked by a BEAUTIFUL MAIDEN: "What are you willing to pay for the cup of life?" (Never "The Grail.")

The drum beats again, like a heart.

"Everything," he replies.

The MAIDEN's eyes turn to fire. "So you shall."

Black.

Dissolve to: an OLD MAN, fishing. He is bedraggled but has a mysterious aura about him. PERCEVAL approaches warily. The OLD MAN struggles to stand. PERCEVAL lends him an arm but says nothing. He notices fresh blood on the other's worn breeches.

"Is there something you wanted to ask?" says the OLD MAN.

PERCEVAL replies in the negative. Seeing the OLD MAN's disappointment, he says quickly: "I was wondering who lives in that castle."

The OLD MAN hesitates. He winds in his fishing rod. "You'd better come with me."

Fade.

Okay, it's a little light on detail and I didn't observe "trad" screenplay format, true, but you get the idea. If it comes across as cliché, that's because arguably the story of Perceval invented cliché itself. Before him, pretty much all heroic tales involved not only the human protagonists in jeopardy but a bunch of angry meddling gods and monsters in the mix with them. In Perceval, it's down to the humans to scribe their own fate. Sure, there's magic and magicians and supernatural occurrences, but everything is answerable in the here and now, in this life, and all characters in the story are bound by the rules of the game.

The Fisher King, as you may have guessed, is the OLD MAN fishing in the above scenario. He is a wounded king, and the guardian of the Grail, which resides in his castle. In some versions, the castle is invisible to the outside world, until the Fisher King invites any would-be seeker to enter. In others, two kings protect the Grail. Later versions are highly Christianised, with angels replacing maidens and other superimposed symbolism, but although the conventional cup of Christ/Joseph of Arimathea connection is at the base of most of the Grail legends, this is not all about The Big JC. Put whatever filter you like over the story, the colours will shine just for you: Christian, Freudian, Jungian, mystical, Romantic, initiation story – the tale of Perceval works on all levels, from all perspectives. The reason it does so is simple if not immediately obvious. That is: we each of us contain all the characters of the story within us. And each of us is searching, consciously or not, for our own personal Grail. Which is to say, the thing that makes us whole.

Who is this Fisher character who guards it?

We cannot say definitively how or why the Fisher King was originally wounded. (Scholars, start your arguments.) Does it represent the Christian concept of atonement for original sin? Some stories have it down as the Fisher King's punishment for breaking his vow of celibacy by marrying; others assert he just put it about a bit once too often. In any case, the implication is that he was once a good knight and noble warrior who has failed in his duty to serve the Grail. Most versions have the wound placed in his thigh, but that's coy medieval euphemism: everyone knows it's his man parts that are damaged. He is thus unable to continue his line, and the land about him is similarly devoid of fertility, a barren wasteland. Hence the title of Eliot's famous poem.

"You and the land are one." As the King suffers, so does the land. If he flourishes, the land will be healthy and wholesome also. Alone, however, he cannot put an end to his suffering. This is our clue as to where Boorman hid the Fisher King in *Excalibur*.

At the moment of Perceval's ultimate ordeal and symbolic resurrection, the spectral Grail-Arthur silhouette asks him further questions: "What is the secret of the Grail? Whom does it serve?" The question "Whom does it serve?" is lifted verbatim from the medieval text of Chrétien de Troyes. In Boorman's film, King Arthur by now is three-quarters of the way through his 1981 retelling. He's lost his wife, his best friend, his fancy blade, most of his knights, and his wizard. His sister has tricked him into having sex with her (the young Helen Mirren could do that) and has borne him an Evil Son/Nephew nemesis known as Mordred. Mordred, understandably, has severe unresolved psychological issues and now wants Arthur's castle, kingdom and crown. On top of this, Arthur has been struck by lightning, his people are starving and revolting, and all the Quest Knights appear to have failed. At this point, he's longing to be back in the Disney version. He is also, unarguably and in all senses, wounded. He lies immobile, emasculated, wasting away in his castle. He has lost himself.

Arthur, the once new hope, the great uniting symbol, has himself become the Fisher King. He sends his knights on a quest to find the Grail, but that's a cover story: the Grail is his own identity, his spirit and his truth. It is his very reason to exist. Which he has forgotten.

It might appear that Boorman has blended the strands of the earlier tales out of convenience. Unfortunately, I missed my chance to ask him why. This is in itself an irony. For in the medieval versions, it is not the Fisher King that asks Perceval the question, but the other way around: he must wait for Perceval to ask *him*. The very act of being asked is the key that will unlock the Fisher King's healing and restore him to a state of grace. It will also satisfy the knight's quest by rewarding him with the Grail. As in the film, the first time that Perceval has a chance to ask the question or "receive the Grail", he fails to do so. In some versions, he never gets a second bite and dies unfulfilled. In others, however, on the second attempt, Perceval measures up and ascends to the status of becoming the new Grail Guardian.

In *Excalibur*, Perceval is the last knight left alive after the final battle. His final task for the dying Arthur (spoiler alert) is to throw the sword back into the lake from which it first rose. Always a slow starter, Perceval baulks at the first attempt. On his second, the Lady of the Lake receives the sword, Excalibur disappears from human view and, to mix up film metaphor, the matrix is reset.

"One day, a King will come and the sword will rise again."

Perceval is the hero who completes the cycle. What makes it possible – the only thing that enables the play to run its course – lies in Perceval's capacity as a healer. Wittingly or not – and indeed Wagner himself in his own adaptation portrayed Perceval more as the innocent fool – he provides the cure. The elixir that restores the balance. The miracle hangover remedy. Reconciliation.

Now it's our turn. That's right, Kin: it's up to us.

That was a long chapter, right? Phew! It's not over yet. Thanks for hanging in there, Kin. The Wi-Fi can be patchy in my tower. When my treasures are asleep and the Livebox is on the blink, sometimes I just groove on. Was a time I'd type till dawn. Idea-visions streaming, inspiration reaming, ahhh – the early days of the fellowship. Here we are.

Did we find the Fisher King? I don't know. Did we: did we find the Fisher, Kin? He can be pretty good at hiding. Even in a film in which he has a crucial role, for the central heroes, he can be hard to spot. Where is he in us?

Maybe, he's not that concealed. Perhaps he's easy to see, for family and friends, sure, but even strangers catch a glimpse from time to time. An angry comment to a fellow passenger, or someone who cuts in front of us. An overly emotional reaction if someone disagrees with us on a point we know we're right on, an opinion we'd rather not shake. If we do something we consider kind, and don't receive the appreciation we feel is merited; if we don't get the money we think we're worth, or the job, or if the date we've long been dreaming of goes sour. For some, the Fisher King is there for all to see on Instagram, FB or TikTok. For some, that wounded figure has millions of followers. Do those millions heal the wound? Do they know the question – the question for which it is fishing:

What ails you?

That's another version of the question. It's the question we are required to ask our world, having first individually asked ourselves. This was the enquiry that released the Fisher King from his suffering and the land with him in Wolfram von Eschenbach's telling, but choose whichever you like, or another story completely, go on, Kin. This is your choice, to find the avatar which best reflects you, on *your* quest for the Grail. Trust me, it's important. We can run with Perceval, or Bruce Wayne, or Frodo or Katniss or Anna: Lear, Hamlet, Othello, Cleopatra, James Bond, Django, Sarah Connor, Roger Rabbit or The Girl with the Dragon Tattoo – which of the stories from your personal history most resonates with you? Chances are, the spectre of the Fisher King is there in all of them. It's in all our heroes. Dressed up oftentimes, no doubt: hiding, crouching in the castle, creepy/invisible/shining with bling, doesn't matter how you try to shroud it. It's in there. It's in everyone.

It's in you, Kin. In you.

Maybe John Boorman is smarter than we thought. Showing Arthur becoming the Fisher King teaches us a valuable truth: we're never set. We play a role we think that's us, who we are, what we represent, how the world sees us. For life. It's done. That's "me," that's WHO I AM – hah: we kid ourselves and anyone else we can, we're such damn fine actors. Then something happens. Externally, internally, doesn't matter where, in-out, it all flows. Something changes. "The old wound" surfaces. It causes pain, which in turn prompts us to become other than ourselves. Lancelot, too, the champion: even he must don, for a scene or more, the heavy costume of the Fisher King.

Do we think we're still in the movies? That all this is irrelevant, or fantastical? Mind the intersection, we're arriving at the crossover.

Do you remember Robin Williams? I don't know when you're reading this. It's the future from where I'm sitting, Kin, that's for sure. Maybe in your present, the humans have fixed things. Friction-less vehicles criss-cross the planet on a thimble of bio-science to the grateful applause of dolphins, emitting carbon-reducing agents and a pleasant whiff of potpourri. There are no nations beneath your perfectly equilibrated biosphere. We've also consigned disease, poverty and money to the Virtual History Dome experience. And conflict? We've done all that for you, right? No more disputes or bloody, senseless wars. The Howl resolves all.

Don't panic. You'll get your slot. It's in the cloud, format 7DX, coming soon to some consciousness near you.

If you haven't heard of him, look him up. Williams was a gifted entertainer. He had a talent for playing roles that were at once extremely comical and extremely poignant. Overly sensitive, even sentimental at times, maybe, but that was his thing. He was a hit, that's for certain. During his life, the roles he performed found affinity with millions of his fellow human beings, and made the producers of the movies he starred in mucho potpourri. What is interesting for us is that if you distil his filmography, there are two roles he predominantly portrayed. One, was a doctor. The archetypal Healer. The other, in various guises, was the archetype of the Fisher King. Sometimes, the two are combined in the same story, as befits this symbiotic world of complementary opposites. You can see them, either solo or in tandem, in Good Will Hunting, and in Dead Poet's Society, and What Dreams May Come, and Awakenings, and Patch Adams, even Aladdin, and – hey, wait a minute: THE FISHER KING. And, rest his beautiful soul, he played it in real life.

I'm not talking about his suicide. Let's not bow to conjecture, sensationalism and hysteria, the Furies of our age. It was most certainly brain disease that pushed him ultimately to take his own life. How much of the existing state before that story contributed to the act – the divorces, AA history, depression, declining career and straightforward ageing – is not quantifiable. Not by me, certainly. Even for those close, who ever really *knows*? As ever, though, stories contain if not the truth itself, then clues or signposts to its mercurial omnipresence. In his biography, entitled *Robin*, we find this paragraph:

> *Robin's children had always been a dependable source of some of the purest, most natural joy he had experienced. But when he saw them now, they were also a reminder that he had chosen to end his marriage to Marsha and break up their home; it filled him with shame to think that he had inflicted the divorce upon them, and the shame compounded itself as he came to believe he had taken something perfect and corrupted it.*

Which is, in a sobering nutshell, the psychological profile of the Fisher King.

Wounding. Shame. Failure. Blame. When we step up to play an active role in life's ceaselessly unfolding docudrama, we almost inevitably pick up a crippling dose of one or even all the above. It's the price of consciously taking part, as opposed to being passively swept along by a plot you figure is somewhere written down in indelible ink. Trust me, that script never dries. Answer: would you rather seek safety in the belief that everything will be resolved if you just keep your head down, say your lines on cue and follow the peculiar stage directions?

I should have been a pair of ragged claws...

The happy news is, everything is temporary. The Fisher King *can* be healed. The sword *will* rise again. All will be roses, roses.

Boorman didn't call his epic 'Arthur'. Or 'Perceval' or 'The Search for the Holy Grail' or 'Merlin'. Not simply, I believe, though I failed to ask, because there was another movie released in 1981 with the title 'Arthur'. (With apologies to Russell, the original is far better than the remake. The 2011 version does star Helen Mirren, though, who was also in *Excalibur* – see how it's all connected? Go, conspiracy gremlins, go.)

Boorman named his film after the sword. The talisman, the magical gift, the Great Symbol. It stands for more than any of the characters in the story, king included. It is intended to be used for the justice of all, an instrument to balance the world's conflicting forces, not to serve the desires or vanity of one man. It is not a possession to be wielded, but a duty, often onerous, to be served. Once its mission is accomplished, it returns to its maker.

Do we dare accept the talisman? If we do, we must do so with eyes open, with our nerve and sinews primed. For we are about to enter a story that is far bigger than we are, that has existed forever and will certainly outlast us and, most probably, the memory of us. Perhaps our role is that of Perceval: to serve a king who serves an ideal, who is noble in the deepest sense, having walked all paths and realised his inevitable fate. In serving so, we may not hold the power, but we can heal the wound that corrupts or diminishes it, destroying the land to which we belong.

Perhaps, in time, we will play them all. One thing is sure: to have any chance of integrating our inner heroes, of attaining wisdom, of becoming whole – of receiving the Grail – we must risk stepping beyond the threshold. It can be a daunting prospect. There are often guardians, traps and monsters. "There be dragons." The penalty for not doing so, on the other hand, is heavy for any who have made the journey this far. To catch a glimpse of the path beyond only to turn back on account of fear will diminish us. For if we do not choose to play our role in this life, what will we become? What then will be our reward?

Come closer, Kin, whisper it: before we leave this world, we become the very thing we despise.

OF C.U.N.T & K.I.N.

DO YOU KNOW WHAT NEMESIS MEANS? A RIGHTFUL INFLICTION OF RETRIBUTION MANIFESTED BY AN APPROPRIATE AGENT, PERSONIFIED IN THIS CASE BY A HORRIBLE CUNT, ME.

- BRICK TOP IN THE 2000 FILM, SNATCH

Are you still here, Kin? I knew it was you. Here: take my hand. This is where the ride gets a little gnarly.

We're going to take an unexpected detour. I mean from the whole "superimposing our lives and the present narrative onto the classic Hero's Journey, with illustrations" trip. Not because it isn't valid or valuable. Verily, it requires no vaulting validation. It's just that, before we get vexed by our own individual version of *V for Vendetta,* we need to smell the coffee.

Breathe.

There are plenty of excellent books, and inspiring movies on YouTube et al., and indeed blogs and podcasts, about this undertaking. You know: the Journey to Self. There are even books specifically about Perceval and the Grail Quest, explaining with exhaustive references the evolution of the path and explicitly dedicated to realising your heart's true desire to become a Better You. They're good, too. Try them. It's partly why we're here. Partly. But there's a problem with this road.

You know when you're driving, say on the school run, or the shopping run, or the daily run home from work? You get back to your hutch, turn off the ignition, prepare to open the car door and head inside.

Stop.

What did you notice on your way home? What will you notice once you're back inside?

Process. Nothing comes. Right? Nothing, at any rate, to make you pause or suddenly realise, in intellect or feeling or bodily sensation, a profound new awareness or insight into your existence. A game-changer. A life-changer. Something that might make you want to alter direction, shout "Eureka!" or spontaneously dissolve into laughter or tears. Why?

Habit.

You're so used to that journey. You're so used to that scene. You've driven it, walked it, hitched a ride on it, lived in it for so long, so many times, you don't see it any more. You don't experience it, not for real. Like social media, or even language, you get so habitulaised to usnig it taht yuo'd hradly noitce if the from or meinnag cahnegd.

You're so used to the "you" that's apparently doing it all that in your current default setting, the information from the original transmission that created you is literally filtered out of your consciousness. In the words and sweet growl of that most saintly of Kin, Leonard of Cohen: "You live your life as if it's real."

There's no point in continuing on this road together out of habit. Depending when you're reading this, that's part of the obstacle we've arrived at. The very stories that are meant to help us see and know ourselves by presenting a mirror to our lives have become ubiquitous. Obvious. Diluted. Trite. Commercialised. They have been told and retold, some bright sparks have analysed what makes them tick, the template's been formalised, cash-tills go ker-ching! and everything from NY Times Bestsellers to Netflix-come mimics the outline. We all know the script:

"Yeah, yeah: ordinary world, hero gets called, hero refuses, mentor appears, hero is tested, hero crosses the threshold, special world, new allies and battles, approaches the cave, supreme ordeal, the reward and the road back, apotheosis, returns with elixir, masters both worlds and nine films and forty-two years later, Rey buries the light sabres in the sand. I get it." Just like Excalibur is thrown back into the – "Yeah, in the lake. We get it. So now?"

Now, we hop off the merry-go-round. Find a freezing cold pool. Not to offload the talisman. Like our fabulous crazy kin, Wim Hof, we jump in. Give each other a slap in the face. To wake up, yes, for sure.

Moreover, to remember: why we're making this journey in the first place.

What do you want from this, Kin? Why are you still here? Are you hoping to gain something from this story, this book – this life of yours? Do you want something further added to your experience of being before you die? Is that what this is all about? Maybe you genuinely want to be "better". Interpret that as "healed" or "upgraded", whichever you find more apt. Either way, who or what do you think you want to be better for? Be honest, now. So you can save yourself? Heal the world? Be the hero – for the glory, perhaps? Not even: just the riches will do. Help neutralise all those shadows you gathered as a child. It's okay, Kin. I get it. I'm not judging here. I don't have answers for all of this myself. Nothing set, at any rate.

Thing is, whatever we want for ourselves, we can't escape our circumstances. We're bound here, with our species, to the Earth on which we dwell. We *are* one with the land. A part of the main. (Thank you, John.) As the posthumously trending Alan Watts lucidly observes, we don't come into this world – we come out of it. Leaves on the tree – perceive it as you will. Did you ever see a bunch of leaves fighting over who's top leaf before attacking their own branch with chainsaws? We have now.

I'm reaching out to you, Kin. I can't do this alone. Neither can you. We've been fishing this wasteland for too long. If you're still here, it's because you recognise some truth in this madness. If you're still here, then there are others here, too. It's time we stepped up. There is nothing else. It's what we are here to do.

When I was younger and less occupied with children, home maintenance and arthritis, I spent a certain amount of time in Central Asia. I say 'certain' amount as it followed time in Western Russia, where everything between the first *ryumka* of vodka in St Petersburg and crossing the Volga estuary on the Caspian Sea much later remains to this day a somewhat beatific blur. Ahhh, the fellowship... Once in the 'Special World' of the former USSR (Turkic/Mongol/Farsi oblast) my colleagues and I had our consciousness jolted by many experiences. Officially, in those days, you were meant to have your tourist visa stamped at every hotel or guest house you visited. This would give the still Soviet-flavoured authorities a paper trail with which to chart the integrity of your 'vacation' when you left. We took Eddie Murphy's endearing '80s character Axel Foley as our inspiration while 'on vacation' in the ex-USSR. Abusing our tourist visas to the max, we stayed with local contacts, families of friends and random allies we encountered along our route, and many total strangers. We figured there's always a way to sort the paperwork later. Whenever officials stopped us to check our documents, as happened often, we would convincingly plead ignorance and repeat the mantram: "We're on vacation". If the worst came and the officials weren't buying it, we bought them back. Cheaply, usually. In this way, unlike the regular western trawlers we saw being led through bazaars and up minarets, perspiring only slightly less than their wallets, we were granted access beneath the skin of this rich and diverse heartland.

There are plenty of tales from this soul-feast era of my life. Some we may visit later out of necessity to our current predicament, which is: getting us through the gloop and into the light of the Howl.

You remember the Howl, don't you, Kin? If you're missing the hero's journey thing, you may consider it our talisman. It's there on the cover, I promise not to disappoint. It's here, too, of course, right now. But everything in its right place.

One of the moments I recall which I shall now conjure for the benefit of present elucidations is an evening with Bakir and his family, at their home by the old railway line outside Bukhara. We were cooking the local *plov*, an oily, meaty rice dish, in the distended hubcap of an old *Gaz* truck, drinking tea and soaking in the otherworldly sunset. There were four generations of Bakir's family present, starting with his own kids and swelling through the generations to three of his own grandparents, as well as his folks, sisters, aunts, uncles, cousins and neighbours all. There were kids in shorts playing in the courtyard and out towards the train tracks; women preparing ingredients and soups and side-dishes; men pretending to cook the *plov* while talking with their dusty foreign interlopers in about half a dozen languages; old-timers, helping if they could, being respectfully attended to by their scions if their honey-making days were done. A hive in harmonious movement, indeed.

I often recall Vonnegut's description of the modern western family in his last treatise on life, *A Man Without A Country*. He writes: "A husband, a wife and some kids is not a family. It's a terribly vulnerable survival unit." I shared with our host my view of the disparate definitions of family as experienced by our respective cultures.

'That is because you come from a vertical culture,' responded Bakir without flinching: 'In your culture, you are brought up to rise independently above everyone else. Even if that is not your education, it's what your society imposes on you as individuals. Get going, get ahead, build yourself higher. Everyone is trying to be above everyone else, it's about getting to the top, am I correct? If other people cannot keep up, who cares? Less competition, so much the better. We, on the other hand, live in a horizontal culture. No one advances without everyone else around them also coming with them to some degree. It's like a net, we're all connected. Of course there are rich people, there are greedy people, we are humans. But even them, you can see them pulling the net forward with them, even if they don't like it. Something filters across, for their family, or their town, whatever. If they don't behave like this, if they cut the net' – Bakir flashed a bright smile – 'here, they do not last very long!'

'Yet you live in a police state,' I ventured cautiously, 'ruled by a dictator.'

Bakir shrugged. 'The fish rots from the head down. It's not so black and white.'

Cryptic native proverbs aside, just looking at the architecture from where we stood supported our host's assertions. The dwellings all the way to the walls of the old city were one or two storied at most, all abutting up to each other with notional private gardens out back that in actuality were shared by the children and animals of surrounding households. Even in the inner city's old quarters, private homes maintained a respectful altitude. Aside from a few modern hotels, the only edifices visible above the ancient rooflines were the old university, the mosque and its fabled minaret. I thought of London, and Paris, of Moscow and Manhattan, and how those cities' skylines have influenced the catch-up cultural shifts in modern metropolises such as Abu Dhabi, Seoul and Shanghai. Florence – not South Carolina, the other one, in Italy: in the 13th century, there were so many towers, and so many private feuds and bloody atrocities committed in and around them, that the local government passed a law forbidding the wealthy families (= extended survival units) responsible for their construction to build them any higher than ninety feet. That was back in the days when governments still had some clout. Remember those? The Florentine *Commune* watched the play from the stalls and the narrative was plain: too many heads in the clouds meant too much blood on the streets. A dark twist for fans of early psychogeography. Here, of all wondrous places, in the crucible of the much-lauded Renaissance: was this where its evil twin, our inherited vertical culture, also began its ascent through our very social fabric?

Beats me, Kin. I'm tired of trying to explain echoes I didn't live to understand. Here's the thing: can you feel it? Do you see what all those towers represent? What's happening within them? Who are they really for? For you and me? Can you taste what's filtering down, through the net, from the "fish's head"? I'm sorry, I'm ahead of myself again. Towers and feelings and all that fragile lonesome jazz, we'll get there, if you're game. Maybe it's not your bag. Okay, then, Kin. You hang in your tower, I'll just type on down in mine. I'm not looking for a feud. We'll call it a stalemate. Just a heads up: towers have a habit of coming down.

We're not here exclusively for ourselves. You agree? That's great, isn't it? We can all tap "Like". But do we actually know it?

In the same breath, we're also here for ourselves. Right? Otherwise, why still be here? You're just another young mouth to feed and an old-aged arse to wipe. Are you really so valuable, so worthwhile, so indispensible during those brief moments in-between? Hm.

We're back at the Duality Trap. Before we step forward and make it go 'Snap', let's give ourselves that quickening slap.

A while back (before kids, for sure) I came across a notion online that interested me. Lord knows how I found it. You know how it is when you're surfing the web and, as often happens, you suddenly wake up and go 'How the hell did I get *here*?' Anyway, somewhere in the search engine between 'Reptilian elite conspiracy' and 'brunette milf interracial double' (I was researching a new book, trust me – I would *never* look into conspiracy theory otherwise) it popped up: STS vs STO. On first glance, I thought it might be a guide to recognising the symptoms of some new strain of venereal disease, which is to say, it would qualify alongside interesting as potentially 'useful', with a dusting of solace. One can be lonely when fucking, but at least one is never alone. In any event, it turned out to be something unconnected, at least superficially.

STS and STO are acronyms which sit at the core of a certain worldview. Like many of our 21st Century worldviews, the viewing is done mostly online, and the pages under scrutiny by and large become the world. This too shall pass. Still, the concept merits attention. Those minds behind the fingers that via the keyboards postulate said notion submit that the human race can broadly be divided into two types: those who look out for themselves (Service To Self) and those whose priority lies in taking care of the rest of the gang (Service To Others). So far, so simple. We can all immediately think of people who fit into either category, I'm sure.

The porridge gets thicker, as ever, when we turn that lens of infallible perspicacity, with which every net surfer is undeniably blessed, on ourselves and look within. Which one am I? Example: I want to make money, sure, and buy some new threads, those sick shades with the bottle-opener-in-the-arm design and maybe even have enough left over to HP the new mid-engined 'Vette; I also want to have enough dough that I'm not a burden on the state, I can buy my own house before losing most of my sweat in interest to a bank, and provide for my abandoned Mum and the rest of my family in these uncertain times. STO or STS? Example 2: I just want to take care of the ones I love. I want to help the homeless and the poor and those less fortunate than myself. I feel genuinely aggrieved when I look at our world today and I have all of this energy and compassion to give. I also want people to know it. I want to be recognised, however modestly, as that special healing light. The one in the group of friends of whom all say in hushed reverence: 'They're just on another level. I'll never be her/him. #gratitude for being their friend.' And I want Justin to realise that I'm The One and pledge himself and his pink-sweet tongue to honouring my profoundest carnal fantasies, forever.

Self – or Other?

Example...3,946,284......

What are we saying? Of course: we're both. Obvious, nah? We're an inner blend of selfish and selfless, of the dark and the light; an ambulating, psycho-spiritual Ben & Jerry's Cookie Dough S'wich Up, often as cold to the touch and rarely quite as tasty. We all know our Solzhenitsyn, don't we? *The Gulag Archipelago*'s most oft-quoted line (abridged): "The line separating good and evil passes...right through every human heart." Or, as that other great philosopher and human commentator, Edmund Blackadder, succinctly puts it:

"Sometimes I'm nice – and sometimes I'm nasty". Well, quite.

Only it's not so simple. There is also a theory, which I checked while my treasures were sleeping, that almost all of us fall predominantly under the STS umbrella. That is, as long as we are being either selfish OR selfless, we are aiding and abetting in perpetuating a duality-based lifecycle. Confusing? Imagine we are fish. We all know this metaphor: the big fish eat the little fish. Now, some big fish are predatory loners. And some little fish stick together in shoals. Cue the obvious government/banks/big pharma/corporations/dictators vs "we the people" analogies. The little fish stick together to protect each other from the predatory elite and their henchfish (medium sized), sacrificing themselves if necessary for the greater good, while the evil snaggle-toothed swimmers above pick them off at will or, during savage frenzies, by the million. By preserving themselves at all, however, the little fish in fact perpetuate the system. Selflessly looking out for one another, especially those less agile in the water, whilst simultaneously trying to appease their persecutors, they ensure only that the insatiable killers on high have something to snack on further down the line. Said killers are themselves savvy, of course. They don't decimate altogether the supply that feeds them. On occasion, they cut the little flappers some slack. Maybe even show them a new feeding ground so they can thrive. For a time. Before it's chow-down massacre again.

This is a snapshot of just two adjacent levels in the food chain. Food Diagram, if you're into your Fourth

Way shenanigans. There are of course predators that prey on the predators, and even the prey have to eat something below their own station. The point is, STO and STS are both contained in this self-regulating and self-perpetuating duality-based system. The Duality Trap is embedded in the play. For the fishies, there really is no way out.

What's our trick?

Well, it's sweet and it's sour. In essence it's this: we are not fish. Whatever Pixar might want you and your progeny to believe, the human realm is a far bubble away from the quaint aquatic world of *Finding Nemo*. We have an extra brain. Maybe two. This is the nub. Anthropomorphic childhood overload of our era aside, by so-called adulthood many of us have an awareness that we are not regular animals. In the standard issue, biological carbon-based life form's 'Visit Planet Earth for One Lifecycle' kit bag (non-refundable once opened), homo sapiens got an extra multi-tool. Not just opposable thumbs. Even pandas got those. No, we got something you can't trade with fellow primates: a higher state of consciousness.

Let's play a classic children's game: find the antonym. What is the opposite of "high"? Easy. The opposite of "fast"? Ditto. Opposite of "good"? No-brainer, right, and we had that already in chapter one, dang. What about the opposite of "alive"? Right again, there's a reason I'm not offering a cash prize on this show.

What is the opposite of "conscious"? Wait, there's a condition: you're not allowed to say "unconscious". Okay, go.

How are you doing? Did you say "unaware"? Wait: did you Google it? Definitely no cash for *you*. But look, it's the same deal: it's just awareness with an "un" stuck in front of it. To negate being aware, being conscious. But what *is* it, the experience – the essence of the opposite state? Define it. Envisage it. Try again.

"Comatose"? Like how we're thinking here. However, we can argue that as long as there is neurological/ biological activity in the body, to a degree the human subject is still conscious. They are just a lot lower on the scale than in your everyday scenario. (Unless by day you're a tax inspector. Just kidding. Maybe.) In actual fact, contrary to the seemingly inert exterior, there can often be a lot *more* consciousness happening on the inside of a coma patient than they experience in the ordinary world. Trust me on that. Tbd later.

What about "incognizant"? (I can Google, too.) "Ignorant"? "Oblivious"? Hmm, maybe the last one is closer.

What I'm attempting to hone in on here is not the state of being unconscious as in: "Being from Iowa, he was unconscious of the fact it was poor form to fart in an elevator, and in any case, with so many others around him, who would know?" That's just knowing something, like a rule or a custom. Or not. I'm talking about the sense of being conscious of one's very own existence. The opposite of that. What do you call your *non*-existence? Dead? Now that's a can of worms, isn't it? Okay, let's stick with this life, for the moment.

As we saw with the selfless/selfish pairing, or the good and evil duo of Solzhenitsyn, there appears to be a line that shifts – "It oscillates with the years". You can apply that to pretty much any opposing principles. Where high becomes low, or hot becomes cold is of course relative, to the local environment and to the observer. What about consciousness? Where is its defining, if movable, line? It appears to function in a caste of its own, along an uninterrupted sliding scale, at the bottom end of which is – what? How can we express it without losing the capacity required to define it, and indeed everything else we experience while alive? What if consciousness is indeed itself subject to the law of polarity, only in our environment, from our perspective, we cannot experience a relative position?

Hoo-hah. There are many more words scribed by far brighter and undoubtedly more conscious beings than I on this matter, dear Kin. I'm also forgetting that aside from keeping us out of rabbit holes, I must paradoxically where necessary play the white bunny. That is to say, remind us we are short here on time. We have to join the road again sooner or later. The show must go on. Let's rinse our grey cells and take a deep breath, for we are now going to dive into brisk and choppy waters. I am talking, of course, about C.U.N.T.

'Mais ç'est terrible, ce mot.' Yes indeed, Michel. My apologies: it is a terrible word. Though terror, too, may

serve a valuable purpose, *mon ami,* if it awakens us fully to the perils of our imminent journey. The readiness is all.

Is this where we part company? I'll understand, dear Kin, if you don't want to continue on this road together. I wish only to say this: if you're shocked, for your own sake let it be intentionally. Don't allow it merely because you are passively outraged that someone should write this horrible word. "There can be no justification for its employment in our open and egalitarian society." Really? Who taught you that? Are you especially sensitive? Do you hold a monopoly on outrage and refined sensibilities? Get you, Kin. And fuck you. Yeah, I said that.

What kind of hero do you aspire to be? If you want to be the kind that cleans up the world of dirty thinking and oppressive language and attitudes, here's the newsflash: you're going to have to toughen up. What – you think I genuinely want to offend you? For you to stop reading, stalk off dramatically and pan this monstrous endeavour we've begun? Have you forgotten the parable of the Swallow? The one who puts you in the shit isn't always your enemy, Kin. I'm being harsh in order to help you survive. If you want to protect your valuable ideals, sometimes you need to defend them with rings of steel. And take your head out of your own arse while we're at it. Arse/ass, I'm not picky right now, you choose.

CHOOSE

Choose not to be automatically reactive. Not to be triggered (that's the word doing the pop. psych rounds these days, isn't it?) Choose to see the Duality Trap before it takes you. Choose to be free, in every breath, every action that you take.

Those in the G-wagon a.k.a. The Work or the formerly secret admissions club known as The Fourth Way™ (© G.I. Gurdjieff expired 1949) will recognise what's going on here. After three harmoniously flowing chapters, the law of seven requires us to make a choice. Either a) we keep reading with the consciousness scale dialled back to – *"meh..."* – and fall into a habitual descending pattern of intellectual feeding; or b) we administer a conscious shock to the system, and ride that ever-ascending elevator back towards His Endlessness, holding our gas and singing Hallelujah (Rufus Wainwright version – sorry, Leonard and Jeff) all the way.

Too much too soon, honey? No problem. Let us return to that terrible word.

We're too hung up, especially at the time of writing, on the whole "Us vs Them" hysteria. Everywhere you look, it's natives vs immigrants, red vs blue, black vs white, male vs female, right vs left, young vs old, corporate vs independent, environmentalists vs deniers, scientists vs believers, "these" believers vs "those" believers, conservatives vs reformists, remainers vs leavers, democracy vs any system that isn't a democracy, goddamn it! Etcetera, etcetera, history's lumpy wheel turns over. At these peak moments of fervour, every camp is scowling at their opposite number and, quite naturally, targeting the very worst elements they perceive in the other's value or belief system. Let's not pick examples here, we're not about that and we've got some controversial vocabulary to explore, besides. Don't want to offend any further than is absolutely necessary. You can find all the contrast you want by simply choosing a different search engine and typing something atypical into your search bar. "Down with corporate algorithms!!" – you see? Thus the wheel lumps onward.

If you sniff the air and catch that whiff of percolated caffeine, you'll notice that there are "Good" and "Bad" individuals on either side of any fraught dialogue you care to investigate on this planet. Depending on the day and circumstances, you can track, if not with absolute precision, Solzhenitsyn's oscillating line as it wavers back and forth in response to events as they unfold. A visionary politician one day becomes a tyrant the next; a well-informed scientific observer one year turns into a zealous proselytiser to shame any religious nut counterpart if they don't get their annual grant renewed. And we, the normal folk: our opinions, beliefs and fears bat back and forth amid the wuthering bombardment of information, driving us into frenzied keyboard crusaderism and from acts of charity to acts of violence in almost the very same breath.

We need to draw our focus and our personal egoic investments out of the issues. We need to concentrate instead on their drivers. The glitch is not "them". Nor is it the opposing "us". It's all of us. Our collective reckless driving is what's sending us spiralling towards oblivion. Whatever that may be. Or rather, it's the information we're allowing to be transmitted through us as a species.

So here's the plan: we honour Nietzsche's ramblings and junk the "good vs evil" dichotomy once and for all. It's been gnawing at our perinea since Genesis 3. Next, we take our sliding scale of consciousness as a yardstick. We now replace the traditional notions of good guys vs bad guys with a more flexible and visceral concept with which we can engage and to which we can organically respond. Finally, rendering unto the age in which we find ourselves, we give our players acronyms.

Let's be clear, speaking confidentially, Kin, what we mean when introducing the concept of a C.U.N.T. If you remove the caps and punctuation marks, we're left with a word unmasked that is, even in this enlightened epoch, often a source of tension in our ordinary world:

Cunt.

Not so bad these days? Say it loudly in the morning queue at Starbucks next time and watch the result. It'll be more rewarding than the stuff in the polystyrene cup.

I pretended only briefly, before my screaming essence caught the nineteen year-old me and dragged him mercifully out into the long dark night, to begin a career in law. I never got to shoulder the burden of proof in a courtroom, or persuade a hostile jury and turn a trial on a technicality, so indulge me one moment in the imagined limelight. When I type the word "cunt" into my search engine, I get two definitions (powered by Oxford Languages, no less):

1) A woman's genitals
2) An unpleasant or stupid person

"The accused is appropriating the *second* meaning for their business of shaping a new and shinier worldview, Your Honour. As Charles Manson stole the song *Helter Skelter* from the Beatles for his own deluded and nefarious purposes, so our similarly afflicted proto-patriarchal society stole the inherent feminine beauty from the *first* definition of this word several thousand years ago. This sullying over millennia of a perfectly expressive, innocent, even mystical word by billions of sadly uninitiated boy-men, whilst lamentable, is not our focus here today. Suffice it to say, where the Beatles relied on U2's Bono as their paladin for the feat of recapturing their creation, I believe certain feminists active presently are so tasked with the return of this word to its rightful lexicographical position. Ladies and gentlemen of the jury, I trust your educated sensibilities and innate powers of discernment will permit my client to continue in the pursuance of his noble task."

Yeah, I bailed at the right moment. Sorry, Dad. Moving on.

We need to train ourselves to discern not between our inherited and often skewed notions of "good and evil", "hatred and compassion", "understanding and ignorance" and so on and so on. We need to be able to assess how conscious we all are. At any given moment. As we – individually and collectively – make potentially far-reaching decisions. That's conscious in every sense. Only then do we have a chance of interrupting the mechanical cycle of our existence to choose a new path for the future.

How do we chart this? By spotting when we and our fellow clothes-toting bipeds fall below a critical level of consciousness relative to any given environment or circumstance where a decision must be made. If we fall below, we must be called out. As a C.U.N.T: a Critically Unconscious Negativity Transmitter.

That's the meaning we're employing here. How do we spot it, in ourselves and others? Well, definition 2 is a good place to start: unpleasant and obnoxious – chances are that if you're behaving like this, you're being a C.U.N.T. We have to be savvy, though. C.U.N.Ts who are sufficiently self-conscious of their own C.U.N.Tishness can often come across as quite other. They've studied the moves, put on the guise. You've heard the expression, "Well, he was a charming C.U.N.T, wasn't he?" and such like. But in our actions, ultimately our conscious level is revealed. As is the remedy.

Want an example? Consider the swallows.

I was watching them the other day, this most magnificent of earthly creatures. Swooping and soaring and gathering by the dozen on the telegraph wires. There was a group merrily twittering and clicking away at each other, probably sharing notes on the best pickings over the donkey shed and advising the young 'uns not to drink from the swimming pool – those C.U.N.Ting humans and their chlorine! – you know, the usual telegraph banter.

Suddenly, a new swallow barges in among them on the wire and, obviously a male, starts trying to have a go at one of his fellow birdies next to him. Now: I'm not great at sexing swallows, not from the other side of the courtyard at any rate, but what was evident was that whatever its sex or inclination, this other swallow was not in the mood for an amorous high-wire ruffle just at that moment. In under a second, the party was over. Every other bird on the wire, and even some that were flying in the vicinity, piled in on the would-be Casanova and chased him pretty much away into the clouds. You could almost hear them, if you imagine the R-rated Disney version, screeching and chattering the chant: "C.U.N.T! C.U.N.T! C.U.N.T-C.U.N.T-C.U.N.T!"

In nature, animals call it. They know, innately, when one of their own is out of line. They act on it immediately, comprehensively. Now, you might say, if the above scenario were translated to the human domain, that there would be a similar reaction to such an assault taking place on a bus, or in a crowded park, for instance. Hopefully, for the majority of cases, you'd be right. But this is where our higher level of consciousness can also work against us. It's the inevitable sour that must come with the sweetness of heightened insight. To satisfy our desires, be they for sex or food or power or land or money, we take that special multi-tool out of the kit bag. We look for the device we need to satisfy the craving at hand, and then employ it to fashion patience, and cunning, and menacing, and dividing and conquering, and playing poor me, and ensnaring, and aggressing passively, and bribing and all the things becoming of the most gifted and advanced creature on the planet. From nicking your diabetic French teacher's chocolate to invading another continent, we come up with these excuses for our desires. We create names for them, such as ideologies, or morals, or vision, or evolution, or progress, or protectionism, or crusades, or the interminably cloudy collective "mission".

But let's be honest, shall we? Mostly, it's just being a C.U.N.T.

We'd better get out of this puddle, Kin. My extremities have gone numb.

What about K.I.N? Hah, no, it's not the antidote. We're aiming to get beyond duality on this journey at some point, aren't we? It will serve a purpose at the right moment. I hope. Christ, I'm only 21,000 words in. This could still go anywhere, my brave and kindly companion. While we're thinking of Friedrich, balance this on the palette of your mind as we head off: "What compels us to assume there exists an essential antithesis between 'true' and 'false'?" Don't go crazy, now. No more shock treatment.

Best foot forward, then. Is that the right – or the left? Dualities, eh? Fuck it.

One...

Two......

Any Way – As Long As It's Fourth

Who lives like dog will die like dog.

- G.I. Gurdjieff

They were the best of times, they were the worst of times.

How old are you, Kin? Teens? Twenties? Thirties? Over the hill? Hah. That oscillating line. By the time I was fifteen, I knew something was wrong. It wasn't just my parents' marriage that signalled it. I was already aware that their outwardly sanctioned social contract and its co-dependent private relationship was flawed. Perhaps it's the same with all marriages, I figured, what could I know back then? As the eldest child, I'd already been granted reluctant access to the conflicted inner circle of their tussling binary world. Yet it was something more. That "splinter in my mind", to borrow from the as yet unreleased social game-shifter, *The Matrix*, was busy burrowing. There *was* something wrong with the world. My education for said mind – one of the best, according to the standards of many – was out of tune with another less definable, more potent frequency growing within me: the evolution of my heart. Like the dutiful, privileged kid that I was, however, I kept on swallowing it down. I knew that a point was coming. Like the stomach beneath it, a human heart contains only so much space. If it can't digest the food that's being piled into it, there's going to be a moment where it pops.

That happened when I was nineteen.

I'd made the grades and filled in all the right application forms. "I want to be an actor," I replied when I asked myself the inevitable question the authorities always pose to young people who are struggling merely to be: "What do you want to do with your life?" Actor, writer, director – something arty and creative that didn't involve advertising, that was pretty much all I knew. Well, that didn't count as a proper career choice. "You need to choose a vocation: something useful that will earn you money. I don't want you to have to struggle like..." Blah blah. I didn't have a ready repost, however. It was years before I would pen the line:

"If you deny a man his struggle, you take away his only true birthright."

Could've been a contender. In any case, there's nothing more annoying than a smart-arsed adolescent, so I went for what I thought was a fair middle ground. I'd apply to read English. At Oxford, of course. Follow in the footsteps of Lewis and Tolkien et al.

Well, that still wouldn't wash. The nearest I could get to a compromise was to go for Politics, Philosophy and Economics. The middle one at least was of some interest. It wasn't enough. They saw through the thin veil of poorly applied enthusiasm (was it my acting, or was my heart already in rebellion mode?) and a few months later I found myself studying Law at a second-tier university. In a pub. Drinking whisky. And getting stoned.

What a cliché! That's the worst part. You know how it is when you're angry, and young, and so damn justified: you read all the stuff off the syllabus, and find Wilson's *The Outsider*, and Hesse, and Gibran, and Tolstoy's *The Cossacks*, and Goethe, and Kerouac, and Camus, and Ginsberg, and all those other howlers. So great, you're not alone – and now I'm in the same class as all of these heroic losers? Fuck.

I drank more, smoked more, started on other things, pestered women, hit the gym, got in my car and drove fast. All in the same day, oftentimes. I think I made just over half a dozen lectures in two years. Somehow, the over-stuffed grey matter in my head kept on gurning. To my wrath and heartrending disappointment, I passed my first year exams. I didn't make the same mistake second time around. The most fun I had in my entire academic career was the 'essays' I wrote to my invisible examiners. My situation wasn't their fault. As humans, though, I swore as I scrawled automatically through gritted teeth, the least they could fucking do is notice.

"I failed my exams," I told my father when I finally crawled home for the holidays.

"Let's wait and see," said he stoically, puffing on his Havana. I picked up my guitar and smugly belted out Dylan's *The Times They Are A Changing*, with emphasis on verse four. He smiled at that. "You know, I saw him at the Troubadour? London, 1962." I could've smashed the guitar, but I knew the line was drawn. I'd already won.

Then I was free. Free of that system, anyway. Out of the frying pan. Into the volcano.

If I'd actually gone to talk to someone that year, my road would have no doubt been quite different. In hindsight, it's clear that that was when I had my first proper mental breakdown, as the episodes were called in the social sector I inhabited. I was also into self-harming – scissors and hot knives and cigarettes were the standard game. Mood swings and depression were my daily bread and water, washed down with cheap Scotch and an amino acid shake. Part of me still wants to be the one to listen to that young guy; at the least, give him a big hug. Ask 'The Question'. I can do that now, of course. The readiness is all. Back then, I'm pretty sure he wouldn't have wanted it. You can't always save a life.

I wasn't alone, much as I often tried to be. There were people who cared, strangers and close friends, fellow outcasts and all in-between. Some have remained: if you're reading, you know who you are. If I ever forgot to thank you, I hope you know that in remembering your kindnesses, I do so now. One of them, closer in essence than my own skin, I have not seen again. Some disappear for a time. Others leave for ever.

Where are you, Kidal, my brother, my Kin? I am Jasur – can you see that you will always be my friend?

I'm writing you now just to see if you're better. Sincerely...

o

The trouble is, the older you get, the harder it is to change course. What say you, Kin? Let's not worry about the whole "change the world vs change yourself" debate just now. In the constant bid to both become and kill the Buddha, maybe it's fair to express once more the inevitability of change allied to the wish that it happen in consciousness. By choosing another path, the right change may visit you. With grace. Maybe? Bygones. It's bloody, tough work to alter your own programming. With the cycles of years, it gets tougher still, and not necessarily more sanguine.

What about you, Kin? What stage of the road were you at when we met and commenced upon this spontaneous, tumbling road trip together? What station do you find yourself at now? Are you still young? Do you have hope, and vigour; anxiety and resolve? Is there too much life, running through your veins, going to waste? (Thank you 'the other Robbie' Williams: like dog roses on a dung heap, our guides can appear in the most unexpected of places.) Whatever you're feeling and contemplating about your lot in this crazy scheme, know this: **never give up**. Yes, my Beloved Kin – that's you I'm talking to. Seeing as we're back on the trail, now, and this rocky path of ours can be hard, allow me to share another moment from our tattered map, *Excalibur*.

It comes after Perceval has narrowly escaped death by hanging from a grisly tree at the hands of Mordred. Alone with nothing and reduced to animal survival in the wasteland, one day he witnesses another Quest Knight, the convert and profoundly loyal Uryens, being hunted down by Mordred and his posse. He is the last of Perceval's companions, and he is left for dead with a spear wound at the edge of a misty lake. When Perceval finally reaches him, it is too late. Close to death, Uryens recognises his brother in arms and says: "Perceval, never give up the Quest."

"I saw the Grail, Uryens," Perceval replies. "It was in my grasp. I failed."

"You are the last of us," the other beseeches him.

Perceval lowers his gaze. "I am not worthy."

"Try again. You must. You...must. Listen! Follow. They call you." With that, the older knight breathes his last.

Whatever has happened to you so far, my Kin, whatever is yet to come: as a battered older knight to a younger flame, remember this: *try again*. You must. You can. They are always calling.

And what about the rest of you, hey Kin? How do *you* find yourself? A bit battered, like your limping companion here? A bit beaten, or wounded, or grudgingly set in your ways? Are you simply low on fuel, and patience, just too jaded to take any path now than the one you already know? Tell me: are you still breathing as you read these words, the ones I'm transmitting especially for you? If you are, stick around, and be ready. Your play's not over yet.

Maybe you think you've won your Grail? Perhaps you're still reading this out of simple intellectual curiosity. I know, crazy isn't it: all that juicy stuff online and still you'd rather be here? You must be missing *something*. Are you content? Did you win, have you really fulfilled all your heart's desires? Could be you're merely a cynic. "Yeah, yeah, I've been through all this psycho-spiritual crap before. Welcome to the real world." Well, it's what you make it, Kin. Too obvious a platitude? Careful – I'll quote Wilde or Einstein at you. That'll piss you off.

Fifteen to twenty-five: I reckon those are the best and the worst. They are the years when you really get to explore and test your extremes: physically, emotionally, mentally. Spiritually? Haha. There's a final graduation exam for that. Depending on your mythology, it involves either nothing, angels, or an emaciated mugger in a hoodie with a scythe.

Whether you choose to remain within or exit the system you were born from, as a human at some point you're likely to search for a sense of either significance, meaning or both as you navigate your environment. These are the best years to do that. You can have kids if you want, or by accident ("But you said it'd be all right! Dang...") but your biology isn't making it a top priority. Ditto a permanent partner – depending on your society, of course, some start young (very young), though in the western world and other places where change mottles the evolving demographic, being in a monogamous relationship isn't an intrinsic social obligation anymore. You can try any job you want. Every job. Get fired, get another – grouchy bosses will always be looking for fresh feet and the blind will to serve. Canon fodder. You can live anywhere, go anywhere, kill your body all night and resurrect like a newborn each morning. Fall in love, study, make mistakes, be forgiven. Above all, yield to that enviable belief only gilded youth can afford: that you have time.

For me, those days were heady and impassioned and high. Low, too, of course. The old DT – a useful acronym, especially when blurred. Moving to the city, through a series of bedrooms I found my way to lodgings in a hive on the same frequency as mine. It was a four-storey townhouse on the perfectly named Grimstown Road, and all the characters Prince Hal could have wanted were there. It enveloped my abraded nervous receptors like a tenderly soiled moleskin glove.

The chatelaine was a refugee from marriage, as magnanimous as she was broken, and she opened her heart and her home to this collective of waifs and strays. We called her Mama Bear. My bunk was the sofa in the living room – it would have been condemned had we not burned it on the street outside when the house was eventually sold – and I couldn't have been happier in the Emir's own damask chamber. Mama Bear's two sons were my essence Kin, as howling and unruly as I, and we walked and staggered and danced on the razor's edge through dusk and through dawn till night and day lost their hold on our plans. Not that we didn't have plans. Amid the capering and the music and the girls, we set out our attack on the status quo. Kin One was a mad genius architect and landscaper, to him fell the task of remaking our sprawling, groping physical environment. Little brother, Kin Two, had a brain for The System: he would play the City and its overlords in the financial darklands at their own monstrous game, win, and so provide the chthonic marching fuel that would take us to our goal. And me? My job was the mission statement. Propaganda. Transmit the message, rouse the awakening dead, unreal city, revive the walking corpses and outwit the Devil with his own devious hand.

Well – you've gotta try, don't you, Kin? If you want to hit the moon, sometimes you have to target the stars.

The Fellowship. Yes, we succumbed wantonly to ideals. That didn't mean we were lazy. We had off-weeks, sure, when the vine was ripe, we squeezed and gratefully guzzled all this life can offer. But the Quest cannot be abandoned solely for pleasure, too much of it tarnishes even the holiest of cups. We worked shitty jobs. Used and schmoozed and abused every contact. We had our own resident house angel – the level-headed roommate, we called her aptly "Nanny" – who dragged us out of our sybaritic pits in the morning and force-fed us solids in the twilight to keep us grounded. I wrote my first novel. A children's book, for adults, it mined the seam of my early heroes: Lewis Carroll, Richard Bach, Wilde, St Exupéry. In it, a small grockle, named Someone, goes in search of his Tale. He meets an old veteran mentor, a pelican, who takes him under his wing. His name? Of course: Perceval. Travelling across the Desert of Information and into the Land of

Knowledge they eventually arrive at a castle. There, to their surprise they find – but wait. I got myself an agent. Deals were discussed and timelines established. I started browsing the classifieds for the latest Kawasaki super-sportsbike. I waited some more. The gun had obviously misfired.

If you're a page-to-screen commissioning editor working at Disney, reading this in a coffee break or on an airplane to meet with some dubiously touted new breakout Y/A author, look me up. There's a print-ready version knocking around somewhere in the vaults of this Death Star on which I type. Back in the day, I should have followed up on the call from the kindly senior editor who took the time to offer her experienced observations on some of the overwrought sections of the text. Should have responded to my agent's suggestion that there were often too many conflicting voices for the target reader demographic. Perhaps, I should have contacted the illustrator I was recommended by a young publishing friend, rather than try to seduce her and then go out on a 36-hour drinking binge. But what did they know?

I was young. What did I?

Damn it. I'm off again, Kin. You've got to stop me sometimes when I'm rambling. You know that tune, *Rambling Man*, by our beautiful Kin soul Laura Marling? Ah, now there's a way... Check the video. Look at the birds. I have to say, in a sense you're lucky. When I started the first version of this draft, over a decade ago, it was going to be a novel. Or a memoir posing as a novel

– something across the boundaries. But then Will Self, a real novelist, said it: the novel is dead. Actually, he said it twice. These days, I try to listen to those who know more than me. They're not hard to find.

So I gave up the novel idea. I had to reach you, Kin, you see? Fast. What about a memoir? Narrative non-fiction? I got about eleven thousand words in. Still too much about me. What am I saying?

Balance, Kin. Our stories can help us, sure. If we invest in them too heavily, though, they can also bind us to the past – a past that need not dictate our future. We need to keep focus on what is essential: the transmission. It's the living element in the tale, the part that is ever changing, ever seeking a new direction, pointing us towards our ultimate goal. I'm keeping this tight as I can. Like I said back when, I'm not trying to show you a "way". The stories I'm sharing are not your guide. They are just a companion, a touch on the tiller, a light hand on the wheel, as you follow yours. When we wobble, I'll show you the practice. I'm not saying it'll get you to Eden, or make you rich or famous. But when you're up there on that razor's edge, alone, it could save your life.

A learned man once said that when you're tired of London, you're tired of life. Amen to that, brother.

Five years after I'd first arrived, liberated and brimming with ideas, the city still looked the same. My new brothers and me no longer felt like fresh cadets serving a noble revolutionary cause. We felt like bloodied veterans. Kin One had made some advances through green-fingered fringe skirmishes, but was succumbing to alcohol-infected wounds. Kin Two had hit a wall in the financial campaign and, following consensus advice, gone back to university so that he could hone the engines of war deemed indispensable against the dragons of Mammon. And me?

I was nearing empty. My inner demiurge kept spewing words: drafts and mission statements and midnight visions and some decidedly rotten egg poetry. I was living with my wild Kin soul buddy, Alex, in once smart-bourgeois digs that by consensus had now gained the honorific title of "The Dog Pit", and with our Kin we railed against the monotonous urban aspirations of our fellows and bowed to Bacchus and danced with maenads through the nighttimes' sodium-toxic glow. By day, I'd been through at least a couple of dozen jobs, from retail to warehouse packaging to courier to indie TV researcher, handyman, waiter, tutor and production assistant. The latter meaning I made the coffee, cleaned up the film studio and wiped the mouth of the actor as she spat out the cold soup at the centre of that month's national ad campaign.

Do you know what they call that perfect soup tin we see in the commercials, Kin? The unparalleled bowl of cornflakes that receives the milk of heaven at 360 frames per second? The exploding fruit and nut chocolate bar that starts us involuntarily drooling and makes us suddenly drop everything and rush out to the corner store? On set, they call it "The Hero".

'Bring in the Hero!' shouts the first assistant director. Hours in preparation, the holy chalice that bears the 3-day stale crunchy wheat and raisin elixir is borne with reverence and laid on the altar beneath the studio lighting. Positions are marked. Cameras and light levels are checked. A hushed and awed silence settles over the assembled cast and crew. The mythical talisman – one of several gleaming new spoons from Ikea – is primed and held steady at the rim of the bowl. The director, high priest of the planet's most pervasive cult, is reclined in his foldaway fabric throne with an Italian espresso. He looks sombre, for as a conduit of divine power he bears unfathomable responsibility, and he strokes his chin thoughtfully. No doubt, he is wondering how best to share among the church's faithful the day's 5-figure collection. Then the first AD calls action. The pre-digital camera turns, a wheel of photographic fury capturing every frozen moment and turning it into narrative ecstasy. A few seconds later, apotheosis is achieved. The Hero has become a god. And woe betide the lowly production assistant who trips on a cable, bumps into the jig and spills the deified bowl of cereal before another shot can be taken.

Yeah, I was burned with London. London was bored with me. And inside, a thousand dreams were softly burning. Then came the call.

"Come to Florence." The voice was a thread in the labyrinth. We miss so much, in these digital days, with our amusingly labelled Smart Phones. A former flame and star sister – we shared the same terrestrial birth date – she had moved to the world's art capital (Italy, not SC) to learn traditional figure painting.

"You're not happy, you need a change of scene. Come out for a weekend, get inspired." Sometimes, we are wise to heed the council of the enchantress.

That was December. I stayed for a fortnight. The following May, having got a certificate to teach English as a foreign language (isn't that what every writer does?) I packed my faithful steed with every inanimate object I cared for and drove out there. Fast.

Don't worry. We're not going to detour again. I could easily relate an entire mini-series on the two years spent in this worshipped Renaissance Capital of Dreams. And nightmares. The characters, the ghosts of legends, the studios and bars. Of the Bukowski-quoting Balkan bar owner turned lifelong essence friend; of Apollonian sunsets and Dionysian nights; of screaming from deserted stone bridges and psychedelic conversations with world-famous statues; of conquests and rejections and botched attempts at threesomes with the wife of an absent industrial tycoon and the life-sick love child of Jim Morrison. More stories, more fables, more myths. We don't have an unlimited luggage allowance on this trip, do we, Kin? How much substance does it require to distil the lesson: it doesn't matter where you go, you only carry yourself with you?

I loved my time there. I loved our moment – the Second Fellowship. For the first time since teenage awareness of my innate sense of social separation, I felt I belonged somewhere. But something still wasn't right. The inner gremlins were still gnawing, still whispering, making ambushes. Saboteurs. As hard as I tried – oh man, did I try – I could not dance and drink, read or fuck or write them away.

Let us make use of our art to compress pregnant years into birthing paragraphs. While I was in Florence, *The Matrix* was released. You may love it, or loathe it, or it may slide off your Teflon-slick skin. It doesn't matter. What makes it relevant is that as a cultural signpost, the film stuck. As a reference, a meme, it's become part of our language in the ordinary world. "Stay the night, have a drink, you'll only hit traffic." "I'd love to, but I've got to get back to The Matrix. Big day at work tomorrow." Whether you feel it or not, it's in our present collective psyche.

I watched that film first one hungover afternoon and something went 'Boom'. Just as it had with *Excalibur* a decade before. I wasn't alone. Never mind the bullet time and the sets and the kung fu and the oh-so-cool Nokia banana phone (have you seen the eBay prices on those things?), never mind the occasionally cringeworthy lines and wooden acting: the film transmits a truth. What is it? I got mine. Remember, Kin: don't let anyone try to tell you yours.

What was uncanny – coincidental, fortuitous, serendipitous, freaky, pick an adjective, I felt them all – was the book I was reading at the time I first watched it. Since the great University Legal Fallout, my father and I had become friends. His acceptance of my atypical life path and tacit newfound support of my literary attempts both surprised and impressed me. How could the old boy have become so zen about things? He and my mother, and Mike the carpenter and his wife, among others, were still having meetings out in the small hours of Wednesday mornings. They gathered at his former boss's house, a retired orthopaedic surgeon I had always respected and admired, as a practitioner and human both. They weren't discussing traditional carpentry techniques. It was another work altogether they were involved in. As I prepared to leave my homeland, between playing Pink Floyd's *Mother* and Cat Stevens' *Father & Son* on our gently weeping guitars, we talked about it. I felt no pressure. But I was curious. Before I left for Florence, and with full consent, I liberated from the secret bookshelf in the library a select number of titles. Among them was the book that accompanied the Wachowskis' trending offering. You may have already guessed it. In any case, we can cut the literary foreplay: it was *In Search of the Miraculous* by P.D. Ouspensky. Don't know it? Put it on your reading list, Kin. It's a trip.

Through the pages of this revolutionary Russian-penned tome I entered into the world, as many have before and since, of Gurdjieff and The Fourth Way. Hold that automatic Wikipedia search for just a second, Kin, let me tell you what Gurdjieff meant to me at that moment: *a way out*. The system he elucidated – by admission not his own but simply "fragments of an unknown teaching" – claimed to make us realise our own helplessness in our sleepwalking life and show us a way through it, and beyond. A way to awaken. To become the real "I". To understand and experience for ourselves the truth of just why the world is so, well: fucked up.

Naturally, there were ideas I resisted. Some of the things Ouspensky claimed on Gurdjieff's part were outlandish, unscientific, apparently gibberish. When you're drowning, though, and someone throws you a life jacket, do you argue with the instructions or remonstrate that it's not your colour? Exactly. You tie that inflatable device around you just as the nice lady in the cabin tried to show you and pull like hell on those fumbly little toggles. Besides, beyond all educated reason, so much of it made sense.

Unlike the Bible, Gurdjieff's central tenet is not that the world is a mess because we humans are a sinful and wanton species, heedless of our penance to our creator or love to our fellows and due any minute for divine retribution. Nor even is our society a computer simulated programme run by a hyper-aware machine empire that is using our psychic-biological chemistry to replace the sun as an energy source. Though, in all fairness, there are marked similarities and that's closer than much of the aforementioned sacred book. According to George Ivanovich, the reason things are so F.U.B.A.R. down here is pretty simple: accidents. The history of our planet is littered with the fallout from some extremely dicey cosmic driving on the part of forces further up the universal food chain, and our lopsided, myopically egotistical view of ourselves and our place in the scheme of things is the result. Imagine Robin Williams playing the title role in the biopic, *Gurdjieff Hunting*, and you can almost hear him telling us: "It's not your fault, Kin. It's not your fault."

Which isn't to say it isn't our duty. The possibility that God was in the restroom when the Milky Way was being signed off for production is no reason to abandon all hope, break out the cyanide capsules and make like a lemming with two fingers waving at the stars. Even if that's what we feel like doing, what we're drawn to do when our self-magnifying structures all crack and we stare openly into the abyss, our calling is to struggle.

If you could choose only one, would it be work, or would it be leisure? Ask yourself truthfully. We all know how Camelot falls.

So why the Fourth Way? What about the other three? On the journey to self-awareness, self-realisation and self-mastery, Gurdjieff tells us there are three traditional ways we can take: the way of the fakir, the way of the monk and the way of the yogi. Each of these ways corresponds to focused work on oneself through a different part of the human system. The fakir works with the physical body, the monk with the emotions and the yogi with the intellectual brain. With correct effort, and depending on the individual's type, all of these ways may bring about the aforementioned self-mastery or, to avoid too much hair-splitting between different flavours in the homogeneously branded spiritual smoothie refrigerator, The Big "E" – enlightenment.

The trouble is, we tend to live in societies. The above ways are all well and good if you have a private mountain to hand, a monastery to hide in or a bunch of disciples who are happy to carry you around all day like a table. If, however, you prefer to take your slice of Samadhi with a shot of ordinary world and a daily planet chaser while you're here, they're not the most practical. In addition, Gurdjieff maintained that work on one element of the human being alone could result in a 'lopsided' individual. Thus, he proposed a fourth way to work on oneself. It was called also "The Way of the Sly Man". Or woman. (Yes, early 20th Century though it was, ladies were indeed most cordially invited.) On this way, the individual continues to live in ordinary, everyday life. It is the very experiences of being in the sham and drudgery of it all that gives us the friction required to melt down our programmed, habitual systems and, employing various techniques that promote within us a heightened level of alertness to and awareness of our machine-like selves, re-crystallise ourselves anew. Life is verily the teacher. We work simultaneously on all parts of the human organism – body, emotions, intellect – and, with right guidance and sustained effort, awaken from egoic slumber to break our spirit out of prison and back on the road to full and conscious being. Known to this day by students the world over as The Fourth Way, it is also known simply as: The Work.

I tell you, Kin: I was giddy as a double-hung hound. I found all the literature and devoured it whole. At school, as a typical angry young thing, I had gotten into weights. The frustration and the vexation I felt was pumped through blood and muscle and sinew, and when that fell short of turning me into the superman I wanted to be, I began to simultaneously feed my mind. All those books I've mentioned so far – tip of the iceberg. Classic philosophers, history, alternative history, religious texts and commentaries, new science, radical thinkers, all the usual suspects, lunatics and more in-between. Then Florence, and to art: painting and sculpture, literature and poetry, wine and women and song. The arts were my muse, my emotional centre the target. Do you see? I knew what it was to work on oneself. I'd been trying to all along. These three different bodies, they were crying out to be fed, and I'd nourished them as best I could. Blindly, without a guide or a mentor. Throwing them scraps, a whirlwind smorgasbord of young instinctive frenzy – a midnight service station feast. Now, I'd found a system. It was there, tried and tested, minutely described in detail, with a host of learned and often renowned observers over the previous century providing content in a clandestine world library.

Yes, I saw it all now: I *had* been living like a dog. Don't we all for much of the time? Loving whilst fearing our masters, reacting only to desires of the senses, territorial, defensive, blindly obedient to codes of which we have little understanding, constantly desiring attention, terrified of being abandoned, desperate to be allowed up on the bed one minute, the next biting the hand that feeds us, and generally pissing all over the place. I didn't want to be that creature any more. I wasn't going to die that way. This life was nothing without full, untrammelled, waking freedom.

I was going to take The Fourth.

EAT - AND BE EATEN

LEARNING IS EXPERIENCE. EVERYTHING ELSE IS JUST INFORMATION.

- ALBERT EINSTEIN (POSSIBLY)

Whoaaaaa! Easy now, Kin. Let's rein in our steeds for a moment. I can see the threshold up ahead. The weather's turning, we'll call a rest and camp here. You make a fire and I'll cook up something tasty and sustaining for the imminent challenge. We don't want to rush at it unprepared. The readiness – remember? An army marches on its stomach, after all.

Did you think we'd arrived already? I'm sorry to disappoint you, Kin. Life isn't always like the movies would have us dream it. Hollywood has a couple of hours to tell the whole story. You've got a whole life. It's very rare that the Hero's Journey unfolds in a scripted and linear fashion. We may reject the call a dozen times or more. Meet mentors and guides, face tests over time and cross what we think are great thresholds, then to find that we've only just scrabbled past level one. Often, we fall back again. We get a taste of some special world, the one we thought we wanted, only to find we don't like it there. Or we get scared. Or dismissive – "Hey: this isn't what I signed up for! Where's my promised Grail? Didn't I earn it already? I want enlightenment NOW!" So we return to the state we left in. Very often, we never see Wonderland again.

I've had that on my path with cities. First London was a threshold, then Florence. Paris was a base camp for a time – *ah, merci, la belle époque!* – and then I really went out into the cold. After the whole Gurdjieff underground movement fizzled out – we'll get to that, dear brother, sweet sister – I spent a frosty season alone on the mountain. I had to reset the compass. Steady the needle. It pointed me in the direction from which Gurdjieff and Ouspensky as an entity had first arisen, more than a century ago, now: Saint Petersburg. "Mother Russia." Unreal city! If you've not been, imagine Florence, substitute red wine with kilos of Vodka and jack the skyline up on steroids. Yes: St Petersburg was quite the gateway. But even that didn't usher me beyond the final veil.

How are you feeling? Are you enjoying this journey? I have to tell you, Kin, I'm impressed you've come this far. That's not blowing smoke up your donkey. Really. There are many who haven't reached this point. Why they haven't is not a matter with which to overly concern ourselves. Live and let live, and all that. It could be because they're not ready to surrender to the Quest. Maybe, it's a simple case of TMI – Too Much Information. More likely, and I'm happy to confide in you and share this, I expect they just think I'm a C.U.N.T. And they wouldn't be wrong in that assertion. We all wear that mantle on occasion, sometimes even when we're trying to be the opposite. Unless...

Maybe this whole essay so far is just a test.

?

Bygones. How's that fire? That's it, Kin: build it up and then burn it slow. There's nothing like a good campfire with your buddy. Seeing as we're going to take a breather here, let's talk about that other issue. I alluded to it briefly above: TMI. It concerns us very much in our present predicament, and I've cooked us up something juicy to chew on. Are you ready to chow? *Bon appétit...*

It was the age of information – it was the age of dumbass: I wonder how future generations will define the times we now find ourselves in? Assuming there are any. Let's bring ourselves up to speed: since I first entered the subterranean realm of The Fourth Way at the turn of the Millennium, over twenty years have passed. Back in 2000, there were somewhere between 360 and 415 million people online, depending on where you look from January through December. Worldwide. Most of them were in the US and Europe. Even there, less than a third of the population was actually using the web. In 1997, there were 10 million email users signed up to a free email service. Or about the equivalent of one large western city. In 1999, there were just over 3 million websites on the internet. You couldn't look at them or send emails on your phone, however. The Smart Phone was still a few years off. Here's the one I like: in 2000, the total percentage of the world population online was just over 7%.

Today – well, we can check it now, can't we? Instantly. Today, there are nearly 2 *billion* websites on the net. Not all of them are live, but it still leaves plenty to choose from. Over 57% of the world is online. So little? Well, it doesn't all look like Kansas out there, Toto. That's still well over 4 billion human beings checking out their screens on a near daily, if not hourly, basis. Number of email accounts? Despite it being widely considered old technology and 'seriously uncool' among the new generation, there are 3.9 billion email users worldwide. In the US, almost 90% of the population has an account, and the average American worker receives more than 120 emails per day. You don't have to be home or in your office to reply to them, either. Over half the humans on the planet these days are mobile internet guzzlers, with just under 3 billion of them being registered Smart Phone users. Oh, and should it come as a surprise, China has the most users in the world: almost a billion, up from 22.5 million in 2000.

No doubt, by the time you're reading this, these statistics too will be well out of date. Time, like an ever rolling stream, my friend.

What is the currency in which this colossal network trades, on which it is built, through which it functions, for which we mine it? Of course: information. On the internet, we find this information carefully laid out for us to make it easy to assimilate. It comes to us, borrowing a system from a supposedly obsolete technology, in the form of pages. Lots of them, in fact.

Do you know how many pages Google indexes at the moment? 35 trillion. Which seems a lot. However, all things being relative, it isn't. From a study earlier this year, it was estimated that there were extant 17.5 quadrillion pages on the internet. We're talking about a thousand million million. How does that look? Something like this:

17,500,000,000,000,000 pages.

Michel, *mon ami,* I see your library, and I raise you...

How much of that is useful? To us? To me? To you?

Let us pause for a while in Montaigne's medieval skyscraper. Going up – Level 3 – Penthouse Suite. Welcome to the writer-philosopher's beautifully curated bookshelves. We said earlier that it was estimated he had in his possession around 1,500 volumes. At the time, for a private collection, that would have been considered pretty extensive. If we Google quickly for a point of reference, we find a study from a few years back of 2,500 of the New York Times' bestsellers and notable books list. The average length of said books was 400 pages. Now, many of Michel's prides and joys would undoubtedly have been what we would consider in our own time to be pamphlets or short treatises. Nonetheless, if we extemporise with a nod to our modern era, that would put Montaigne's browsing limit at a maximum of 600,000 pages. From these, and from his own life experiences, deliberations and downloads from the ether, he distilled and concocted 1,344 pages of mental fodder. (*The Complete Essays,* Penguin Classics edition) Out of which, around 5-10 pages worth are probably trending in quote form on the internet currently, covering, as I maintained earlier (debates invited) illustrations of and pointers to the overall state of our human condition.

How many words do we need to live by?

Of course, as with our Egyptian building contractor from earlier, words are often used for practical undertakings as well as merely working out the meaning of life. There are a lot of pages dedicated to trade: stuff and services we buy and sell. 'How to' fixes for everything, from a leaky tap to a recalcitrant interplanetary rocket. Online bureaucracy, and forms, and speeding fines – all of that sexy day-to-day stuff. Speaking of which, there's a lot of gratuitous pleasure on offer, too. Who needs words when we have videos, eh? It's not all live concerts and cuddly animals, either. You weren't aware? Of course you weren't, Kin. Not you. And while there's a strong whiff of the urban myth about 70% of the net being dedicated to porn (figures for now put it at around 4-5%), did you know that 40 million Americans regularly visit said sites? 35% of all internet downloads are apparently related to heaving naked bodies? No wonder there aren't any trees left: that's a hell of a lot of tissues. On an output to return index, porn punches seriously above its weight. If only we could make a business out of it somehow, hmm.

There's an obvious bottom line here (no pun, really): the internet presents us with a surfeit of information. There is too much for any one human, or even enormous group of humans, to ingest and process in this lifetime. Even if 99.9% of the pages online could be canned, written off as unnecessary to human survival, and all the money shots wiped from the servers, you'd still need a more powerful processor than the one between your ears to get through a tiny umpteenth of it before you die. Even if you could, would you really want to?

Let's not talk about the internet too much more. We didn't come out here together to sit at the fireside and discuss what's already being examined a million and one ways online. Should we wish, we can do that when and if we return. Breathe, Kin. We were nearing the threshold. As we do so, what is more pertinent for us heroes is not so much what information is available, nor even which bits of it are of themselves "good" or "bad". On that last matter, as a species, it's unlikely we will ever arrive at a consensus. What is more important for you and me right now is quite straightforward and mundane: the manner in which we eat it.

There's an old parable doing the rounds here at the start of the 21st Century. It's the one about the two wolves. Do you know it? Pull up your poncho and draw closer. I'll tell it again, just to make sure we at least, Kin, are on the same page:

An old Cherokee grandfather is talking to his grandson. "There is a fight going on inside me," he tells the boy. "It is a savage battle between two wolves. One of these wolves is bad: it is anger, it is hatred, it is greed, it is deceit, it is self-pity, it is sorrow, it is pride.

"The other wolf is good: it is love, it is compassion, it is faith, it is humility, it is patience, it is kindness, it is truth. This battle rages throughout my entire life, and it is inside of you, too. It is inside every human being."

"Which wolf wins?" the grandson asks.

His grandfather regards him and replies: "The one you feed."

Lovely, isn't it? The one you feed. We can all relate to that. It's up there with the one about the Swallow, but with more feeling. Pathos, even. The boy – learning that from here on in he will consider his life to be a constant battle. The end of innocence. In any case, he needn't worry. The story isn't true.

How so? Of course: the details are all online.

The grandfather wasn't a Cherokee in the original (it would be tricky, as the word "Cherokee" is a US government invention, there was no such tribe), he was an Inuit, and the tale was invented by a controversial Christian evangelist in a book published in 1978. Some versions of the tale contain a black wolf and a white wolf representing the two sides. Have a guess: which colour represents evil? Bingo. Which, again, is a European invention and nothing to do with Native American culture. Lastly for now (happy browsing after) the notion of all humans being intrinsically comprised of a dualist nature, sinful and good, would be similarly anathema to a Native American or, as they were mistakenly labelled for a little too long, Indian. They had no concept in their tradition of the notion of original sin. Clearly, the author of the tale is on a particular ticket for his own brand of religious insight.

Is the above all clear and correct? I don't know, Kin. I've just learned all this in the last ten minutes. You tell me: which pages should we trust?

This is where we find ourselves. It's so easy to feed off the information at hand. We don't have to hunt for it, earn it, carefully collate it or rely on magical chance encounters with teachers who guide us to it and help us uncover it. It's just there. Cheap. Easy. We hardly have to twitch our thumbs. Imagine Yellowstone Park, or the Black Rock Desert or, I don't know – Africa – laid out from end to end and side to side with contiguous bumper family picnics. Admission to the world's greatest feast is only $2.99 a month, payable to your local network provider. Er, no, we can't tell you exactly where all the information comes from. No, it's not all fresh or organic, there may be artificial colourings, additives, preservatives and GM foodstuffs contained in some of the picnics. Yes, you can count on some palm oil. For some of the hampers there is an additional cost. Erm, we believe the produce is generally sourced from ethically approved cultivators, but we can't be certain. We've laid out some sections with arrows for you to follow, based on an algorithm that notes your habitual grazing patterns: it overlooks the fact that you've probably arrived here already stuffed full of existing programmes, but there's so much to choose from, I'm sure you won't notice. You'll just have to follow your nose. Have a nice meal!

And we wolf it down (pun intended that time), like famished Tasmanian devils on a sheep farm, and proudly tell ourselves and others on social media that, thanks to our participation in this global informational banquet, we now **know** something.

Hooey.

Let's not misunderstand one another, Kin. There's plenty of good stuff online. The internet is an incredible tool; it has the power to connect the world; to reduce our environmental impact – blah blah. The internet is not the problem. The problem is: how do we discern? That which is positive for our being, from that which is not?

Moreover, how do we grow? I mean in knowledge, in understanding. In wisdom. We can all chuckle at the trending Twitter meme that "knowledge is knowing a tomato is a fruit; wisdom is not putting it in a fruit salad", but does adding that to our short-term browsing memory bank actually make us any wiser? Maybe, if we change our habits and take in on a daily basis only positive and educational info, with time our mysterious subconscious processors may alchemically transform our way of thinking and, subsequently, behaviour. It's not a great stretch for us to see that, if information is the food for our minds, ultimately we are in broad terms the result of what we eat. To follow on from the contentious yet also potentially useful parable above, does that mean we can actually choose? That in order to grow ourselves in the manner that we wish, all we really need do is improve our mind's diet?

Gurdjieff thought so. Here is one of his tenets: "All psychic processes are material."

In The Work, students are invited to experience and test for themselves various fundamental assertions about life on our planet. One of these involves the discovery of our place as humans in the grand scheme of things, graphically represented in a theory called The Food Diagram. A concept familiar to anyone who can remember a 5th Grade biology class, the principle is the same as the food chain in the animal kingdom: the little guys eat the plants, the medium guys eat the little guys, great big guys eat the medium guys and, eventually, in the grave tones of James Earl Jones Simba's dad Mufasa in *The Lion King*, the big guys die and become the grass. So the cycle runs.

With Gurdjieff's chain, there are some subtle additions. Not constrained to life on Earth, the universal cycle loops all the way from 'Holy The Firm' or 'The Absolute' at the lowest point of the diagram, to 'Holy God' or 'The Absolute' once more at the top, with 'Holy The Immortal' in the middle. In this middle section, we find man, above plants and animals, behind angels and archangels on a shared horizontal axis. Don't panic, non-theists – there's a lot of allegory in these parts. What's fascinating about this system is that it can also be stripped of all religious allusion and be presented perfectly well in mathematical format. If that's your thing, seek and be merry. That noble and worthy rabbit hole is not one I am well equipped to guide you through.

In base terms, Kin, it's this: we humans have an issue. Our limited historical worldview, at least until relatively recently in some quarters, has traditionally put us on a pedestal at the top of the cosmic food chain, with only this supernatural figure a.k.a. "God", our creator, positioned above us. The Food Diagram – purportedly a "fragment" of this very ancient knowledge rediscovered by Gurdjieff and his buddies back in the late 1800s – shakes that up and breaks it down. Between us and the Big Guy, there are further levels. Just as we feed on those below us, so we are being food for them. We do not say a prayer, pass "Stop" and collect everlasting life. That's just a tale we were sold, way back when lying was first invented.

The Universe eats us. This is not an allegory.

As humans, according to G, as he is also known, we have three kinds of food. First, and most coarse, is the food we eat daily to sustain our meat bodies: solids and liquids, plants and animals (should you wish). Secondly, there is the air we breathe. Thirdly, there are our impressions.

We can live without the first type for days, if need be, until our physical body throws in the towel. The second, air, for minutes at most. If we stop eating impressions, however, it will take only a few moments for the organism to expire.

Disclaimer: don't try this at home.

The Work or Fourth Way is very much concerned with the business of growing our bodies. The reason for this is that, as stated above, what happens psychically also affects us materially, in the physically manifest universe. Cue the sensitive debates around such phenomena as the Placebo Effect and whether it's actually possible to die of a broken heart. In this fluid perceived realm of two-way energetic exchange on which our laws of physics are based, this means that what happens physically also affects us psychically. Example: drugs, music, sex, pain, chocolate. When it comes to putting substances into our mouths and thus into our alimentary canals, that all seems fairly obvious. You might even say instinctive. With air, it's not so clear. However, we know about what happens when you have fresh air as opposed to polluted air for your daily intake, and vice versa. It's no surprise that a lot of meditative and spiritual practices place breathing techniques high on their agendas. When it comes to impressions – now that is a head-scratcher, isn't it?

Lots of philosophers and scientists have played with this notion. Isolation tanks and thought experiments have attempted to give us a clue as to how it would be to be totally deprived of our senses – not as in sleep, where the nervous system is still functioning, albeit on a 'default' setting: we're talking about that opposite of conscious again. Call it oblivion. Perhaps by the time you're reading this, some clever bods have figured it out. I hope they or their test subjects made it back okay. Maybe the closest we can get to conceptualising it for now is to return once more to the world of imagination and film: if you die in The Matrix, you die in real life. The body cannot live without the mind.

Our impressions in life are the food which create and maintain and grow our psychic body. Our minds. If you took two children of the same age, one from a cosy upbringing in, say, Montana, and another from war-ravaged Syria, and charted their growth into adulthood you would no doubt, even without a specifically defined scientific scale with which to measure it, be able to observe clear differences in the composition of their respective psyches. The impressions, the information, the food their minds have received, absorbed and excreted have resulted in their mental bodies having a very different makeup.

Back in the mathematics class, The Food Diagram shows us how these three levels of food and body creation all interlink. The physical food takes us so far on our journey up towards the top of the chart, then its cycle reaches its limit and descends once more. Our physical body eventually dies and we once more "become the grass". Air can extend a part of our existence onto a higher plane, till again we reach a limit, a ceiling, which we cannot surpass.

And impressions?

Via the inner processes we engage when we consciously harness our mind to the rest of our earthly bodies, the information from impressions is transmuted to create our soul. In the world of The Fourth Way, we don't automatically get one of these with our terrestrial welcome pack. This is where the lauded and nebulous notion of choice enters the fray.

We can, and most of us do, pass through this life simply "letting the programme run", that is: we spend our lives essentially asleep. We believe ourselves conscious – to a degree, we are – but on our sliding scale, it's a low level thereof. To look through a glass darkly, we live below a required threshold of consciousness to move further up the food chain. To get beyond it, we have to wake up. We have to shock ourselves out of our inherited and conditioned state. It is not our birthright, but it is our destiny to develop a soul in this mortal life. Whether we determine to or not, however, ultimately is up to us.

If we accept and adhere to the process and do it well, we can get beyond being cosmic bar snacks for the ravenous echelons immediately above. "Hands off, Zaqiel: let the Earth eat my flesh and you can nibble on my astral crust, but this soul is reserved for something higher." If we don't decide to step up and get our soul growing, well: we're Moon food, as G would have it. This majestic being, this human, so noble in reason, so infinite in faculty, is returned to the dust of the terrestrial realm. We lose it all and, if the judges are generous, come back down again to give it another try. A thousand times or more, if necessary.

If you're a Buddhist, that will sound familiar. If you're not, well, this is the 21st Century: we can find the expression of the notion everywhere, from perfume brands to the Internet of Things. It's called Samsara.

Maybe our obstacle isn't the limitless internet feast of information on offer per se. Our brains can only handle and process so much information, true, but that's nothing new. Over the centuries, many a learned scholar has suffered the consequences of reading too many books and listening to too many high-brow lectures. Witness *The Incredible Book-Eating Boy*. It may not even be TMA – Too Much Analysis – that stands between us and our Grail of an elevated and wholesome sense of being, though that could be nearer the mark. When we examine something in too much detail, we invariably compare it to all kinds of other related material, until the thing itself risks losing meaning or distinct identity amid the ceaseless acts of cross-pollination. Perhaps our stumbling block is actually, but for our deeply entrenched habits, more simply resolvable. Gurdjieff, again, offers us guidance. What we need to be on our lookout for are the telltale signs of TMC: Too Much Considering.

It's four in the morning, the end of December...

Thank you, my patron Saint, dear Leonard of C. Actually, it's not. It's the start of December, and it's coming up to ten at night. Put another log on that fire, Kin. My fingers are cold in my tower. These battered old bones, eh?

It's great time travelling, isn't it? You may not have moved from our cosy little camp, out on bare mountain, and in truth, neither have I – I'm right here with you still, Kin: huddling down against the threatening sky, sharing a mug of cocoa, or stronger, chattering on about how we can save ourselves as the threshold looms before us. My mind is, at any rate. My spirit – my soul, even, if I have such a thing.

Meanwhile, this complaining meat body of mine, this stubborn mid-life donkey, is busting for a pee. Give us just a second there, my friend. I'll understand if you feel the urge to do the same.

o

With you again. I made the most of that. Four flights down from where I hammer out my love to you – you who, whether you consciously chose it or not, are now also here with me – I found my wife by another fire. It's an old wood stove, you see, in our extremely old-fashioned kitchen. Being the generous soul that she is, a kettle was keeping hot for us both, beside a pot of herbal tea. From the garden, plucked and dried. Here, try: verbena and camomile, with a trace of dried orange. Roll that on the taste buds of your imagination. Tea and oranges – ah, she knows her stuff, this fine lady of mine.

All these words can be vexing, can't they, Kin? There's none knows that better than the wife of a writer, believe me. She bears most gracefully with the condition from which I and my fellow scratchers suffer.

'How is it going?' she asks and, not wanting to leave you out here alone for too long, I give her a quick résumé.

She listens first – a talent she has – and then says: 'The trouble with the internet and social media is how it lulls us into believing we're walking some path. But actually, we're not.'

I told her, sincerely, that that would do to complete the present chapter, and asked whether she'd like to finish the rest of the book. We'd have it on the editor's desktop well before Christmas. Sadly for you, she was happy at that point to call it a day.

I'll attempt to keep this concise now, Kin. We'll need our rest before the final chapter of Part One. After all this winding way, there's no putting it off any longer: the assault on the threshold. Towers will shudder, too, I'll warrant.

My lady is now snug in her bunk beneath us. Let us wish her sweet rest. It is a tumultuous world, outside. The winds are keening. I shouldn't be surprised if we have a storm before morning. So it is.

With that in mind, I'll not say too much more about our Mr Gurdjieff today. My task, as ever, is not to prescribe some way for you, Fourth or other, whatever its credentials. You can find all you need about it in a library, or online. Maybe. What I will say is this: without my meeting him, we wouldn't be here.

What my experience of The Fourth Way taught me was that if we want to get ahead on this Quest, we must learn to use all the tools at our disposal as we find them at the outset, even if on first acquaintance they appear suspect or frighteningly inadequate. When life's traps spring and enemies appear, it's extremely rare you get through with a perfect, rehearsed, heroic stroke of whatever talisman you may carry. The external world's "perfect" is seldom aligned with our own. This is where we must pay particular attention to one of the most dangerous, double-edged blades in our kit bag: the practice of Considering. To sign off on G's behalf, here is one of his aphorisms:

"Consider outwardly, always; inwardly, never."

When it comes to information contained in impressions, the potential – *potential* – ambrosia for our soul, this is the crucial distinction: focus on what that information wants of you first before you allow it in. Our habitual way of being is to just eat it without considering what it is, and *then* begin chewing it over once we've received it and started to absorb it into our very fabric. Once we've ingested the information into our system, we begin to compare it with what is already percolating around inside us: all our habits, our education, our natural predispositions, our experiences and beliefs and prejudices. That's where we judge it, criticise it, like it, try to reject it, or it gives us a tingle in the right spot so that we just go on licking, like Pooh inside his honey pot, but it's already too late. We are not eating: we're being eaten. From both above and below. If we make it to the special world, this is going to be of supreme importance. It is a practice to help us discern.

If the story of the two wolves is helpful to you, as it has been to me in our duality-encoded realm, then use it. There is even an excellent podcast named after it called The One You Feed. I don't personally know the guys who created it, but it's helped me along my way at times. In this, and with everything you find online; in broadcasts, podcasts, on TV, in lectures, the news, commercials, in books – even this very one: never forget to consider outwardly what the information wants to achieve in you. Everything that is moving in our universe has an agenda.

How can you tell before you swallow it, you say? Same as you do with all food. Smell it. How does it smell? Taste it. Is it sweet, or sour? Does it have a chemical tang? Does it make you want to retch? Is it familiar, your daily bread, only you're so used to it that you forget it's packed full of extra sugar and preservatives and is damaging your health? Crucially, does it taste too good to be true?

The aphorism on Considering works especially well for people, too. This should come as no surprise: after all, we people really are just a bunch of constantly shifting information posing as multi-cellular living organisms. So it's the same deal: consider others – but out there. See what they are seeing. What their agenda is, and what their need. Empathise. Don't bring it all inside. It's not all about you: your opinion, your view, your judgment, your current programme, your entitlement, your projection. That's where all your "bad wolf" comes from. Lest we forget: wolves are great howlers.

As my very dear wife so economically observes, let's watch ourselves carefully as we traverse the marshes of self-belief. By all means, like #wordstoliveby. Follow Echkart, and Rumi quotes, and Ram Dass and Tony Robbins and Brene Brown and Oprah – Sam Harris, Joe Rogan, Marianne Williamson, God, Justin Bieber, Kate Upton, POTUS and Beelzebub himself, if you must. Some of whom, no doubt, may be wonderful, insightful and solace-giving guides. Just beware: as we surf the boundless oceans of the web and scroll through our social media feeds, when they leap out as us, don't automatically let them in. Lest we are tempted to say to ourselves (and others): see? I know something. I'm on the path. I mean it modestly, but I have the insight, I am initiated, I am a cut above. I'm connected to The Source.

I #eatwisdom.
I refer you to Michel's quote in the first chapter.
Hashtag.

Demolition, Man

He who can go to the fountain does not go to the water-jar.

- Leonardo Da Vinci

Morning, Kin. This is the day. Our day. We're just a howl away.

Breathe...

From my tower, I see storm clouds over the trees. Worn doors on neighbours' barns are battened down; cattle outside low sharply beneath ribbons of rain, calling for lost calves. They will not find them. Like the swallows of summer, their children are gone. Unlike the birds, they will not return. Eat and be eaten. Not everyone can choose.

Inside, all is quiet. My treasures are at school. My wife tends the fire downstairs. Inevitably, some heat will slowly rise. But there is a cold, up here, in the ruins of these old battlements: a deep cold that will not easily be thawed.

"If to be warmed, then I must freeze and quake in frigid purgatorial fires..."

Thank you, Thomas Stearns. You're such a blast to have around.

Remember the film, *Fight Club*? "I am Jack's complete lack of surprise..." The first of the eight rules about Fight Club are:

1) You do not talk about Fight Club
2) You do NOT TALK ABOUT FIGHT CLUB

This is The Fourth Way. At least, it used to be, until the internet came along and blew all the doors off. Almost all. You did not talk about The Work. In the ordinary world, you went about your usual business. Your everyday job, everyday friends, everyday downtime, everyday issues, everyday family. Your everyday you. You played your role in society as though nothing were different than ever it was. Inside, however, you were in The Fourth Way Club. Which meant that nothing outside could ever look the same.

There were several ways you could join. Your family could be in it. This didn't give you an automatic rite of passage. It simply meant you were in the immediate view of the those already involved. If invited, which was at the discretion of individual group leaders, often the would-be adept had to first try it on for size. Not everyone was a fit. If it didn't work out, they simply left, or the leader would ensure that they went. There was nothing dark or intimidating or cult-like about it. Not in most of the groups I encountered, at any rate. You didn't have to swear allegiance to a high priestess dressed in black goat skins in a candlelit chantry, there were no rituals or ceremonies or symbolic blood drinking or sacrificial virgins. Understated, you might say. Almost disappointing, in fact.

Another way to discover The Work was through the books. If you somehow found out about this mysterious chap, Gurdjieff, and decided, as used to happen in the last millennium, to look for more information about him in a bookstore, there would sometimes be a contact address tucked discreetly inside one of the classic Work tomes. When you got home with your costly and heavy edition of *Beelzebub's Tales*, as you flicked through the 1,200 or so pages a calling card dropped out on your lap. "If you would like to find out more about The Fourth Way, write to us at..." Which could induce a mild state of excitement.

The other way you could become involved was by what might often mistakenly be called these days The Law of Attraction. As many disillusioned individuals may corroborate, this does not mean the law of gathering together a load of desperate people in cheap suits at an airport Holiday Inn and convincing them that by thinking positively and focusing on being rich and smug instead of fat and worthless they will somehow take over the international marketing pyramid they are vainly trying to ascend. No, thank you. Rather in this instance it represents the action of a genuine mutual magnetism, ingrained in our collective unconscious, of like seeking like, of self calling to self. We do nothing to actively activate it. It's there all the time. By stepping aside, we allow it to happen through us. In Work terms, when an individual has exhausted the apparent paths available to making themselves feel 'better' – healed, wholesome, healthy, practically perfect in every way – and/or integrated into the society in which they live, they often reach an exquisite crisis moment. This is when the ego or accidentally fashioned "I" gives up. Just for a pause. We fully perceive, and step off for a few beatific moments, the habitual merry-go-round of "I **know**/I just don't fucking know" and understand it all for the illusion that it is. The one we've been riding almost our entire lives.

"Every heart to Love must come – but like a refugee." No prize for guessing who.

In that moment, through that window, a messenger calls. They can come in many guises – the collective unconscious has a hell of a fancy wardrobe. Anything from a cataclysmic career breaker or split with a partner or bereavement or sudden health issue, to a child stranger saying unprompted "You're not so happy, why does God want to punish you?" can do it.

What is the message?

Give it up, pal. Let it go. You know you're faking. You're trying too hard. You're not walking your truth. You don't mean what you say. You don't act what you mean. You're out of line. You're hiding your light. You're grasping at straws. You're taking what's not yours. You're stuck in the waiting room. You're lying. You're unreal. You're not true. Let it go.

In that precious moment, you stop. You wake up and become more conscious. Enough to stop being a C.U.N.T. at least. As G said, one awakened person will always recognise another. Two people come together, and show themselves – not as they want to be perceived, but as they are. That's when the Work happens. And someone, a complete stranger or somebody you've known for years, approaches you at a social gathering and, after some obligatory chat, says: "You know, there's someone you should meet."

Mike the carpenter. Bless him. He had a bad back. As I said before, he'd done work at the folks' place for years. By the time Florence, the great enchantress, had brought me back from the brink of the abyss, from purposelessness and self-destruction – from literal disenchantment with the world – the spell had worn off. I was renewed and ready and hungry for something else. A station further up the trail.

Mike was a gifted artisan. He created beauty out of seemingly unremarkable lumps of matter. Pieces of wood my father adored for their age and history and patina, but which most would have deemed useful only for the fire, he patiently and gently removed of their external ugliness and transformed into works of art. Doors and cabinets and lintels, panelling and shelves, floorboards and ceilings and banisters. Mike was unflinchingly modest about his art. "I'm just a chippie," he would joke, sipping his umpteenth cup of tea and stretching his tired bones. Anyone, and there were many, who enjoyed times in the library he created at my parents' home would disagree.

When I returned from Florence, I found myself back there for a spell. The eternal prodigal son. Having read the books and trawled the exploding but still relatively inconclusive internet, I had The Fourth Way on my mind. I discussed it with my parents, but – well: they were my parents, weren't they? You can't be a reactionary and follow in family footsteps, however unconventional they may secretly be. We all know the tale of the circus child who runs away to join an accountancy firm. One afternoon, I found myself helping Mike with the garage doors. "You're a strapping young thing," he said. "Could you give me a hand? It's not the lifting, it's the holding steady that hurts." Prophetic words.

We had always got on well and the lively banter was pleasurable and natural. I told him about my time in Florence, both the architecture and art as well as the nightlife and the characters and the girls. As a father to four daughters, Mike found it entertaining and worrying in equal measure. "When I was young, I always wanted to be surrounded by women," he quipped: "Be careful what you wish for." Banal male humour aside, we shared our insights, such as we had them, into the bigger picture. It was when getting onto mechanics via the medium of cars, a mutual passion, that the subject of Gurdjieff arose.

There is an analogy made in The Fourth Way of the human being as a Hackney Carriage, that is: we are made up of the horses, the carriage, the driver and the passenger. The horses are our emotions, the carriage our physical body, the driver is our intellect and the passenger – well, that's the question. Many would argue that on the observable scale of consciousness on our planet, the human intellect is highest on the chart. Forsaking argument for the time being, we'll stick with the current programme and simply relate that in general the passenger in the carriage represents the soul. Gurdjieff stated that in a healthy or objectively normal world scenario, the team works as follows: the passenger gives instructions for where, and how, to proceed; the driver obediently relays the instructions via the reins to the horses; the horses, well trained and in fine fettle, provide the energy for movement; thus, the physical vehicle moves along, carrying the soul on its terrestrial journey. Perfect. Only, of course, being in the sphere we've inherited, it doesn't usually work that way.

For most of us unfortunate three-brained beings down here, this is how we tend to roll: the driver is drunk in a public house. He or she is intoxicated on various substances, the most devilish of which is probably imagination. Outside, the horses are starving. Or the driver beats them. At the least, they are virtually untrained and so incapable of properly performing their duty. They wander where they will. Meanwhile, the carriage is in a poor state. It has missed most of its service intervals, hasn't been repaired properly after long years of neglect and numerous accidents, or has simply been pimped whilst underneath everything is ready to fall apart. And the passenger? Even if the passenger issues instructions, the driver is deaf to them. Drunk, angry, bitter, depressed, generally wounded or just too busy telling a rapt audience at the bar about his or her daring past exploits and their incredible plans for the future. When they do take charge of the reins, they drive like maniacs. Or just fall asleep. Often, they are completely unaware there is a passenger in the carriage to begin with. So passes a life.

Mike and I were chatting this through, as you do when you're trying to be Atlas holding up a solid oak lintel while an aging man with a dodgy spine is drilling holes around your head. Like most concepts, this one is not new. You can find a similar analogy in the two-and-a-bit thousand year-old Bhagavad Gita. Gurdjieff, you're a thief. I was putting it in the modern context of a car, where the chassis/body is the physical human, the engine the emotions, the driver still the driver and the passenger, well, the same. Perhaps, I offered, these days we see ourselves all as drivers – we identify with owning the car and driving where and as we will? It's even harder to conceptualise this soul figure in the back, and it's all about our intellect getting somewhere? Then again, how do we know which voice is the passenger's, with all that racket in our own minds? What if we're still drunk but don't know it because it's normal to us? Because we're imagination junkies? What if we're hearing voices? What if the passenger doesn't exist? Didn't Gurdjieff say we have to grow it? What if...?

Which is when Mike kindly, gently, yet abruptly said: "You should ask Alec."

Dad's ex-boss. The surgeon. And The Fourth Way group leader for the south-east of England.

So I did.

Ah, good Kin. I could tell you tales. Of early Wednesday morning sessions at Alec and his lovely wife's home. Of guided meditations and conversations and warm breakfasts and coffee in the company of fellow seekers and masters and stars. Of excursions to watch Gurdjieff's Sacred Dances and meetings with other students of all ages, races, backgrounds and creeds. Of opening up the many cracks in my tower, of seeing more clearly and of being seen. Of being accepted. Of being loved, oh yes. Consciously. To be loved is not to be desired, not to be eaten: it is to belong.

I could tell you, attempt to show you, through these meagre words what that meant. But that is not your journey, here. It is not ours. I am human, all too human, and I still have the desire to honour through nostalgia that space that no longer exists and the friends who, for a time, dwelled within it. To break an earlier promise – another human trait – what is nostalgia, after all, but the pain of yearning to return home? In every home, we each of us have our roles. In the Work, each student may be seeking something, but the Work also has need of each student. They are assembled carefully, to act as mirrors to one another as much as to fulfil their part in this hive of awakening. Through no fault of their own, if they cease to fulfil this role for the collective, they have to move on.

I did not leave because I was asked to. In a sense, I never left at all. I was thirsty, I came and was invited to drink. There was plenty of knowledge to go around. The little group I attended mostly consisted of veterans. Alec himself had been in The Work almost since Gurdjieff was still alive. He had known many of G's original students and had worked and studied with them, performed the movements with them, practised

The Fourth Way for his entire life. Indeed, in many ways, he was a remarkable man. There were remarkable human beings all around. Still, something else was calling.

Partly, it was the stage we were at. At twenty-something, I was by far the youngest body there. My presence brought the average age down to around sixty-five. This in itself was not a problem – after all, the soul is ageless, right? We see the circle close between grandparent and newborn child and remember Shakespeare's 'Seven Ages', there is a resonance that runs right through us all that age cannot, or should not, dim. They had wisdom, no doubt, and even if I did not directly consume it, I bathed in its glow. I am sure that for them, too, there was something vivifying in having youth in the circle among them. There is something core about witnessing the rise of another generation, the unrelenting cycle of life. But something was nagging.

Gurdjieff was dead. He had died over half a century before. There are many myths and shadowy legends about the man who came from Armenia, disappeared for his entire youth and surfaced again in Tsarist Russia as a middle-aged man, just before the revolution. He bunkered down with his students in the Caucasus for a time until after the First World War, then made an incredible journey on foot across the mountains to what was then called Constantinople. Through shattered Germany, he finally arrived in Paris, there to see out his remaining years. Money was always an issue. He made several trips to America, raising funds for his own school, The Institute for the Harmonious

Development of Man at Fontainebleau, and his group performed at Carnegie Hall, to rapturous applause and thundering donations. He had a car accident that should have killed him. He lost his wife. He aroused controversy and fathered illegitimate children. He closed the Institute, and relocated permanently to a Parisian apartment. Another war came and went. Gurdjieff passed the time sheltering Jews and pissing off the authorities. Old, now, no one knows exactly when he was born, he ended his days hosting meetings and parties and raising "Toasts to the Idiots". On his death bed, some said that his parting words (unverified – there is nothing about the man that is not controversial) were: "I leave you all in a fine mess." According to some, his body stayed warm for many hours. At the precise moment the funeral service ended in the Russian church on the Rue Daru, it is said that all the lights in that quarter of Paris went out.

Bygones. I wasn't there. We weren't there. It was not the singer, but the song that had me enthralled. Yes, it was G who brought the teaching to the West. Undoubtedly, he was a huge personality, and we know how we often need to tread carefully around those. Teacher, or fraud, guru or conman, G was probably all and more; yet in those fragments of a teaching, something in me discerned a taste of something true. An internal compass, uneducated, unconditioned, untrained, pointed at it like magnetic north. Like a swallow heading home. And, as I would later discover from a trusted first hand source, there was indeed a quality of "otherness" about him – a presence that raised him above the ordinary human being, from which no ordinary world abiding person can hide.

The trouble was, Gurdjieff did not appoint a successor. Usually in esoteric schools, which in essence is what his community was, if the master does not appoint a new master to replace him or her, the school dies with them. The work they accomplished in life no doubt lives on, in the students, in the practices and the teachings, but the active transmission – the ever-evolving informational stream that nourishes it – is cut off. Afterwards, we witness the usual story with such schools. The group splinters. Different adepts and former students claim legitimacy. A power struggle of inevitable ego-influenced motives ensues. All promote their own version of the system as the true successor, the heir, the purest line. The message is interpreted, and reinterpreted, and even when it is done so with the best intentions and the highest ideals, the information gets garbled. Changed. However subtly, it no longer bears the hallmark of its source.

After more than five decades since his death, in the hands of successive caretakers of varying degrees of proximity to the master in life, what condition was The Fourth Way now in? How could its authenticity be measured? The society The Work first encountered on arrival in Europe and North and South America was completely changed. "Do not talk about Fight Club?" Who cared anymore? Within in a few years, you had only to Google "Gurdjieff group" and you could take your pick in pretty much any major city, only an Uber away. Never mind all the other "ways" that were trending, from a hundred kinds of yoga to meditation, mindfulness and Shaolin Kung Fu. How do you choose? Who do you trust? We were taught to consider outwardly – are there exceptions to the rule? Hello?

In the end, I did what John and Gaia would soon be advocating: I just said Fuck It. We all knew roughly where Gurdjieff had been on his twenty-year vacation. He even named some of the towns he'd visited, in the regions near these mysterious schools. They were mostly in the former Soviet Union. Which was handy, as after 80 years in lockdown mode, the area was now open once more for business. And tourists. And travellers. What was there to lose? A stellar career in copyrighting?

I went to St Petersburg for a month to learn Russian. I just about made it back. For the next flight, I got a maximum stay visa and a one-way ticket to the heart of Central Asia. My intention was clear: I wanted to drink from the fountain. Maybe Gurdjieff's pupils were all dead (in fact, they weren't, quite) but that didn't matter. I wasn't looking for the diluted version of his fragmented system. Neither was I interested in a vintage that was well over its drink date. I wanted to taste the hooch from straight out of the still.

I was going to find his teachers.

o

Kin – it's time. We're here.

Are you ready – ready to cross this threshold? With me? True, I have been here before. To a degree, I can guide us over. The story I have shared up to this point has brought us to this place: hopefully, it has prepared us for what lies ahead in the special world. At the same time, it is never the same as before. The gateway, and its guardians, like everything else in our universe, is forever shifting. There are no guarantees we will pass through without difficulty. One thing is sure: the act of crossing over will change us. Besides, there is another factor we must not overlook: the fact that you are with me.

That was my story. It is the story of how I first broke away from programmed conditioning and answered a call to discover a new world. To "break on through to the other side", baby. In bringing us this far, it has served its purpose. We can let it go. Now that I'm here again, I want to hear yours. Do you think you cannot tell me? Sure you can. No doubt, my good companion, you have already crossed many thresholds of your own over the years. The hero's journey is never a straight run. How did you get to this one? What has brought you to be here, now, with me? For us to stand together at the gate, when so many others have already turned back? If you think I cannot hear you, don't worry. I may be far away, even long dead, but the magic of words works both ways. Just because my body isn't here doesn't mean I don't know you are here, too. I am listening to your every thought, every feeling. Every beat of your heart. Do you know that the heart of one is the heart of all? If you don't believe me, ask Solzhenitsyn, or Michel.

Take a moment. Close your eyes, if it helps. Remember. Remember how you came to be what you are. Who you were as a child. Do you remember how that felt? What were your big battles? What were your dreams, your desires? Your disappointments? How far did life's unrelenting winds and mercurial hidden currents alter your course? Are you still on target? Are you adrift, or becalmed, without reference points on a restless ocean? Are you forever caught in the storm?

Speak true now, Kin. There is no one here to judge you. Only the winds and the water, the earth and the sky will hear your secrets. You arose from them. They will not burden you. They are waiting for you to tell them. But not in words. They are waiting to hear you howl.

Take your time, dear Kin. Take decades, if you must, as I did. I will always be waiting.

There is one final duty we must perform before we can get into that special world: we have to prepare ourselves for the modification of our towers. For the next stage of our heroic adventure, we must be ready to pare them back, to clean them – to have demolished any existing structures that might impede our progress. The good thing about our towers, unlike those built of earth and brick and concrete and stone, like the one in which externally I now write to you, is how they change. If we allow it, they can be flexible, fluid, liquid silver. With care and practice, we can restructure them to suit our onward journey. To do it, we will use our talisman: The First Howl.

There are three howls in all, you see, Kin. That's right: with this book, you get three for the price of one.

Call it a token of the age from which I write. The First Howl acts on our tower. The Second, if we make it that far, does something equally funky. And the Third – well. If we do not stop, hopefully, you'll experience that too for yourself.

Given our proximity to the threshold, it's probably time to explode this whole tower metaphor. I'm sure you've already got it – please understand that I don't doubt your insight. I just don't want to lose you, after all these words, on account of what may appear to be a bad case of riddling.

Our tower is the structure that surmounts us. In current psychoanalytical terms, we can call it the ego. From birth, as soon as we enter the stage where we interact with our surroundings, its construction begins. At first, it is built by those around us, in tandem with our newborn essence. As we grow, we start to take over more of the building process for ourselves. As we stated earlier, this process is often undertaken at the subconscious level, through our automatic reactions to external stimuli, though we are also often complicit in the task to varying degrees. The form and substance of our tower depends on the materials we inherit, and those at our disposal in the environment around us. Though each tower looks a little different to the next on account of weathering in said environments and the inhabitant it surrounds, we can observe generally definable distinct architectural styles and design blueprints. Yes, we are all individuals. No, there is nothing new under the Sun.

In today's culture, the personal towers we create are reflected in the macro environment around us. As above, so below. Our old cities, and new cities freshly rising the planet over, follow the cues of our inner psyche. They are the expressions of our collective desires, our visions and our imaginings. In olden days, they were built primarily for protection. As time went on, we added status to the remit: to show our neighbours our wealth and power. Today, they represent our dominance over our material environment and the rise of our global virtual world. Their inhabitants and the tasks they perform therein are a symbol of what we aspire to. Success – reaching the top of the food chain. Bakir's "Vertical Culture".

Yet they can represent other things, too. Cheap high-rise accommodation the world over does not embody great achievement: rather, it points to containment, to control. The people that live within them are not the movers and shakers. They are simply raw material for feeding, and feeding off, the system: depersonalised, crammed in. Stacked for economy. Transmitting towers across the planet are used to send across information. We need not qualify these structures as good or bad, positive or negative: we should only be aware, and wary of, the agenda that said information carries. Does it free us? Does it bind us? Does it help make us prisoners in our own private citadels?

One last thing: I am sure it has not escaped you that there is an overtly masculine aspect to this whole tower-building analogy. That is not intentional on my part. The devil is in the design. With the whole fury surrounding the present gender debate in our society, I do not intend to enter verbally into the fray. I do not have an agenda in that regard; moreover, in an arena where many words have become sensitive and anything but neutral, I have no desire to add further charged notions to the fire. All I will do as we continue on this quest is to transmit the essence of any related information as I receive it in as impartial a way as I am able. No doubt, you may have felt that the tone so far has leaned often towards the masculine side of the scale: zealous personality, ribald storytelling – a lot of wiseacring, undoubtedly, as some would have it. That is no accident. If it has offended you or made you uncomfortable at moments, I am sorry. We must begin our journeys where we first find ourselves. To find ourselves, we employ the practice of reflection. Those of you with an eye on what is coming will have noticed the balance may be about to turn.

For the present task, let us make a point of reminding ourselves that masculine and feminine as aspects of our human life should not be confused or be automatically interchangeable with our classification of 'male' and 'female'. Whichever of the latter you are, good Kin, whether you chose it or it was chosen for you, we all find ourselves in towers. As we travel deeper into the special world, even that may change.

Now: let us Howl.

The First Howl

Find yourself a clear space. It can be your apartment, your bathroom, your car or, even better, somewhere outside. A garden or a park or a forest is good. A mountaintop overlooking the receding Earth for miles in all directions is swell. But not necessary. Just don't try this straight off in an aeroplane or restaurant or on the 6:47 home train out of Grand Central. There may yet be a time for that.

Pull in all your attention, your sensations, your thoughts, and feel them in your head. Hold in your mind whatever processes and images, memories and visions pop up on the screen of your mental projection room and watch them flow. Add a soundtrack if you wish. Close your eyes or keep them open, whichever adds more energy to the cranial montage. Breathe in and out with vigour, sensing the air flowing in and out through your nasal passageways and mouth, until you start to feel your skull tingling. If there is anything on your mind at the moment – some aspect of your life that is causing you discomfort, or anxiety, or frustration, or anger, or anguish, or self-doubt – focus on it for a few moments and then throw it in the mix. When you get to the point that you feel like your head is ready to explode, howl. Like this:

HAAAAAAAAAAAAAAAAAAAAAAAAAAOOO OOOOOOOOOL!

HAAAAAAAAAAAAAAAAAAAAAAAAAAAAOOO
OOOOOOOOOL!

HAAAAAAAAAAAAAAAAAAAAAAAAAAAAOOO
OOOOOOOOOL!

Do you feel it? Your head will be ringing. Do it as many times as you can tolerate it, or until the energy starts to tail off. Then take a seat, if you're not seated already, close your eyes, flop your head forward and just breathe. Deeply. Into your chest, and out. Keep going. Until your system resets.

This is The First Howl. Observe how it affects your head physically. Don't try to analyse it. If you find yourself doing so, watch yourself, and let it go. Don't expect anything weird or mystical to happen. Expect nothing. If you do have an unfamiliar experience, feel it, taste it, remember it. If you feel uncomfortable, overly dizzy or lightheaded, stop. Try again later or another day. Observe your mental processes, your overall state of mind. The First Howl can work well in tandem with physical exercise – half way through a run, for example. Try it, but don't push yourself too far too soon. There are a lot of bricks in your tower. Likely, some cracks, too.

Depending on the present state and design of our own respective architecture, we will each have differing experiences. For this reason, do not aim for a specific result. Goals can be useful, but we often obsess too much with the outcome at the expense of learning from the experience of the journey in real time. For this reason, there is no prescribed right or wrong howl. As a general guide, keeping the purpose of The First Howl in mind may be instructive:

To vibrate, resonate and soften the result of years of the habitual building of your everyday "I". In other words: to shake your tower. Make it malleable. For what? Patience, Kin – we've another two howls to go yet.

As you develop your practice, you may wish to hold this notion as an intention. Take your time, and be patient. Rome wasn't pulled down in a day.

If cracks do appear, if you find yourself letting go, fall silent. Breathe. Be still. It is not unusual for laughter or tears or both to make an appearance. Performing the practice with another person is a useful way to amplify the experience, whilst having the security of a buddy nearby in case of full demolition. If that happens, don't panic. Everything can be rebuilt. It may even be an improvement on the original.

If everybody does it together, well: then we'll have a revolution on our hands. Let's start with one tower at a time. The readiness, Kin. Are you ready? I'm going to howl with you.

What? Still stuck on thinking about it? Come on, Kin. Try a little faith once in a while. Some of the best things in life happen to us when we're not too busy thinking.

What have you got to lose? Time? Really: aren't we losing that anyway?

I'll see you in the next world. Deep breath, now:

One...

Two...

Three......

THE CAVE

Cold Mountain

All of humanity's problems stem from man's inability to sit quietly in a room alone.

- Blaise Pascal

There once was a man who lived in a cave...

Hey, Kin. Looks like we made it through. Did you try The First Howl yet? Did it affect you at all? Keep practising. This is the age of everyone wanting instant results: imagine it, produce it, package it, send it out. Consume it, pass it. Want some more. The fast food info culture. The good stuff doesn't come to us that way. Never has, never will. Treat yourself with something beautiful this year: patience. Click **HERE** for an instant download.

Gotcha. Ha-haaaoool!

Ahhh, beloved Kin. We may be over the border, but just as with real overland journeys, the landscape on this side doesn't change drastically straightaway. Let's approach it gradually; patiently, even, if we can. The special world isn't always immediately some fantastical other country, with mountains and forests and glacial streams and waterfalls. Multi-coloured pterodactyls arcing gracefully above the misty jungle canopy. In fact, it can look pretty much indistinguishable from the ordinary realm we just left. The realm that in-formed us, and which we carry with us still, whether we choose to or not. Let's not focus on it too much. Accept a little of the familiar "old tones" narrative voice to accompany us as we make our way deeper into new territory. Have faith that everything will and must change. And remember: what makes a thing special is not necessarily how it is presented, as much as how we perceive it.

There is a lovely Blake quote on this somewhere: something about a tree, I seem to recall. I'm sure you can find it, if you wish. Or let it be. We will encounter new mentors in this phase of our journey. Let's not fall for that old DT of comparing our new experiences with everything that went before. Must we remain attached to all those acquired voices – wrapped up like Gulliver, pulling the heavy fleet of our history into unknown, choppy waters? I feel not. I'm sure dear old William B. will be waiting for us when we return, besides.

Let's go and make our visit.

There was indeed a man who lived in a cave. At the age of 63, he dug a cell out of the earth beneath his dwelling and therein remained for the rest of his days. It was quite a long time ago, and there are plenty of legends surrounding how long he was there and what went on while he lived in his subterranean abode. Some say he died soon after; according to others, he continued to live well past his 120th year. What is undisputable is that, like our earlier hero in his tower, this man transmitted something that lasts to the present time. A living legacy that has survived the complexities and vicissitudes of history and humankind to reach us here, in these very glyphs and the intentions of the words we now share. Unlike Montaigne's broadcast, however, this one was not transmitted so widely, nor so far. Not for a long while. You might say it was on something of a hidden frequency: difficult enough to pick up in the first instance, and if you *did* find it and wish to subscribe, signing up took far more effort than a click and an email address.

What did he tell us? Not much. Not in written form, at least. Some insightful proverbs and profound observations, yes, though nothing like as extensive or as well-travelled as Michel's. But he did transmit something. *Mon Dieu*, but did he. And when it hits you, you can forget about your tower: the whole frickin' mountain trembles.

o

Before we get too deeply into caves, let's acclimatise to our present surroundings in more modest and familiar a fashion: in a tent.

When I was a wee young thing of twenty-seven, I had what you might call a Joan of Arc moment. By that, I don't mean I was sick of watching everything I loved being destroyed, stolen or violated by the English-speaking world. There are enough people out there who can attest to that better than I, one of the would-be transgressors. What I mean is that I felt I was being called by a subconscious force to do something out of my usual remit. At the time, that remit was to enjoy my succulent Italy-based lifestyle, work for a horrible newspaper for way too much money, and generally feel quite pleased with myself. By this point, I had discovered Gurdjieff and entered into the world of The Work, albeit superficially, so also could content myself with the notion that I had 'found a way' and was, in every sense, on it. It was all pretty comfortable. Too comfortable. Life as modest, middle-class art. Obviously, it had to be smashed.

Have you noticed the rise in popularity of extreme sports? It began a while ago on a significant scale with the advent of triathlons. Since the end of World War 2, our leisure-biased society has been subjecting itself to ever greater challenges for body and mind, from cold showers to ultra marathons and free solo speed climbing. It appears to be everywhere. These days, no one bats an eyelid if you tell them you're spending the weekend running though waist-deep liquid freezing mud, crawling through barbed wire, jumping over burning hay bales and then heading for the finish line on your belly through a forest of dangling electrified wires. Back in our grandparents' time, or about .008 of a second ago in evolutionary terms, that would have been sniffed at by the military, let alone your friends. Were you doing it as a punishment for some heinous crime? Because you were training to be the first human being to explore the surface of Mars? Because you hit your head and have patently lost all ability to think, or are raising awareness and money to save a world-famous children's hospital? Actually, no: just doing it for kicks.

Are we flocking to these events as a culture simply because subconsciously we're so damned bored of having a screen stuck in our face every minute of the day? Is it simple vanity – so we can show everyone on social media how cool and tough we are: a matter of base bragging rights? Or does it come from a deeper place than that? The place that tells us that if this life is, to the senses at least, permanently over easy, we're not doing it quite the way we were designed to?

Perhaps it's "d" – all three. TMA. In any case, I needed to tap out. We hadn't even invented smartphones yet and I wanted to put my fist through my laptop. I did, in fact. More than once. I guess there was further work required in every field.

What the voice was calling me to do was to walk out into the wilderness. Right there. Like in some cult indie film where the hero just makes for the door, unprompted, and disappears. Biblical, man. I didn't, of course. But I knew I wanted not only a physical challenge to help me wake up, reset, reconnect with that indefinable yet concretely tangible natural intelligence I felt adrift from in my own body: I also wanted space. Not as in the take-a-cheap-flight-to-a-tropical-resort-and-accidentally-fuck-a-stranger space. Full time-out.

Alone.

The concept of retreat is on the "must do" list of most religious and spiritual hand books. From the lowliest monk or or disciple to the highest of God's chosen, anyone on the path to self-realization or spiritual union or enlightenment – so many descriptions for the inexpressible – is expected to take off and be on their lonesome for a stint. I didn't know about that. I wasn't intending to get somewhere or achieve some incredible altered state. Not as a matter of priority. I just wanted to sort through and silence the chaos in my mental courtroom and tap into whatever it was inside that was adamant that playing the bit-part role of a regular contented human being for the duration of your lifetime is a second-rate sham.

Provisions were packed. Partner appeased. Location chosen. I climbed into my car and – dot dot dot.

I know we're backtracking here, Kin. There is a practical application for you in this, though, so hold that bolt for the horizon. I did my time and, as we've a long way to go yet and the clock is ticking, I'll keep it as brief as I can without diluting the substance. Forty days and nights is a long watch on your own. I'm glad on this occasion to have you near.

I headed for the mountains. Of course – where else? Filled with romantic notions of pre-Raphaelite poets on journeys of discovery across dizzy Alpine passes, or of making like G and finding *Shambhala*, it had to be The Full Monty. Okay, it was November. It would be cold, and my survival skills were rusty. An old school buddy of mine would have made a useful mentor, but he was out preparing to cross the North Atlantic in an inflatable hotdog bun. It would be a few years until *Man vs Wild* first aired and returned one-to-one remembrance and respect for the natural world into our climate-controlled living spaces. Thank you, Brother Bear. In any case, this was modern Europe. Humans had long since emptied even her most primordial environments of vicious beasts such as wolves, bears and lynx. I had a camping stove, a knife and some NASA-spec thermal underwear. How bad could it be?

I arrived at the foothills of the Pyrenees, the mountain range that stretches almost coast to coast between France in the north and Spain to the south. There was a personal agenda behind the choice of site: this was Cathar Country. Long before Dan Brown turned the Templars and their friends into a bestselling career project for Tom Hanks, I had been seduced by the many underground tales and publications surrounding this medieval society or "sect". In hindsight, most of the ensuing notoriety and hysteria was probably the usual media conjecture bubble being inflated far above the subject's natural capacity. Yet there was and still is something magical, mystical even, about this rugged, red-earthed remote region of France. A pregnant silence, full of pain-stitched memories of historic suffering and injustice; of the land lying dormant, not fully wasted yet dare not breathing; abiding, waiting for some ancient spirit in the rocks and woods and streams to stir and move across it again.

Imagination can be a precocious companion. Then again, would you rather be seated next to reason for the duration of the dinner party? Beneath a ridge above a stream near the forest, with a village half an hour's walk downhill and a looming, craggy peak dominating the skyline above, I made camp. I sent a last SMS to my girlfriend and took the battery out of my pre-Matrix Nokia. In one corner of the 2-person tent, I stuck a bottle of red wine, a pack of cigarettes and a jar of coffee. They were to remain unopened until 6 weeks later. Well – what's time in the wilderness without a little temptation? For sustenance, I had a load of couscous and instant noodles, some kiwis, 6 tins of something fishy for Sunday special, some carrots and a couple of dozen chocolate bars. I'd read Jim Crace's *Quarantine* and wasn't going to embrace the chutzpah required for bargaining my mortal cage against the whims of the Holy Spirit. Body's gotta eat. Still, my habitual daily calorific intake reduced by a half to two thirds. If you're convinced you hunger and thirst for truth, as Gurdjieff put it, I figured there could be something gained by matching the talk with the walk. And I would be walking.

The fun of exploring without a guide is that you have no expectations of what you might find. Without the pre-coloured mind putting an anticipatory slant on your cognitive faculties, you experience your surroundings more directly through unfiltered senses. Everything is more immediate, especially if you've been fasting, detoxing and assiduously meditating and are already feeling – how is the best way to put it: a little weird? The peak in whose shadow I'd chosen to camp was not one I'd ever heard of. I had stumbled on it whilst driving around some well-known Cathar villages and landmarks nearby. It had a peculiar aspect about it, more like it had landed on the surrounding terrain than sprouted from it, and I figured it would make a great viewing platform as well as provide some proper exercise. I was not to be disappointed.

The downside of exploring without any form of guidance is that you can end up looking like a complete idiot. Even if it's only to your internal audience, it can nevertheless be thoroughly humiliating. That being part of the curriculum during self-enforced isolation, you have to take it with a pinch of salt. Otherwise, you're probably in the wrong occupation. I scrabbled up to the summit on two occasions through briars and gorse, up vertical sections of rock and across overhangs. At one point, I found myself shimmying around a ledge no wider than my thermos flask. For what felt like hours, but was probably only a couple of minutes in real time, it presented a perfectly uninterrupted view of the valley a hundred feet or more below.

It was only on my third visit, approaching the base of the ascent from a different aspect, that I noticed a sign. The sign indicated, via simple colour-coding in case an idiot like myself should finally see it, that there were already three clearly demarcated routes up the peak, with varying degrees of difficulty. Just follow the coloured markers that accord with your ability and hey: you're at the summit. I chuckled to myself and set off up the medium path. Having already made my own 'Fourth Way' up twice, I felt I'd earned it.

The view from the summit was never short of extraordinary. Let's be clear: this was no Everest. Not even a personal one. Nevertheless, it did act as a reminder that you don't always need the ultimate adventure in life to have the ultimate experience. Call it cosmic economy or the universe meeting you halfway or, if you prefer the Mick Jagger version: "If you try sometimes you just might find you get what you nee-eeeed". Watching the amber descent of the winter sun across Spain to the south with all of France at my back was a treasured gift in time I feel still to this day. Namaste, honey, and you can keep your hashtag and your cynicism, just for one precious, fleeting moment. Feel, I did. Howl too, surely I must. It wasn't The Howls as we are discovering them together on our present journey, Kin, methodically and patiently as we approach them, though of course it came from the same source. Whatever the mechanisms that were unlocking within me, all I knew with certainty was that something was, beyond doubt or intellectual scrutiny, feeling better. *Working* better. The moment that sealed it was when, on my fifth and final ascent, I sat on a ledge by the peak's famous 'window' looking out and, as often I would, reached for my notebook and pen. You can take the writer out of his study, but you can't take the study out of – etc. Feeling light and clear as I did after two weeks in natural isolation, I went to record my observations for the day's journal entry. What came out?

Nothing. Sweet, blissful nothing. It was not simply that I had nothing to say, nothing to record. Given the wrong incentive, I know I could have gabbled. Probably an entire essay on the fact that when there is nothing to say, it's amazing what the mind will have to say on the matter. But the awareness was in me that my attempting to define or interpret or even relate the experience would be nothing but a spoiler's act of injecting muddy artifice into a state that existed, just then, only then, by and of and for itself, through me. And so I let it alone. And sat. And watched. Sometimes, when I'm lucky, I still do.

Then the rains came.

What year are you in there, Kin? God, it's merciless, this Heropass – this "Time". Are we still measuring our planetary combustion cycle from the supposed moment a certain Hebraic reactionary first arrived in an urban donkey sanctuary? By turns of the Moon, since the last Prophet (PBUH) was given shelter in the city later known as Medina? Is there a new system in place? Did you dig this manuscript out of the rubble of a former medieval stronghold and, whilst using an antiquated translating scanner to have this read back to you in your own tongue, are now wondering what year you're standing in, and indeed why the English language died out? Here's a tip: if you dig a bit further, there's a few ancient bottles you might find of interest in what we used to call "the cellar"...

Where I'm sitting now, Kin, a little way above you, it's the end of 2020. The world has been even madder than mad this year. The pandemic I mentioned earlier has taken the news by storm, stealing all the headlines from the usual minor existential irritations of politics, economy, war, genocide and exponential climate crisis. It has killed a few of us, too. Out of a global population of (Google...) around 7.83 billion, just over one and a half million are reputed to have died from COVID-19, as the virus is called. About 0.02% or 1 in every 5000 living people. While that statistic may not be up there with the Black Death, the Spanish Flu or even a modest meteorite, the fear generated by the fear of contracting and spreading the disease has resulted in an unprecedented defensive action on a near species-wide level: we have gone into self-isolation. For weeks, even months, at a time.

In spiritual babble parlance: the human race has gone on retreat.

How was it? Were you there, do you remember it? Still on it? How did you find it? Not so bad? Or a pivotal life moment? If the internet is still functioning, and the Wi-Fi and 6G didn't perish in the general collapse, you can look it up. There are a few pages about it. Plenty of videos, too. Millions, in fact. People talking to their computers. Singing to them. Performing little dances. Not all of them sacred. Talking to each other through computers, and phones and tablets and screens, all across the world. Recording conversations. Sharing information. Transmitting, sending, receiving, feeding. More, in many instances, than back in the ordinary world of 2019 and before. Home alone, or locked down with our families, our mental information intake has gone through the roof and into the stratosphere. What would we have done without the internet? Without TV, radio, phones? Without online music and drama series and films? How would we have coped with the kids – *Dio buono*?! Wasn't it almost a massacre as it stood?

Can you be alone? Well: can you, Kin? Can you be in your space without any distraction where you are, right now? Did you find yourself at any point there: locked down in the true sense, without receiving or sending out any transmissions in your tower? The still point of the turning world?

Try it. It's a test. Not to appease or defy me, hell, I'm not going to judge you. I'm probably dead anyway. Try it for you. You owe it to yourself. Here's the game:

Whether you're single and reclusive or in charge of a family of a dozen (nothing personal, Mormons) I want you to STOP. This is not the infamous, full-fat Fourth Way exercise which means that when the Master calls it you don't twitch a muscle, even if you're standing in fast-rising water while across the road your Grandmother is on fire. Just stop using your phone. For a weekend. Friday evening to Sunday night. Go on. I dare you. Switch it off. No calls, messages, browsing, social media. Stop. And your tablet. And PC/Mac/whatever you clever folk use these days in Shanghai. No emails, no TV, no music, no radio. Nada. Tell your friends and family and colleagues you're going to be leaving the planet for 48 hours. Can you do that?

Really? Who's in control of your life?

Life is truly full of great ironies. In 2020, she threw us this: so many of us were fried, and frying Gaia back in the process, and yelling inside if not outside also: "Please, I just want some space! I just want it all to stop! For a second! I need a break!" Then it stopped. Societies, economies, countries – entire continents. The human race went into freeze frame. We were deprived some so-called 'liberties' and granted in their stead an opportunity: time-out. The funny thing is, without assistance in the form of even more distraction than before, we couldn't handle it. The still cave was too much to bear.

I accept that if you're stuck in a small domestic bunker with young children or sulky teens for company, lockdown is another level of challenging. I have several of the former myself and it certainly wasn't all a walk in the harmonious von Trapp paradise park. If you're a single parent, or partner to an abusive partner, or caring for a sick parent, or [insert complication] – it can overload the situation. Break you down. Shatter your tower defences and suck dry or flatten whatever's left inside. It's a torment fit for Job. There is no shame in that. Only pain. Pain and suffering. How are we to respond?

Gurdjieff tells us we must choose our suffering consciously, conscientiously, if it is to serve any purpose for us to grow and evolve as humans. That may sound well and good, but what happens when the world throws so much on you that you can't bear it? When it bursts you apart at the seams, murders any hope you might have had left, devours your resistance and leaves you empty of will, of hunger, of desire? At that point, either we collapse and die or, against all odds, we get back up. It may take what feels like an eternity, but if we stay down, eventually we will be eaten. The alternative is to stagger up one more time. Drag ourselves up by tooth and nail, if need be. Just as in the wonderful opening paragraph of the novel *Shantaram* when the narrator, Lin, is chained to a cell wall being beaten by prison guards and realises for the first time he is free: "...free to hate the men who were torturing me, or to forgive them." We can still choose. Between hatred and forgiveness, courage and despair, love and loathing, oblivion and life. We all get the demon we need. As with information on the earlier part of our journey, when suffering comes – as inevitably it does in this life – we can choose. Not necessarily the form it takes. But how we eat it.

So here is the question: how do we eat the silence?

The rain did not stop for a week. As if on cue, after my ecstatic moment of natural high, the organic world's special effects department went into overdrive. My little tent, stuck like a barnacle on the mountain's underbelly, might as well have been cast into the sea. You want howling? The sky provided wind in relentless, frenzied abundance. I placed stones and tied extra cords on the flysheet: twice it was torn away, recovered, repaired, and ripped further again with each thundering assault. Day on day, night after night, the sound of rain, now abating, now drumming, now hurling once more against nylon and dribbling through feebly taped patches, became omnipresent, outside my skull and within. "Blow, winds!" yelled me, crouched in a primate squat to attend to nature one raging morning, as the hurricane greeted my paltry existence by grabbing the umbrella that vaguely protected my matins ritual and hurled it half a mile down the hillside. Ten minutes later, I returned to my battered temple with what was left of the umbrella, made an inventory of the complete absence of a single dry article of clothing, and stared like a hunted maniac for several minutes at the illegal stash in the corner.

"You shall not pass!" I finally bellowed at the innocent collection of inanimate objects. I laughed, stripped off, lit the stove – to hell with the rations – and sat down to write.

"Reading, thinking, is also prayer." This from the book of *Proverbs* attributed to our man in a cave of earlier: Khodja Ahmad Yassaviy.

Let's be real with each other here: I wasn't really suffering. In hospitals, the nurses ask you to inform them on a scale of one to ten how much pain you feel you're enduring. Pain is, as with most things here, by and large a subjectively measurable phenomenon. In my own story, intimate knowledge of that scale would be a treat reserved for later. Back in my sodden little piece of independent heaven, my self-declared Autonomous Republic of One, all that weather and fasting and sleep deprivation and lack of coffee and human contact etc put me probably around a two, or two and a half at most. Otherwise known as: minor discomfort. When it came to my mind, I was on the scale by the narrowest of margins. Most of my friends in London were in a far worse situation.

What was the point? Why did I choose to spend over six weeks in isolation, halfway up a French hillside with enforced radio silence?

You could call it answering the subconscious human need for initiation. In a culture where the word has lost any real meaning, at least none we can constructively envision, the persistent subconscious request for external confirmation of our ascension through levels of maturity is quite evident. Whether it is being corralled into downing relentless litres on top of stupefying shots of alcohol, taking drugs, stealing totems, making sexual conquests, getting that contested place in higher education or sharing the details (and contents) of your first major paycheck, what passes for initiation in our world these days can by and large be flushed down the pan, along with the kebab that didn't make it home via Google Maps' preferred route. Initiation, ordination, test – whatever works, just use it. The question is this: do you have the resolve?

Well, do you? Do you, Kin? I need to know. Now. If we're going to proceed through the special world together, do you have what it takes? Have you been weighed and measured? That's what all this tent narrative and regressive storytelling is bringing us to: can you walk the walk? You need to know, for yourself, that you have that resolve. Maybe you were just a kid in 2020. Christ, you must have an entire lobe in your brain dedicated to animated films. It's not your fault. Move on. Your parents were getting through the only way they knew: distraction. That won't help us now. Won't help your companions, or your planet. It won't help me. You need to know you can rely on yourself. That others can. Some day, even if not this day, it will be necessary.

Writing helped me. That's not because it's my profession. Hell, I was trying to get away from any notion of work with a diminutive "w". It is an expression of thinking, and a natural companion to reading, and as our mysterious *Khodja* above points out, isn't it all a kind of prayer?

Prayer vs mindfulness or meditation – we're not going there. Not right now. Too subjective. Just like pain. Hopefully happier. Another distraction.

Can you sit with your suffering? Can you sit with silence? If you don't know the answer: try it. Try it for 48 hours. Screens are out of bounds. Be tough on yourself. If you live with family or roommates, get them to help out. Ask them to cut you a break. Bring you food and water and otherwise leave you alone. Shut yourself in your bedroom, the attic, the basement, the garden shed. No alcohol or other kinds of drugs unless medically necessary. We won't go into the anti-depressants debate today, either: if you feel you need 'em, keep taking them. For now. This is not designed to make you panic. This is designed to centre you.

You are allowed to take one book. I had three, but I was there longer. It must be an old-fashioned one – made out of paper. Why? To be limited. Screens are a portal to the limitless mines of information out there: this exercise is designed to reassign your trajectory, if only momentarily, to the limitless mines that exist already inside you. You don't need to do any digging. Just witness that they are there. A physical book can also be a more present companion in the dark hours. There's a reason we imbue objects with veneration sometimes.

It's reassuring to know that other voice you've come to know won't disappear with an electronic glitch or low battery.

One book, then. Choose a good 'un. One pen or pencil. One notepad. Paper, again. Oh, and lastly on this subject: you can read or write for a maximum of four hours each day. Time it. Be strict. If nothing else, it will give you a taste of what it was like for our ancestors back in the day when information was inherently valuable. Trust me. You are going to LOVE your phone again on Monday morning.

I completed the quarantine. Forty days and nights on the mountain. After the rain came the snow. Everything became magical overnight. *Into Great Silence*, ahh, my brothers – my sisters. If you haven't seen the movie, rack it up. I wrote a book I hadn't envisaged writing. It took ten days. It's probably still the purest thing I ever wrote, or ever will. Want to call it channelling? Too dangerous. It minds not me. The word "inspiration" is honour enough for whichever muse was on watch for those cold, advent hours.

Thinking on strange encounters, years later I discovered a fascinating coincidence: the modest yet peculiar peak I had climbed, bonded with, in whose shadow I had clung, was well known. Geologically, it is a genuine freak of nature. The theory goes that it was an extremely large segment of rock that got blasted out of a super-volcano 65 million years ago and landed back on the earth upside down, hence its weird appearance and constitution. The entire region around it is known for bizarre magnetic activity and, naturally, there are more tales and superstitions about the mountain itself than even Scheherazade could drum up. Everything from the resting place of the Arc of the Covenant, to Mary Magdalene to an inter-dimensional portal to a terrestrial UFO base to an alien transmitter to Armageddon 2012. Well, that's one down, at least.

Does it matter? Not really. Not for us, Kin. We're looking ahead and side to side, now. Right? Whatever experiences we may have had, let's not be overly zealous in comparing them with where we are heading. Keep it fresh, eyes of a newborn, and all that. All the same, it could say something for the power of magnetism. That force that pulls us, pre-consciously, in spite of our ensuing intellectual misgivings, to take a different fork in the trail. A new path – one which after even a few steps, feels more familiar than it has any right to feel. Whether the signpost has a colour code or not.

Enough chatter. Get on, Kin. Then we can get on. 48 hours – right? I'll do the same. Flashback is over. It's time to remember: WHO YOU ARE. I'll meet you back here for the main motion feature: the beginning of The Descent. You be ready, now. No cheating. Remember, if doubt should come: I love you. I will be waiting.

Ustoz

A Sufi is one who knows that nothing matters, yet acts as if everything does.

- Murshid Fazal Inayat-Khan

If it's signs we're after, our Hero's Journey is full of them. They are rarely colour-coded, granted. Sometimes, they are hidden or disguised, to put off the superficially curious and the non-committed. We may miss them entirely, and have to find out the hard way there are infinite ways up the mountain. One of the surest signs that you are really getting somewhere on your journey is that all at once everything appears to get harder. An investor pulls out, the market crashes, you get refused entry, your mentor dies – the forms this gauntlet can take are endless. Or you simply get tripped up. Not just by any old trap, no: by something specifically concocted for you.

In the 2012 film *Flight*, the Denzel Washington character's chief flaw is his addiction to alcohol. Aware of its grip on his life, he vows not to drink in the run up to a hearing where he is due to give evidence of a plane crash in which he was the pilot. The night before, Denzel a.k.a. 'Whip' Whitaker agrees to stay in a guarded hotel room so there can be no chance of him falling prey to his old vice. But – shock horror: someone has accidentally left a connecting door to the vacant next room unlocked. In it, would you believe, is a fully loaded minibar. For a decisive moment, Whip resists. Hesitantly taking a bottle of Vodka, he smells the contents, then replaces the cap and sets it down. He closes the fridge door. For an instant, it appears that he has walked away. Then a hand seizes the bottle, and – cue the montage.

For some, it's the distraction of sex that prevents them from achieving their Grail. More specifically, it is a perfectly timed encounter, on which decision hangs the entire outcome of the story. In *The Wrestler*, Mickey Rourke plays the aptly named Randy 'The Ram' Robinson, a once popular but now ageing and little remembered fighter. At one point, Randy finds himself approaching a potential moment of reconciliation with his estranged daughter, Stephanie. A part of him genuinely wishes to 'make good' on his past errors, as he feels emotionally connected to someone again for the first time in years. But a rejection of his advances by the messenger figure that initially fashioned the reconciliation sends him back into a spiral. Angry, he falls into an old pattern and runs into a young temptress, who is more than happy to help him release his frustration. Randy sleeps through the next day and misses the special dinner date with his daughter. This is the turning point in the hero's narrative arc, and he never gets the healing, or the prize, he desires.

Real life, unlike art, is rarely so linear. Back in the early 1980s, a young boxer from a broken Brooklyn childhood was taken under the wing of an older mentor figure and the two began their journey. The older man was reinvigorated by his stray prodigy, and for a few hard but mutually rewarding years he watched as the young man became a fearsome warrior. He predicted that one day his pupil would rock the world of boxing and become heavyweight champion of the world. He lived to witness the 18 year-old turn professional and win over a dozen fights, most by knockout or TKO. Then he died.

Distraught by the loss of his mentor, his role model, his legal guardian and all-round father figure, the young boxer nevertheless dug in and focused on his training. He continued to win fights and, two years later at the age of just twenty, became the youngest ever heavyweight world champion. But it was too much, too soon. Something had not healed. The young champ's brutal reputation in the ring was quickly overshadowed by his behaviour outside it. Eventually, he brought his demons to work with him. In no particular order, he was banned from boxing, lost fortunes, lost marriages and served time in prison for rape. By his own admission, it would be years before he managed to start getting a handle on what it could be that might make him whole. The last I saw, now in his mid-50s, Mike Tyson is on that journey still. Safe road, brother.

"Whip"? Randy "The Ram"? Fighters? Rape? Heavyweight champ? Wait a second: what happened to all that 'feminine focus' we were tipped off about earlier? Isn't this supposed to be The Cave – the balancing principle for The Tower and all that macho BULLshit?

Indeed, it is. These fables, fictitious or not, indicate that we are nearing our goal. Just as with the old Yin-Yang symbol where the seed of one principle arises only within the fullness of its opposite, so we observe the approaching limit of the 'masculine story', above, as it fails in its solitary desire to achieve isolated greatness. This is the maxing of vertical culture: the false Grail of western capitalism; the spiritual poverty of the ego's quest. In fiction, autobiography – in tale form. For now.

I knew I was getting somewhere when the legendary secret monastery I sought turned out to be a Soviet-style concrete compound on the edge of a two-bit desert town. The "Mad Max" Volga taxi that dropped us there on New Year's Day was driven by a baccy-chewing, curse-spitting homunculus with a blade in his boot and a Russian service pistol jammed under the seat cushion. Being somewhere close to nowhere and several degrees below frostbite, our volatile but entertaining helmsman spent the night and left on the morrow a convert to our hosts' life example.

I missed him at breakfast. I was too hungover to move. Well, my Kin: signs don't come better than that.

Patience – or the lack thereof: a big flaw of mine among many other psychological fissures. It had taken me six weeks to get there. Six weeks of searching, asking questions, following cold trails that led to dead ends and generally reassuring myself, not always successfully, that I wasn't clinically delusional. The flight into Tashkent had been exciting – up to the point of landing. I had already experienced ex-USSR style bureaucracy, but the three hours it took to get through customs and into the country in the small hours of a winter's morning knocked the polish off any romanticism I might still have been hoarding. No matter. This was business. A long time in coming. Expectations were not my allies. When I finally got to the hotel, I told myself I might be the first person to attempt this particular crazy mission in almost a century.

Gurdjieff had left clues. In his writing, and verbally to his pupils. I hadn't met any of those, not directly. Not yet. But in his book *Meetings With Remarkable Men*, an autobiographical travelogue of sorts, he had dropped the names of towns and regions he visited, and some of the people he encountered. The city that interested me most was Bukhara. At the time he visited in the late 1800s, it was still notionally an independent Emirate 'under the protection of imperialist Russia'. Ie: a vassal state. Soon after, it was swallowed by the nascent Soviet Union and all but lost to the outside world. Political history, however, was not at the focus of my enquiries.

In Fourth Way lore, it was known that Gurdjieff had met a certain dervish in Bukhara at the central *Lab-i Hauz* complex, the square that was built around the public pond. After a few days, the dervish agreed to show the young seeker to a special place of learning outside the city. According to his story, Gurdjieff was saddled on a mule and blindfolded so that he could not subsequently show others the way. He was then led on a fourteen-day journey through the unforgiving surrounding countryside until finally they reached the infamous monastery. What he learned there, the initiation he underwent, contributed a large body of knowledge to the eventual system as it was transmitted to the West.

Via Samarkand, at the crossroads of the Silk Route, the heart of Asia known also as "Heaven's Mirror", I arrived in Bukhara. The old city is tiny by modern standards, in a footrace you could cross it in under five minutes, but that would be rather to miss the point. Even after centuries of turmoil, and Soviet domination, and the blight of modern tourism, this defiant yet humble desert fortress still holds innumerable jewels in its heart. I found my way to the central pond, practically empty of other travellers at this time of year, sat down at an adjacent *chaikhana*, ordered tea, and waited. A modern statue of the famous Mullah, Nasreddin, on his equally renowned donkey, saluted from across the square. Gurdjieff's writing is full of the Mullah's exploits, at once amusing and sage. It felt like a personal welcome. To pass the time, I read the guide book I had picked up in England before leaving. The antithesis of the usual touristic patter, it had been written and revised by a couple of guys who evidently had fallen under the spell of what in the current age is known as the Republic of Uzbekistan – the country in which technically I now sat.

Like so many regions in the area, or anywhere that is repeatedly invaded and parcelled up by that year's top megalomaniac plus cavalry, Bukhara and her environs had belonged to a seemingly endless succession of dynasties and rulers over the millennia. After the collapse of the Soviet empire in the early '90s, the city became part of the newly declared independent republic. If you look at a map, you will notice that with the exception of the mountainous eastern provinces of Fergana and Andizhan, Uzbekistan's borders are drawn, Africa-style, in straight lines with the habitually sightless nibs of oppressors' pencils. Tribes and peoples and families are divided. Previously harmonious or at least coherent cultures are separated, mashed together, scattered to the wind and forgotten. Almost forgotten. Ruin and rule. "Let the past die," as the First Order's Supreme Leader, Kylo Ren, insists: "Kill it if you have to." Indeed, Bukhara was almost killed on many occasions, not just by the Bolsheviks, but by Arabs, by Genghis Khan and a host of other squabbling would-be Emperors. Try as they might, however, and under whatever political pretexts our so-called leaders may claim to operate, there are some traditions that will not die.

An hour passed. I ordered lunch. Delicious, *rahmat*. Another hour. I was heartened that, according to the guide, the lovely mulberry trees surrounding the pond were in many cases centuries old. I was looking at the very same trees that Gurdjieff would have seen, sheltered under, when the square was a bustling marketplace with men and women in traditional flowing dress, merchants traded spices and animals and tales, dervishes hung out by the dozen before the 17th Century *khanqah* – the lodge for itinerant Sufis – across from the exquisite *madrassah*, and all was, well: just roses, roses.

Mid-afternoon. No sign came to me. What did I expect? A hundred-and-fifty year old dervish to appear at the table and tell me in broken English: "This way, Aka – your mule is ready." I took a walk through the frozen city. Wandered the old bazaars and trading domes, discovered hidden workshops in old *madrassahs*, stared up at the majestic and elegant lines of the famous 900 year-old Khalon Minaret, scarred by the shells of the Bolshevik Red Army, and met friendly people everywhere. There were children in the streets and the squares. Heedless of the sub-zero temperature, they were eating seeds and sweets, running, shouting, playing football: "Manchester United!" they would invariably yell on discovering my native country. Others were selling goods, from dried fruit and spices to tourist trinkets and ceramics. I got talking at one stall to a boy in his early teens, he trying on his impressive if broken English to my basic Russian dusted with a few syllables of Uzbek. I bought a *piala* – the local form of teacup – and he invited me to dinner with his family. I stayed with the Minaret Mafia, as they fondly became known to me, for ten days.

Can you imagine that where you're living? An out-of-towner turns up, looking kind of lost and foreign, evidently not some fat-cashed tourist, so you decide to move into the sitting room and put them up for the best part of a fortnight. I insisted I would be happy sleeping on the floor in the salon of their modest but charming home. They wouldn't have it. I said I'd been paying fifty bucks a night at the hotel and offered them the same: they were visibly horrified. How can such places charge so much, and with such terrible food on offer? There were the parents and four children in the house: two biological, one adopted and one cousin. Could I help with the food? They laughed and ushered me to sit on the plumpest cushion on the floor where they ate. What did I think: that they were starving?

In the evenings after dinner, the father, a tinker by trade, offered me brandy to drink. "*Chut chut*" – just a little. The family was ethnically Tajik but, as with everywhere in the country at that time, especially with the older generations, we always spoke in Russian. I accepted, though was confused by the apparent conflict of their outwardly Muslim lifestyle and this major taboo. When I woke early, I would always find my host solemnly performing his morning prayers. What was the deal?

'It *is* a deal, Jason brother,' he told me confidentially. 'You see, Allah knows that I drink, because Allah knows everything. I work hard all day to look after the family, and in the evening, I have something after dinner. Sometimes I even have too much. Well, Allah is always watching. Early in the morning, I feel a finger on my cheek, here' – he showed me – 'and He says "Orif! Get up. I know you have been drinking again. Go and perform your prayers, and I will forgive you." So I do. Every morning, I repent, then go and do a day's work. In the evening I drink again, and every morning, He wakes me up and then forgives me again. It's not for everybody, but for me, it's a good deal.'

They were generous and playful and always respectful. When I explained, as best I could, what I was doing in their city, it elicited many tales and questions, but no concrete pointers of how or where best to look. I had already made my visit to and paid homage at the tomb of arguably the city's most famous esoteric teacher, the 14th Century Sufi Master Baha-ud-Din Naqshband. I had sniffed around for some scent of present activity there but found nothing to twitch my nostrils. Why should I? You don't go to Poet's Corner at Westminster Abbey and expect to find a secret creative writing class in progress. A guide I had met back in Tashkent told me he had studied with the present *Naqshbandi* group, and that while the training was intense and profound, they were very strict on observing Islamic practices. Indeed, it was not feasible for a non-Muslim to practice with them. I wasn't sure about becoming a Muslim at that point, moreover, in spite of my naturally rebellious disposition, I felt it would not be respectful to try to be the exception and gatecrash the transcendental party. I would look for my ticket to nirvana via another agency, fascinated as I was by what little I knew of the *Naqshbandi* tradition. Our paths would cross further up the track, besides.

As often happens, that ticket pretty much fell into my lap when I had just about given up all hope and enthusiasm. I was camped down over Christmas in Samarkand, staying with another magnanimous family at their beautiful courtyard B&B near Tamerlane's final resting place, the Gur Emir. The family home-cum-enterprise was managed by two highly educated sisters and the elder sibling's polyglot teenage daughter. Having graduated from university under the old Soviet system, the sisters embodied an already vanishing demographic of Uzbeks who bemoaned the eroding of certain qualities in society since the break from the Communist system. For them, independence came with a high price. As an Indian friend used to be fond of telling me, "At least the British left us the cricket when they finally went home". We chatted about and agreed on many things, but they found the notion of seeking for mystical or esoteric schools and teachings in their back yard faintly absurd.

'What is wrong with you?' Ziza would ask incredulously. 'You have a perfectly good brain: why are you looking around Central Asia for fairytales? This is all just crazy stories.' Then we would share a huge dinner, and they would find me some local wine, and we would sit snugly by the heater looking out at the snow-covered garden, while their mother vainly attempted to teach me old Tajik songs, and we would laugh until tears rolled.

Being excellent and knowledgeable hosts, and with the desire to humour me, the ladies did make connections for me. On one excursion, they took me to see a local *folbin* – wise woman or fortune teller – they knew of. We spent the homeward journey trying to come up with convincing reasons to Ziza for why the chicken had to die just so I could know my future. Another time, a neighbour of theirs, a veteran from the military in Cold War times, dropped by and explained to me the precise details, with drawings, of a UFO crash in Siberia at the beginning of the 20th Century.

'At least there is some science to this,' Ziza shrugged while regarding the hastily sketched cross-section of an alien propulsion system. I conceded that logically it was more plausible I'd meet visitors from outer space than blindly stumble upon the hidden kingdom of Agartha any time soon.

Then, late one evening, I heard newcomers in the courtyard. Apart from one Japanese student on sabbatical, there were no other residents for Christmas. To be specific, there was no Christmas. I was therefore intrigued, no less because between themselves, a man and woman, they spoke in German.

I had already eaten breakfast the following morning when Ziza tapped excitedly on the door of my room. 'You must meet these people,' she insisted: 'He is a German diplomat working in Tashkent and she is a Swiss tour operator from Bukhara. She is showing him around Samarkand for a couple of days before he goes home to Germany, but listen: the lady is coming back here next week on her way to a special centre for natural medicine. The town where it is located is really nothing, but apparently the head of the centre is a well-known healer. They are Sufis there. Come, come, I have made some special chai with lemon.'

That, dear Kin, was how I ended up awaking on 2nd January 2004 in the middle of frozen nowhere, Uzbekistan, with the mother of all hangovers. The night before, I met Ustoz for the first time. For once, the hangover was worth it. Nothing has really been the same since.

Have you ever had a great teacher, Kin? Someone who truly inspired you, whose memory continues to inspire you to this day? What did they teach you? By that, I mean more than just their chosen subject: Science or Mathematics or Art or Music, Carpentry or Basketball. What was it about them that made a difference to you and your overall perception of life – of yourself? That engaged you, connected with you, in-formed you to the point that the effect lingers even to the present second? Take a moment. Remember them. Recall what it was to be in their presence.

Taking up from writer Muriel Spark's earlier observations, a great teacher for me is not just someone who is simply proficient in the technique of uploading information onto the internal filing systems of their pupils. While the transmission of information is necessary for constructing knowledge, it is this latter process that is at the heart of an educational foundation. How to transform one into the other? A drill sergeant has a critical role in training cadets, certainly, but he or she alone does not shape the faculties that result in a fully formed soldier. Those finer qualities that may in time differentiate the average private from the excellent future brigadier must be breathed on, given space to crystallise, carefully honed and led out to meet with the external environment, where they can be trialled and refined in the field so as to accomplish their purpose. This is in itself an art as well as a science. Raw data input is just the coarse material that feeds the growth process.

George Bernard Shaw came up with the rather cruel idiom: "Those who can, do; those who can't, teach." Cruel, yet undoubtedly accurate in many cases. I'm sure we can all remember supposed educators who we would pin, perhaps with satisfaction in hindsight, under that label. For me, though, I would say that it is some of the very finest of those "doers" who make the greatest teachers of all. They do not merely transmit their subject: they embody it. Whether a seamstress, a nursery teacher, a swimming instructor or a professor of nuclear physics, they live and breathe and emanate their passion, their obsession, their Grail. You cannot but help be transformed by it, captivated by it, infected by it in a positive sense – you want to know what it feels like to know what they know, be able to do what they do. In turn, they know where you, the student, now stand. More, they know how to build and navigate the bridge between the two stations, sometimes with an apparently eternal gulf to traverse, and see you safely over to the other side, with your own bridge-making programme installed.

My privileged education had introduced to me to some fine teachers. Many were extraordinarily knowledgeable, true experts in their respective fields. Some were undoubtedly wise. None more so than Alec, my father's former boss, and his kindly wife, my Fourth Way teachers. Above being leaders in their chosen professions, they were truly masters of life and lived their philosophy, always perceptive, empathetic, and compassionate to the end. At the same time, they and all the other lights that had illuminated my journey thus far were to varying degrees bound to the systems, the societies, in which they lived. Consciously or not, they seemed unable, or unconcerned with, moving beyond the boundaries that inevitably define our everyday lives which, as individuals, we adopt as a matter of course. Could it be possible to live a 'life unlimited'? Was there anyone who existed in such a free state that they were able to actually live in this duality-based world without being a slave to its inherent, paradoxical blueprint?

I recall the story from the Hasidic tradition of the seeker who heard of a famous *Zadik,* an enlightened teacher, and after many years of failed attempts and struggles at last managed to find himself in the master's presence. After mere minutes, before any words had been said, the pupil bowed and turned away to begin the long journey home. His companions rushed after him. "Where are you going?" they asked in amazement. "We've only just got here – don't you want to hear him speak?" Their friend smiled. "It is enough for me to see the *Zadik* tie his own shoelaces," he replied. With that, he set off home.

When I was growing up, I remember that at my grandparents' house there was a grand, quite stuffy looking Victorian writing desk. Being a kid, I delighted in climbing on it and opening the many little drawers, some of which contained old letters and black and white photographs. They depicted children in long dresses being held by severe women with what looked like eagles on their heads. My grandmother would usually catch me, gather up the scattered images and then gently but firmly close everything up once more. "This belonged to your great-great-great Grandmother," she told me. "Be careful: this desk was a gift from grateful ladies, and those letters and photographs were sent by the Queen." Much later, I discovered that my ancestor had founded an organisation called The Mother's Union. It did just what it said on the elegant old hand-crafted tin, and it exists to this day. One of her famous sayings was this: "Remember – be yourselves as you would have your children be."

Be yourself. "To be – or not to be." Make your life your message. Hashtag. Hah!

Easy – right?

How the hell had this happened? I rubbed my face and sat up. Some kindly murid had covered my comatose form with blankets during the night where I lay, on comfortable floor cushions by the gently woofling gas fire in the meditation room. Outside, I could hear the hum of the human hive as the centre went about its daily work. I ran the previous night's events through the clouded space inside my aching skull.

After a five hour mission from Samarkand through freezing fog, seeing scarcely another soul on the snow-sprinkled highway, we had been greeted at the centre by several students, male and female, and shown into the guest apartments. My companions, being the friendly Swiss tour operator and a couple of her local young employees in the company of their sick mother, seemingly found our new environment as unfamiliar as I did, in spite of the habitual customs and the typically warm Uzbek welcome. Nothing definitive set it apart. It was just a taste.

We had been seated at a large table in the dining room, which was unusual since as is typical across much of Asia most meals at home are eaten sitting on the floor. I was to learn that this was in deference to the many European visitors who came regularly to stay at the centre. We were presented with an enormous spread, with homemade bread and soup and rich salads, followed by the inevitable mountains of *plov*, eaten by hand and offered repeatedly until the bowl between diners is picked clean and the cotton oil is running off your elbow. Then sweets, and desserts, and tea, and on and on. A little way into the meal, a tall, well-built man with pronounced features, apparently more Mongolian than Uzbek, entered quietly into the room. One of the murids – simply 'pupil' – took his hefty winter *chapan*, that is long Uzbek coat, and the man sat down next to me at the table. As is customary, he offered thanks, and started eating.

'Where are you from?' he asked me in English. I told him. 'Hm, that is good.' He considered. 'The English are very sober,' he said. 'A lot of very good people from England. Shakespeare.' He clenched his fist, and smiled. He was looking at me. Through me. His eyes didn't flinch for an instant. I realised, all at once and beyond any thought I could muster at that moment, that he saw me. Fully. There was nothing I could – and nowhere to – hide. Then he laughed. He patted me on the arm. Turning to one of the boys, only just a teen, he asked for a fresh pot of hot tea. He returned his gaze to me.

'What is your name?'

'Jason.'

'Jay-son,' he repeated slowly, weighing the word. He thought for a moment. 'In Uzbek: *Jasur*.' He nodded. I smiled back. Obviously, I had just been bestowed with the mother of all names and wanted him to know I appreciated it earnestly.

'What is your name?' I asked him in my best St Petersburg Russian.

'Oh – you speak Russian?' He was visibly pleased. 'Please – eat, eat.' I did as I was instructed. 'What other languages do you know?'

I told him I knew French and Italian and some German.

'Ah, I love to speak Italian,' he said, in Italian. '*La Dolce Vita*.' Then, switching to French: 'But I have to say that my French is better. Can we speak in French? Then we can have a free conversation. *Bon appétit*.'

So French it was. He told me his name. It was not one I knew. I noted that the boys and girls serving us and the young men and women seated among us, whilst saying very little themselves, always addressed him as Ustoz. I asked if I should do the same.

'Yes, if you like.' His eyes, like his smile, never wavered. 'Tell me: what brings you to Uzbekistan?'

Well, Kin: I don't need to tell you again, do I? You, who have been such a patient and loyal companion on this interminable journey. Allow me to thank you for having made it with me to this point. Truly, without your continued presence beside me, I could not have come this far.

I showed Ustoz the little notebook I carried with me. In it, among the scraps of journal and ideas, I had scribbled a few images and diagrams. Graphic representations of esoteric systems and concepts, designed to help keep my compass needle pointing in the right direction during my Quest. One of them was a faithful representation of a key symbol from the Fourth Way teaching: The Enneagram. Like so many ancient symbols, it has in more recent times been appropriated to work as a foundation principle for other systems: in this instance, as a kind of psychological personality test. It has been developed to serve another school of practice in its own right, and is often employed in psychology, even, unsurprisingly, for use in highly lucrative business guidance seminars. There may be merit in that. You can make your own enquiry. I knew nothing of this at the time. For me, it was an obvious litmus test. Did Ustoz recognise it?

'This is a very powerful symbol,' Ustoz said. He gave nothing away. 'My son,' he continued, indicating a strong and impassive young man seated further down the table, 'knows a lot about this. You can ask him tomorrow, if you wish.'

I couldn't help myself. 'Was he here?' I blurted. 'Did Gurdjieff come here?'

Ustoz regarded me for a few moments with that unflinching stare. 'Are *you* here?' he asked. He held my gaze a little longer. Then he smiled once more. 'Would you like something else to drink? Do you like beer? Or wine?'

Snapped out of my reverie, I was unwilling to let it go. I considered it would be respectful to follow my host's cue, however. There was always tomorrow. I looked around the table and noted that, with the exception of our vociferous taxi driver, no one was drinking alcohol. Who'd have figured – in the midst of what could be, at least in my excited imagination, the Grail Castle for an Islamic-based hidden esoteric mystery school? I declined respectfully. Ustoz asked if I did not drink alcohol, and I answered that usually I did, sometimes too much, but that I was happy to fit in with the prevalent local custom. He nodded and we chatted some more, about my profession, the natural medicine that was practiced at the centre, and about travels in general. Ustoz, who I put somewhere in his early fifties, had evidently led a varied and unusual life.

He then turned his attention to the rest of the assembled guests, and the language switched back to the lingua franca: Russian. One to one I could just about get by, but in a lively exchange of many voices I struggled to catch a lot of the details. Rumil, who's mother had come to the centre looking for relief from an internal complaint, did his best to translate the gist of the conversation, but it was largely hijacked by our driver who, fuelled by beer and the satisfaction of a colossal free dinner ticket, made voluble interjections every other sentence. Eventually, having collected wads of the local currency from his clients, he made a toast, repeating over and over in stoned awe: 'This is no joke –

these guys are serious, it's no joke,' at which point Ustoz signalled to one of the murids, who scampered out on an errand.

'We will all toast,' whispered Ustoz to me. 'As is the custom of our guest. But not with beer.' He winked.

Two large, old-fashioned bottles were placed on the table, one at each end. *Pialas* were brimmed before the master and the guests. None for the murids. They did not appear to mind.

'To our guests,' toasted Ustoz, 'who have travelled so far. You are all very welcome. I hope you find here whatever you are looking for.'

Pialas were drained. I blinked rapidly. Across from me, I'm pretty sure I heard the tour operator gasp. I looked at the bottle in front of us. It contained a clear liquid, inside of which was what looked like some old plant matter and a small, black stick.

Ustoz smiled. He indicated it was my turn. *Pialas* were refilled. It might help you to know, for your envisioning, that the average *piala* holds approximately the liquid volume you'll find in a regular quadruple Scotch. I said something along the lines of thank you and how honoured we were to be at their table – the usual fey European diplomatic gabble – then tentatively dispatched the contents of my vessel to go and wreak havoc with its predecessor. This time, I noted, our friendly tour operator actually spluttered. It was now her toast. Empty or not, *pialas* were refilled. Oh well, I figured. Back in the USSR. Whatever was in this hooch, it was starting to give me a buzz. I couldn't think of anywhere I would rather be right at that moment. I made a note to self not to remove any items of clothing – a couple of the female murids had already caught my eye – and lifted my ceramic chalice for round three.

Things are pretty blurry after that. More French-Russian-English chit-chat. A lot of laughter. A video presentation of some of the things that were practiced by the group, professionally shot in-house, containing a mixture of the beautiful and confounding and downright bizarre. At some point, Ustoz made a respectful exit. Apparently unaffected in either mind or body by the mysterious elixir, he hugged me and said something about an excursion the following day. 'It's New Year,' he said, smiling. Then, he and the murids were gone.

The last conscious entry for the night is of me and Rumil, eating Russian chocolates and drinking beer, in front of the original version of the film *Titanic* at around two in the morning. Rumil lay on the floor, laughing wildly as I shouted 'Jack's dead! Let him go!' over and over at a shivering Kate Winslet. Afterwards, unable to find my cosy and well-appointed room, I must have crashed out in the tranquil and no doubt sanctified space of the meditation hall.

So it was, dear Kin, that your not so humble companion stumbled into the realms of the enlightened.

La Dolce Vita

The organism that's evolving is the super-organism called Human Civilisation. And right now, humans are fighting each other and killing each other, and if I say: 'Well, what would that look like in the body if the cells fight each other and kill each other?' And I say, 'Oh, well that's called autoimmune disease - self-destruction.'

- Dr. Bruce Lipton

Well, Kin. Happy New Year. Is it happy where you're sitting? Sure, it can be. Not out there, perhaps. If the external world seems scary, that's nothing new: just stick with me a while. Where I'm sitting, back in my tower for to continue scribbling this love letter to you and our Kin, things are pretty good. I've a heater to stop these hands getting too cold, and a mug of hot green tea, while outside the land is dusted white by the morning frost, twinkling in the light of the winter sun. From the window, I can see smoke rising from the stacks of the neighbours' chimneys, and even the breath from the cattle in the valley below. My treasures are at school, save for my wife, who is putting this old house back in order. Here we are. I breathe and I'm glad.

Of course, were we to look at the news today I've no doubt we would be informed otherwise. Despite the initial moment of gratitude for leaving a terrible year behind, this new beginning is not without omens. Notwithstanding the creation of more than one vaccine, there is still a global virus on the loose. One that is already mutating, according to some. Then there is the little island where I first began this terrestrial journey: after great difficulty, it has apparently at last succeeded in severing itself from the maine. Will the new start herald a grand renaissance – or a steady continued sinking into a mire of its own making? The metaphor you choose no doubt depends on which of the 17.5 quadrillion pages you read. I tend to stick with the Zen master: "We'll see." And of course there's the exponentially warming climate, the ongoing farce surrounding the US presidential handover, the claim that the Iranians are enriching uranium again – on and on the lumpy wheel turns.

In the emboldening words of Bob Newhart: "We don't go there."

There is a bar in St Petersburg that is famous for celebrating New Year's Eve. Not just on December 31st – pretty much any establishment in that city will fulfil this task to requirement – but in fact on every night of the year. When my soul brother, Simon, and I were on our way to see Ustoz, more than a year after my initial contact, we got stuck there for a while. For three or was it four nights in a row, towards the end of May, at around ten o'clock we'd walk into this club on the *Fontanka* Canal and be attacked by grinning guys and girls in full white bunny costumes. Every night, just before midnight, the countdown started, to be followed by a joyous eruption as the chimes struck, corks popped and everybody got, well: how do you get when you're young and it's New Year's? Exactly. I guess that around day five, waking up in the back of the Land Rover in a warm, sticky sweat with another credit card gone, we remembered that fun as it was, this wasn't the true purpose of our mission. With grateful hearts and throbbing heads, we waved goodbye to Groundhog Bunnyland Night and pointed our lumbering steed south. Not all white rabbits are there to lead us home.

What we're coming to is this: it's not just that we can create our own reality. We've all heard that "New Age" meme enough, right? More soberly, it's this: we can't help but create our own reality. If we don't get ourselves conscious enough to create the one we want – the one our true heart desires – then we're already busy creating its opposite. The one we fear. That we did not want. The one we try to reject, and which ultimately will surround and then become us. If we live asleep, we die in sleep. Like dog. If we live in fear – both feeding off, and feeding to others – in and through fear we die. If we live on love...

Ah, words. So easy. Here I am, Kin, seventeen years on. Seventeen years almost to the day. Dang. Since I woke up in that meditation room and knew – *knew* – I could do it. I *could* live a life that was free, that I chose, that I made, with grace, if I willed it. I knew now what before I had only suspected because, at last, I had witnessed it. I had met a human being who did exactly that. All I had to do now was to watch, listen and learn.

If I could just get myself out of my own damn way.

I've never been great on fish. Real fish, that is, not the processed tinned stuff that's currently mutating entire species and emptying the planet's oceans. It's the bones, you see? As I already said, I'm not good on patience. If I can smell the meat, I want to eat the meat. I can't be doing with picking morsel after tiny mini-bite-sized morsel off almost imperceptible but potentially lethal biological ossein poignards. I'm not partial to nibbling. Not on dead flesh. It is, I suppose, a fair truism that we tend to find not so much the teachings we seek as the lessons we need.

The morning after my meeting with the Ultimate Mentor – call it Gandalf, Elrond and Galadriel rolled into one – we went for a drive. In a battered yet unbreakable old Russian army jeep, driven by Ustoz's son and protégé, we toured the town and the immediate countryside surrounding the centre. Rumil's mother and sister had stayed behind for treatment, which left just myself, Rumil and the tour operator, Andrea, to accompany our hosts. Ustoz pointed out various landmarks and told stories about the town and how its people survived the harsh seasonal extremes, all the while happily answering Andrea's questions about how feasible it would be to bring other paying guests and what they might be able to offer them. At the mention of a special Sufi massage, Andrea was delighted. Rendered silent for once by my pounding headache, I caught our driver's eyes for a moment in the rear view mirror. I was sure that for the first time I saw him smile.

After the tour and a walk through the snow-bound terrain, Ustoz announced we would go to a special restaurant for lunch. We would be his guests, he insisted, for his group it was one of the favoured local eateries. It served only one type of food: fish. I tell you, Kin, by now I was sure the Fates were real and they were laughing themselves silly backstage. Uzbekistan is a double-landlocked country. Its most infamous body of water is the tragically barren Aral Sea – not so long ago Earth's fourth largest lake and a self-contained fishing industry for the infant Soviet Union, now a poisoned puddle. The fishing boats and villages can still be seen where they were abandoned, a hundred or more kilometres from the present shoreline. Irrigation for cotton of the similarly waning rivers that now only just feed it, the once mighty *Amu Darya* and *Syr Darya*, has altered the water cycle, and the climate, of the entire region. It was the middle of winter. We were in a desert town. And we were going to a fish restaurant?

Very well. I indicated my enthusiasm by not manifesting any of yesterday's comestibles into our lurching, diesel-rich environment, and with bright and jolly faces we chugged our way across town and into yet another Soviet-style concrete courtyard, almost indistinguishable from any other we had yet seen. Received and welcomed with great familiarity and respect in equal measure, Ustoz and his latest crew were shown to a table. We were offered water with which to wash our hands, and almost at once the food began to arrive.

To be fair, it was pretty good. Deep fried, meaty and rich, wherever the mysterious pescatarian pleasing menu had been sourced, there could be no doubting its inherent quality. On a normal lunchtime, the incongruous local platters would have made a refreshing change from the typically mutton-heavy Uzbek diet. The trouble was, I was feeling anything but normal. Encouraged by my hosts and by the restaurant's genial owner, as always when a guest at a Central Asian banquet, to eat, eat, and more eat, my system's warning signs advanced speedily through amber and red to "get ready to scramble". Excusing myself as casually as I could, I half-staggered, half-ran towards the obligatory hard-to-find tiled cabinet with hole in floor and unleashed the full barrage of failed digestive process from the previous twenty-four hours. For a few brief, blissful moments, I told myself, as my trembling hands dabbed the cold sweat and any lingering remnants from my ashen visage, my search for contentment was over.

Back at the table, they were waiting for me.

'Are you okay?' Andrea asked.

I nodded I was fine. My buddy of the night before, Rumil, said nothing. His expression, however, put my stomach straight back in fight or flight mode.

'That is good.' Ustoz looked pleased. He appeared to take me at my word. 'Here: I have had them prepare this. Just for you.'

On a plate in front of my place at the table was what looked like a Victorian museum exhibit. About a foot long, fat and black like an eel, with its head hanging off the dish, tongue, teeth, eyes and all, was your queasy diner's nightmare made fish. A large, wooden-handled knife had been placed beside it. Everybody waited. As steadily as I could, I took my seat and tried to inhale as deeply as possible without offending my fellow diners. Tentatively, I picked up the knife. Where the hell do I start? I prodded the bloated corpse. My Oscar Wilde came back for my gallows amusement: me or the fish – one of us has to go. Somebody mercifully poured me some tea. I gulped it down.

'Oh, Jasur...'

I looked up.

Ustoz regarded me. He was smiling – not with humour, not with playfulness. He smiled with kindness.

'I think perhaps,' he said slowly, 'you are not so very keen on fish.'

'I'm – I'm not feeling a hundred percent today,' I replied, depleting in one hit any lingering reserves of understatement.

With the lightest of gestures, Ustoz signalled for the offending leviathan to be removed. He then indicated for his son to take something from a bag they had brought with them into the restaurant.

'Here,' he said, as a shining disc of bread was unwrapped, 'this is *non* bread from Samarkand. Eat some. You will feel better.'

Gratefully, I did so. He then poured something into my *piala* and motioned for me to drink it. I did this as well, noting thankfully that it wasn't the same as whatever had catalysed the present caper the night before. In a matter of minutes, if not quite all roses, my system felt back online.

'Why?' I asked when eventually I had relaxed once more. The dense, thick bread had done the trick down below and my head was clearing. Table conversation had resumed. Ustoz waited for me to continue. I couldn't help laughing.

'I've come six thousand miles,' I cried, 'after years of searching, to try and find the source of all these teachings, the thing I sometimes only just hoped or believed even existed, and when I get here, having tried to leave all those bad practices and habits and vices behind, you get me completely wasted!'

'Wasted?'

I mimed it, to make sure it wasn't lost in translation.

Ustoz was chuckling now, too.

'What did you drink last night?' he asked. 'Did you drink something else, after the spirit?'

Sheepishly, Rumil and I confessed we had tucked into beers and a movie later on.

Ustoz waved a hand. 'There is nothing useful in beer,' he said flatly. 'This is not surprising. Tell me: how does your body receive its information? Mostly, through the stomach and the digestive tract. More than eighty percent of the information coming into the organism goes through and is taken into the body through the gut.

This is base science. What the blood transmits into your cells from digestion affects your physical condition and also your mind, the two are linked, how can it be otherwise? We have so many people coming here, wanting explanations for some philosophy, or miracle healing or to know about the real Sufism, to understand secrets – you understand?' I nodded that I did. 'Yet they don't even know how to feed their body properly. What information their organism should or should not take in. How is it possible to evolve or grow spiritually if you cannot even look after the poor biological animal you inhabit?'

'So that's why you got me drunk? To see how I take care of myself?'

'You got yourself drunk all on your own,' Ustoz replied. 'You can say no. That spirit is strong, but it is very pure. It is not used just for getting high. But yes, it can also lead to inebriation. And I like to see what there is to work with.'

He was looking through me again. It was a look with which I would become familiar, though of which I would never be able to say I got used to. I raised my piala of tea and said thank you.

Ustoz chuckled again, warmly.

'Ahh, Jasur,' he sighed. 'What are we going to do?'

I stayed at the centre for a few days. It was a tasting experience rather than the full immersion course, but some of those tastes left indelible traces nonetheless. In the way of Ustoz and his group, nominally a chain of transmission anchored in the aforementioned Sufi saint, Khodja Yassaviy, there were many directions of study. Among various rooms and buildings around the extensive compound, there was the medical centre, for treating patients with traditional Central Asian medical techniques and herbs from the nearby mountains; the gym, where gymnastic movements, breathing exercises and martial arts were practised; classrooms, where murids learned calligraphy, studied the Quran and also anatomy and foreign languages; the garden, with fruit trees and vegetables and sheep for the pot; and the *zikrxona* – the temple for making *zikr*, the Sufi practice of unifying the heart with The Beloved, a.k.a "God". This last, above all, I was itching to see and, if permitted, take part in.

First, however, as Ustoz had already pointedly noted, I needed to check my meat body – G's carriage – in for a service.

Every morning, Ustoz ran a clinic for the local populace, as well as for people who had travelled from all around the country and beyond, sometimes for days, in order to be seen. The appointment began with a pulse diagnosis. I had seen this technique used before in traditional Chinese medicine, though it was the first time I had had it done personally. Ustoz laid and then pressed his fingers on the pulse points of both my wrists respectively, then told me to what extent my internal organ systems were functioning. Unsurprisingly, my liver was low, as too were my kidneys. He pressed again. After a pause he said, 'You have urine in your blood.'

'Urine?'

He nodded. 'There is old pathology here. Something cold, from years ago. You must clean it. I will give you some herbs.' He signalled to a murid, who took down a list and scurried off. On a specially printed list of foods, Ustoz crossed off a number of things I was not to ingest for a period of three months – a diet to maintain in conjunction with my prescribed herbs. Among the off-limits items were aubergines, tomatoes, refined sugar, dairy and beer.

'Only Sufi spirit for Jasur,' he quipped, catching my eye. 'Now, our murid will take you to see Shukhrat. For a massage.' Ustoz beamed.

I thanked him and followed the silent young messenger, out through the waiting room and down the stairs into an annexe. I hadn't figured on being indulged in relaxation therapy whilst out in the monastery, but after the embarrassment of my arrival and the early morning physical exercises, hey, why not? Half an hour's downtime was just what the doctor ordered. The old Soviet *petchka* or heater in the corner made this zone of the centre particularly toasty. Maybe one of the shy and pretty young female students would be looking after me? I was feeling better already.

I was first alerted that this might not be your regular Swedish-style, warming body rub by the shouts of pain and alarm. They were coming, at far too frequent intervals, from the cubicle where Andrea was having her massage. To her credit, the cheerful and driven business entrepreneur was managing to swear with vivid expression in at least three languages, in between outbursts of sheer animal-in-pain intensity. The young murid who guided me indicated I wait on an adjacent chair outside. His expression never changed.

'Wait,' I said as he turned to go. 'Is that...Shukhrat in there?'

The boy nodded. 'Shukhrat very strong,' he confided. He trotted off once more.

A new culture, a new language: new names. I had learned many since my arrival in Tashkent. I now knew another one and, if I wasn't sure five minutes before, it would be imprinted into me over the following half hour that in Uzbek, Shukhrat is, indeed, a boy's name.

In the cubicle across the hall, the screaming finally stopped. There came a ringing series of "Bangs!" like canon firing, or meat on a block being axed, followed by a low and drawn out groan, and then the curtain drew aside. I appraised my imminent destiny. The man was little taller than myself, about three times as wide, with no neck, dark iron paws and a grin that went from ear to ear. He was, bar the infamous top hat, the Uzbek version of Oddjob. With a bow and a show of one of the lethal weapons attached to his arms, he invited me to go and wait in a nearby cubicle. No need to strip off, just lie face down and relax the body. He'd be with me as soon as he had dealt with what was left of our Swiss Tour Operator next door. Weakly, I did as he asked. From the adjacent abattoir, there was another muffled moan and the sound of a body being righted, followed by the distinct crack of bones and a final piercing shout. Through the curtain at the foot of the table on which I lay, a flash of bedraggled long blonde hair indicated that Andrea had finally managed to flee, though whether or not under her own steam I couldn't tell. In my mind's eye, I saw Shukhrat carrying the body out into the courtyard, where a murid with a shovel waited by a ready-dug hole in the snow. Then, it was my turn.

The agony and the ecstasy: never one without the other. Right? Well, I figured, as the colossus that was Shukhrat pushed and twisted my limbs and torso into positions I hadn't seen even in Yoga books, the ecstasy was going to have to be pretty damn explosive if it was going to balance up with the sensations I was experiencing now. It wasn't that he was brutal – all force and no direction. The force that he possessed, which was considerable, was directed perfectly.

First, using a gold tipped metal pen, he drew lines down my body's energetic meridians. This, I learned later, was to 'open up blocked channels' and facilitate the natural flow of energy that a healthy organism enjoys. Judging by the pressure of the metal tracing down my muscles, and the ensuing electric jolts that shot through my whole nervous system, I guess my channels had been silting up for some time. Next, it was stretching out limbs and joint flexion. Three rounds of MMA with King Kong, including takedowns, would have been my preferred choice.

'Hold this,' said Shukhrat at one point as I felt my hip socket about to pop. He handed me something just in front of my left temple: my foot.

'Oh, very good, Jason aka.' He grinned expansively. 'Here: the other one.'

'Thank you,' I wheezed.

Having turned me into Elastaboy, the bludgeoning then started. First, it was the kind we recognise from all those lovely '60s movies: a good-looking, Nordic-type white-clad man or woman, gently and rhythmically pitter-patting the edge of their hands up and down the smooth, tanned skin of our smiling heroine or hero. Only (CUT TO): Shukhrat, with the power to fell a healthy average-sized tree in each blow, his synapses firing off rounds of perfectly irresistible karate chops like a Gatling gun over torso and limbs, till it feels like you've been assaulted by an enraged octopus wielding a cosh in each suckered arm. He then used those same indefatigable biological machine hooks, working like a pair of pneumatic pincers, to "tenderise" me. Prising and squeezing and knuckling into knotted sinew and gristle and subcutaneous places I didn't know were there, soon it felt like all my tissues had been Magimixed into a homogenous pulp.

Next up: the thumps. This is open-palmed, full-on symmetrical assault of the patient, like a pair of synchronised jackhammers moving down the body, expelling negative energy that may have pooled anywhere in the organism and literally forcing it out through the limbs, hands, fingers, feet and toes. Which are then clicked, crunched and snapped back for good measure.

'Breathe,' said Shukhrat – fortunately, otherwise I'm sure I'd have overlooked it. After a brief respite, he sat me up on the table. Placing my right hand on my left shoulder, he put me in a kind of a bear hug and twisted me around until my spine cracked. He then repeated the move in the opposite direction. Finally, indicating that I let my head hang forward and relax completely, he twisted it quickly and expertly to the left and right, before landing a final double thunder slap on my back.

'Finished, Jason aka.' Slowly and tentatively, I came out of Rag Doll pose. 'How do you feel?' Perfect, I told him. Absolutely...amazing.

Shukhrat smiled. 'Very good,' he said, pleased. He placed his hand across his heart. 'Now rest. Tomorrow: again. Goodbye.'

Later, in the guesthouse, Andrea and I compared notes. Over herbal tea, we laughed and tried to fathom among who exactly we had landed. While we both agreed that soon after the massage we had experienced a great sense of lightness, energy and general good vibes within our respective systems, and while she felt there was certainly much to learn and be amazed by here, Andrea could not in all conscience recommend a stay at the Sufi centre of medicine for any of her upcoming Swiss tourist groups.

'If I brought my clients here,' she told me confidentially, 'I don't think I'd have a business for much longer.' She laughed, but she wasn't kidding.

I, conversely, had other ideas.

o

"Looking at the cake is like looking at the future," Merlin warns a young King Arthur, enraptured on encountering Guenevere for the first time: "until you've tasted it, what do you really know? And then, of course, it's too late. Too late."

Remember the Quest, Kin? That Hero's Journey we started, way back around, oh, fifty-something thousand words ago? Me too. Does it feel like we're getting anywhere together here? Hah. I know, Kin. I know. The bedazzling and often dangerously unshakeable magnetism of stories. Gotta watch them: they can turn even the most determined of travellers off course from their desired destination. A seed in the listener's imagination is all it takes. A little water; pinch of fairy dust. Boom! Once again, Ithaca must wait.

I have related all the above as it happened, in précis, of course, there is always so much more, but to serve its purpose for our journey here on in, it will suffice. For us to find our present Grail, we need not spend too much more time with Ustoz and his tribe, much as a deep and ever-longing part of your companion would like to. Thing is, Merlin is right: when you finally perceive that vessel of beauty, make that connection you may not even have known before that your soul was looking for, you can't help but imagine how it's going to be. This is the moment you can never fashion, nor ever recreate: the moment you fall in love. It doesn't matter if it's guys or girls, sports or amateur dramatics, your firstborn child or a dying stranger; a dog, a house, a car, a country, a story, a job, an outfit, a practice, a mountain, a restaurant, a piece of music or a battered old red violin. A Sufi master and his murids in a two-bit desert town. That cake is in your hands and you can't believe it. At that moment, you're sure: it is all you ever wanted, ever dreamed. Until you actually taste it, though, you still don't fully know. You have not *realised*. So you raise it to your mouth, unable to do anything else, and take a bite. You chew; you swallow. And it's done. The veil has been stripped away, the entanglement sealed, the peak attained. You now know. Never again will you be able to un-know it. Never again will you experience the connection afresh, unfiltered, uncompared, unanalysed, merely imagined. That taste resides in you forever. In our duality set world, it resides for good – and for bad. Depending on the moment, and your station in relation to it. And each moment is just the very first of yet another future we do not know. Until we taste it. So on it goes.

If one thing is for sure, the old saying is true: you can't have your cake, and eat it.

I'm telling you this now, Kin, because the cake is still in your hands. In your present time and accompanying constituent incarnation, that cake is the book you're reading. My meeting with Ustoz, the story we have just shared, represents the moment I finally ate mine. Had I chosen, I could have probably got away with a lick of icing sugar and the hellish hangover. If I had left that first morning, gone back to collect my things in Samarkand, told Ziza she was right, I must be crazy looking for a bunch of fairytales in the desert in the middle of winter, you would not *believe* these people, and hopped back home via Tashkent – for sure, my life would have gone differently. I would always remember the event, of course, but in time no doubt I would be able to present it to myself and others in such a way as not to overly disturb my self-enforcing ego's varied projections. I may even have remained in the Fourth Way, and enjoyed the glow of being able to say, "Well, I met with a group Gurdjieff once stayed with. No, the monastery isn't quite as he described it in the book..." Bygones. Not in this timeline. *Que sais-je?*

But I didn't leave. I stayed, I was thirsty, and I drank. I ate. I fed. I went back to Samarkand, collected my gear, thanked the Gur Emir sisters of mercy and went straight back to the fountain. I wanted ALL the cake, I was so hungry – Kin: it was a feeding frenzy.

Luckily, of course, Ustoz had seen it all before.

'You have too much fire, Jasur,' he observed one day as he watched me, zealously performing an exercise I had recently been taught. 'If you cannot balance it, it will make your organism unwell. Breathe. Calm yourself. You are patient.'

We are patient, Kin. Perhaps we just don't remember it. Need to polish up that practice. It can come. If you've already eaten that cake, though, and fallen in love, it's going to be much harder to be so. If we want the Grail, how much are we prepared to suffer for it?

Do you know what "apple" is in the Uzbek language? *Olma*. The first part *ol* is an instruction meaning "take" and the suffix *ma* is a negation, meaning "not". A "take not". That's right: straight from the Garden of Eden. No Latin to get in the way.

Do you want to eat it? Do you feel lucky? Well, do you – Kin?

Cake or apple – sweet or healthy (save for the unbearable burden of divine knowledge): choose your metaphor. What I'm telling you in all seriousness is this: once you've eaten, there's no turning back. Don't let the adrenaline and the endorphins fool you. At this stage, it's all excitement in the Special World. Luke has found Yoda, Fight Club is up and running. Katniss is hanging with Haymitch, Will and Jeff are checking out the toys in Area 51 and Anna – well, Anna has Olaf. Playboy Bruce Wayne is training in the secret mountain fortress of Ra's al Ghul's League of Shadows. The return to his cave is just a full-pitched Ninja battle and a few explosions away. Your narrator, meanwhile, is already not properly hearing the most influential human in his entire life. Because it's just all too **exciting**. With every high, however, we know what's going to come after. Do you have the resolve to handle the inevitable crash?

Do you have it? That resolve? It may seem you've already eaten most of this tale. We've shared the First Howl (have you actually tried it yet, Kin? Come on: tell me true) and the Second, the more visceral, Howl is not far off. You've done 48 hours in solitary without screens or phones (you have done that, haven't you, Kin?) as a first initiation and a demonstration of trust and commitment to our common Quest. For my part, I'm sharing some things that, taken altogether, I haven't really shared with anyone else before. There's more to come, too. All in all, it's quite the adventure.

But...

This is the turning point. This is where it all goes down. It is the moment that Bruce realises his ultimate mentor, Henri Ducard, will become his mortal enemy. That Arthur asks Merlin if Lancelot and Guenevere have betrayed him and, after telling him that yes, so they have, Merlin too must now leave Arthur to be king, alone. Katniss loses Rue, and her reaction catalyses the rebellion against The Capitol. Miguel discovers Ernesto de la Cruz murdered Hector, his ancestor. Tyler Durden disappears. Meanwhile, in The Matrix, the Oracle tells Neo that he is not "The One" and that he is going to have to choose whether to save his own life, or that of Morpheus. She gives him not a cake or an apple, but a cookie. Which, inevitably, he eats.

If you carry on now, there will be no turning back. My own tale is almost run here, Kin. I've been down in the whale's belly so many times, I don't fear it any more. I'm here again now to accompany you as you make your own way into that foreboding sanctuary, to face your own Supreme Ordeal. You won't be going in unarmed, I will pass on the talisman before I go, but you will be going in alone. There is no other way. We embrace the cave, the maw of the beast, not for kicks or pride or trophies, to prove and show we can do it, but because that is where our treasure is buried. Our secrets. The great things we have forgotten. Once you have tasted, eaten, let your presently-known self be devoured and have *remembered*, in all your being, you can truly never go back to the Ordinary World. Not as you were before.

Neo: "I can't go back, can I?"

Morpheus: "No. But if you could, would you really want to?"

If you want to turn back, Kin, now is your last chance. Once we've entered the cave, no one here gets out alive.

o

In what felt like moments, my visa was out. Before I left Uzbekistan, Kin One from heady London days joined me and we went on a tour of the region. He was interested in finding the once majestic gardens of Babur, founder of the Mughal dynasty, near Andizhan in the Fergana Valley. A production company was keen to create a series on famous gardens, with my rakish if unpredictable brother in arms as the expert host, and along with a pilot filmmaker we made our way through this now wild and sometimes perilous province. A fellow seeker in his own right, afterwards I took him with me to meet Ustoz. He later expressed in hindsight that the meeting saved his life.

On my last night in Tashkent, I received a surprise phone call. It was from Ulug Bekh, the son of Ustoz who had driven us to the fish restaurant. In the few weeks since I had first met the group, he had already become a friend and brother.

'Hello Jason aka. Where are you? Ustoz is in town. He would like very much to have dinner with you. A very fancy place.'

I asked him whether it was another fish restaurant. When he stopped laughing, Ulug Bekh told me to be ready in the hotel lobby in ten minutes.

It was a surreal experience. There were five of us: Ustoz, Ulug Bekh, his younger sister, myself, and a murid whose speciality was martial arts. In total contrast to the mood and their usual presence at the centre, a world away from the country's modernising but oppressive capital, there was a distance, a graveness about them I hadn't encountered before. As if they were screening themselves, had veiled their real selves off from the everyday human realm. Their clothes were modern, crisp, formal and devoid of emotional charge. Smart, and unexceptional. Their movements were clinical and economical, without their usual grace and expressiveness. Calm and quietly self-assured in their personal space as always, they nevertheless gave off the impression of being on high alert. Even the car was tailored to fit: a black, subtly menacing and patently souped up new sedan, with darkened windows and a covert CB radio. We were in the Uz-Matrix, all right.

'I am sorry,' Ustoz apologised. 'The food is not so good here. It is prepared only for business. But it will do. Drink?'

I said I'd be fine with tea.

Over the meal, he asked me what I intended to do. I told him I had to go back to Europe for the time being, make some money and absorb and process all that had happened since I'd arrived in their country three months before. Was it that little? It felt like years and minutes all at once.

'Do you want to come back?' he asked.

'Yes.'

'Good. If you wish, you can come and study. You will be our guest. You understand?'

I thanked him, all at once overwhelmed.

Ustoz smiled that smile. It was the only real thing in the restaurant – probably in all of Tashkent. Surveying the scene, he nodded. With a stroke of his beard, he signalled for the murid to settle the bill.

'Jasur. Maybe we can do something with you.'

They dropped me back at the hotel. 'Next time, you come and stay with us, yes? At my home.' I nodded. 'Hotels are not for you anymore. Wait: did you take your herbs from the centre?' Ustoz double-checked with his crew. 'Good, good. Well, Jasur. In Uzbek, we say *oq yo'l* – white road.' He clenched his fist.

I placed my hand on my heart. Ustoz did the same. A moment later, I was alone.

London was quite the trip. "Unreal city" – in contrast to my recent weeks, it felt dialled to 11 with the "gain" knob turned to max. I had considered myself an outsider living there in a previous life and, as our creative ego will use whatever scraps are at its disposal, used that fuel to make myself feel special and different, whilst justifying all my sketchy behaviour. The truth was now self-evident in its chilling simplicity: we are all of us outsiders to ourselves. I saw it, felt it, in every face and every body I encountered. I could not panic or get down about it, however. My compass had a new setting.

A great friend from my aborted career at university, H, had a flat in a smart part of town with a room to rent. More a glorified wardrobe by the kitchen than a room, it was perfectly suited to my current needs. I set up a copywriting company, writing marketing guff and providing brand strategies pulled from the nebulous depths of my backside, and pedalled these wiseacred words and notions among friends and contacts who had started "proper" businesses and careers in the coal bunkers of Capitalism's frenetic steam-driven engine room. Who cares if you're aboard the Titanic when all the icebergs are melting anyway, right?

In my downtime, I embarked upon a novel, based on characters and events that had crossed and influenced my path in recent years. Set in St Petersburg, New York and Central Asia, it was the story of Christ's return to Earth at the turn of the Millennium: a glorious impromptu mission of mercy that goes wrong the moment he lands in Russia and is gunned down by the waiting local mafia. Being Jesus, he doesn't stay down long. Unfortunately, the repeated killings mess with his terrestrial brain function, rendering him amnesic and a little more confused with every successive resurrection. That's when our heroine, Nadia, finds him, wandering crazy in the Hermitage Museum, and reluctantly takes him home with her to stay. So it begins. It was called *Black Madonna, White Nights* and, like so many other doomed works of genius, it never got finished.

There was another story that had gone cold, which to this day remains the greater, if not greatest, loss: Kidal had disappeared. A mutual friend and soul brother to both myself and H, since I had been off chasing dervishes in Central Asia, he had gone to ground.

'I spoke to his sister a few months ago,' H told me over beers one evening. 'I guess he's still alive. But he doesn't want any contact. From anyone.'

Even now, I wonder: should I have pursued him? Would a transmission through a brother, from an ancient, ever-fresh and flowing well of spiritual sustenance, have provided the taste to bring him back – back to this *life*? Or was that simply his role? We see the Kidal character in the books and movies, in Russian literature especially: the *lishniy chelovek* – "superfluous person" – the one who sees and understands too much to be engaged in the farce of human society, yet cannot make their own way through it. The supreme irony being that Kidal was not only innately self-aware, he also wrote about the state with more purity, more honesty and sublime, pared-back efficiency than any other writer I ever encountered. Superfluous? No - he was essential. He was the unbending reflection the superflous culture that dominates our planet could not bear; that untarnished mirror of self-perception into which no-one from the ordinary world could look, for to do so would rob them of all their jealously prized notions of worth. He was a Bukowski who never made it out of the post office, but who fought inwardly always, outwardly never. Graceful, watchful, quiet, true. Vulnerable. The most precious of dog roses.

"Genius," said Irving Layton of Leonard Cohen, "is the ability to see the truth and express things as they really are. Not to be fooled."

Kidal was a flame from another realm, one which could not find hold upon this coarse hologram we temporarily inhabit. One way or another, they leave us – at least from our uncomprehending standpoint – too soon. Yet something, delicate but ineradicable, lingers for a few. Like Montaigne's Étienne. Out of the corner of one's eye, against hope we are forever seeking after the shadow of a longed-for ghost.

Sometimes, I wonder was he even real? What is left afterwards appears so fragile against the inevitable and merciless, albeit necessary, erosion of change. Traces. Memories. Fragments. Some pre-digital, inexorably fading photographs. The "Extra Joker" playing card he gave me, one of the last times we met. It sits on my desk as I write. The soft but indelible, permanent ache in my heart.

Until next we meet, Beloved Kin.

It was that stage in life when, all of a sudden, all your friends appear to be getting married. For single people, of course, weddings are the ultimate hunting ground. It wasn't long before this inveterate cad, fresh from adventure and living the high life with fellow bachelors, was back to his usual pursuits: wine, women and throng. I'd also acquired a long-lusted after fantasy: a classic, beaten-up '80s Porsche. A silver 944 Turbo, to be precise, for all you petrolheads out there. Knowing that I wasn't going to stay in England for long one way or another, it had the steering wheel on the wrong side, peeling paint, the original Fuchs wheels, quarter of a million kilometres under them, and cost me a whisker over £3000. After a few obligatory tweaks, it went like a crack-hungry honey badger on steroids and was about as easy to handle. I loved it.

At the same time, I felt myself diminishing. Something wasn't right. Having arrived back from Central Asia in what I believed to be the best condition – physically, emotionally and psychologically – of my life, in spite of my finest tricks and attempts at self-foolery, it soon became evident that the state of Denmark was, indeed, heading for a self-generated collapse.

It began with the awareness that I was constantly thirsty. Commensurate with this was the frequent need to piss. As the weeks went by, my appetite also grew noticeably, while alarmingly my reasonably well stacked frame began to shrink around me. I ate more, worked out more, drank more: the weight continued to fall from my bones. I asked my father, the family medic, what might be going on.

'It's probably just your metabolism adjusting,' he reassured me. 'I used to drink a lot when I was rowing. I wouldn't worry about it.' Well, if you insist on asking a carpenter about a medical condition...

The eyesight starting going next. Mornings particularly, it would sometimes take an hour or more for things to come properly into focus. Especially if it had been a big night before. Feeling on top of the world as I had been, deciding that having found the eternal fountain I was now on my way to becoming invincible, Ustoz's careful diet plan and herbs were of course sitting in a cupboard, unopened, gathering dust. It was those tantalising spiritual secrets I desired most: the ones that

Ouspensky and Bennett, Krishnamurti, Shah and maybe even Gurdjieff himself had failed to fully unearth, and through exposure to them via my newly found Masters of Wisdom, I was going to honour poor old mad Friedrich's memory and transform, with tear-provoking humility, into The Superman.

"For he on honey-dew hath fed
And drunk the milk of Paradise..."

Honey-dew or not, Superman was going to need a lot more milk than this if he wanted to stop looking like he'd just been pulled out of the Gulag. What the hell was wrong with me? Now the breath was going, too. Well, that was wedding season sabotaged. Dry mouth, flaking skin. And tired. Not just soporific: heavy limbs, heavy skull. Weak and listless all over. I just need to get my willpower back online, I told myself, having turned down the regular weekend invitation of a pub and dinner somewhere, followed by who knew what nefarious activity the capital's many Lucifer wannabes had in mind. The material process – is also psychic – if I have my mind – can use The Force – just keep – going – forward...

In May, three months after my return, Kin Two got married. In a bid to mask my illness, I had grown my hair and beard and dressed myself up like a dervish. Looking at the pictures now, I can't really remember being there. I drank champagne, played my part as Best Man, enjoyed the feast and the love and the dancing. I think I even pulled. Only it wasn't me. I was somewhere nearby, floating between stage and wings, half-prompting Jason's lines, half watching. One eye on the clock at the back of theatre. Will this be his final performance?

The following day was my birthday. Twenty-nine. I had a presentation to prepare for the following week but I couldn't face it. In a daze, I drove down to the family home of my close friend and landlord, H. Usually, being Irish, he would suggest a Guinness or so at the local country pub, but having watched me during the previous weeks and encouraged me on more than one occasion to see a doctor, he was ready now to be there if I yielded. After tea and the usual homely chat with his Mum in the kitchen, we walked down towards the woods through a bright spring meadow.

We arrived at a fence. Horses were playing beyond it. Suddenly, without any thought arising, I knew the walk was over.

'I don't think I'm very well,' I whispered finally.

'Ah. You think so?' said H.

I turned and looked back up the gentle slope we'd just descended. I turned back to him and smiled. 'You're going to have to carry me.'

As always, things could be worse. It didn't take a genius – or an orthopaedic surgeon – to work out what was wrong. A 5-second blood glucose test at the hospital said it all: off the frickin' scale. So that was my birthday present to myself: Type 1 Diabetes.

Around September, once I'd got myself used to my new regime and had the condition relatively stable, balancing diet, exercise, sleep, routine and 4 injections of insulin a day, I managed to speak on the phone with Ustoz. Straightforward as it may sound, getting in touch with your Sufi master, even in this day and age, isn't always a given. For a start, he has no email, no social media and no mobile phone. He doesn't even have a private landline. Can you imagine being that free? Through some missed windows and much assistance from Ulug Bekh and his sister, eventually we spoke.

'Ah, Jasur. How are you?'

Just to hear his voice triggered something inside me. I started to well up. As ever, I hadn't realised what I'd been missing. I told him how I was, what had happened. He listened carefully.

'Did you take the herbs I gave you? What about your diet?' I informed him I had been far from a model murid. Was there anything to be done?

'I told you,' he reminded me patiently, 'there is too much old information in your organism. Remember? I said there is urine in your blood. This old information must go. Then you can put in the new information. Then you will be healthy.'

'But Type 1 isn't reversible,' I countered. 'Only Type 2 can be controlled by diet, and not always even then.' I had read up on it all, naturally.

'This is not Type 1,' Ustoz said flatly. 'For one set of symptoms, there can be many causes. Treating the symptoms alone will not cure you. The insulin will help for now, you must keep taking it. If you come and find me again, we will do something and you will see. Agreed?'

What else could I do? 'Yes, Ustoz. I'm a bit behind schedule. I don't think I'll be able to make it this year.'

There was a pause as he spoke to someone in the background. 'I am going to Switzerland next month,' he said, returning. 'I have some students there. We will go to the mountains. If you can meet me there, it will be good, for both of us. You can do it?'

There was no time to think. Really, there was nothing to think about. 'Of course.'

'Good. Ah, you are lucky, Jasur. God loves you. He has given you a good test. I will see you there.'

In rose-tinted hindsight, it's actually pretty obvious: Ustoz had me at hello. Back in Uzbekistan, Nowherestan, at the table in the guesthouse, while the freezing winter blizzard whirled outside.

Another friend and Kin of mine, Babu, is a great scholar and curator in the field of Sufi practices and traditions, among many other treasures. As well as drinking in person from the heavenly waterfall, he knows all of the customs and technical language of the various *tariqa* and *silsila*, that is, Sufi ways and chains of transmission. One evening much later, we were discussing Ustoz and his group, and the inner conflict that often ensues, especially in the western-born mind, when the heart makes known its core wish to yield to the sheikh's authority. What if reason, quite understandably, won't permit total submission? What if the ego refuses to step down? Can agnostics, or non-theists, proceed through the many stations of the way, if only through accepting that the limits of their perceived knowledge may be far closer to home than they believe? And what of belief in general – is it the thing believed in, the act of believing itself, or an alchemical melding of the two, that can bring about evolution and, ultimately, transformation and salvation?

'Ah well,' said Babu that night, a little after midnight. He poured us each another measure of cognac, as is his magnanimous way. In questions of the above nature, its gentle consumption often seemed to assist the onset of our mutual inspiration.

'There are many terms,' he said slowly, 'and phrases describing the moment when the murid submits fully to the *murshid* or *pir*. It can proceed through individual or through a combination of the centres – physical, emotional, mental. Even spiritual, but that is grace, not a choosing. In general, the submission marks the entry into a state of repentance. There are three stages: *tawba,* the return from sin to submission; *inaba,* the shift from lack of resolve or sincerity to resolve or high sincerity; and *awba,* which is: returning from pursuit of other than God in favour of complete turning to Him alone.' Babu paused and took a sip of his cognac. 'There is one expression, however,' he went on, 'of which I am particularly fond. I encountered it personally in the tradition that I myself have been involved with for many years. What it is, is this...'

He paused again, and in the low light leaned forward conspiratorially:

'From the moment that you *know* you have met the master – you're fucked.

Cake & Death

Death makes angels of us all.

- Jim Morrison

Do you remember the 1999 movie *American Beauty*? Yes indeed, pre-millennials or even pre-zoomers, it was that long ago. See if this rings any bells:

"I had always heard your entire life flashes in front of your eyes the second before you die. First of all, that one second isn't a second at all, it stretches on forever, like an ocean of time..."

For those who haven't seen it/forgotten it and care to visit, here's a spoiler alert: these are the words of the hero, struggling and sedated middle-class, middle-aged Lester Burnham who, as you may intuit, doesn't make it out of the film alive. I remember loving *American Beauty*. I even recommended it to my ancient Fourth Way group, telling them it was filled with concepts that echoed G's teachings. I was excited by it: the call to awaken is going mainstream! Digging a little further, it turned out the film's writer is a committed Buddhist. Well, go figure. In any case, what's especially touching about the above lines, from right at the end of a deserved Oscar-winning screenplay, is that they're spoken in voiceover by a character who is already dead.

As a collective, humans are obsessed with death. Okay, at a supposedly conscious level you may not think about it every day, even every week or month. But in that submerged, gently vibrating iceberg you unwittingly drag around with you through the apparently limited but in reality limitless ocean of your daily existence, what we call the sub- or unconscious (a relative misnomer – "unconscious" it ain't) is constantly busy making and enacting plans, driven by and anchored in a basic human fear: the fear of dying.

As usual with the peculiar three-brained beings on this unfortunate planet (you and me, Kin ;) we tend to eschew good-old "middle path" balance when confronted with an obstacle or fear and instead react in an extreme fashion. When it comes to death – that sole certainty in life aside from your regular demands and statements from the IRS – we either become infatuated by our conjured notions of it, or we push it away from our minds as far as we possibly can. If we set aside for a second our animal survival instincts, which are there to protect us from expiring prematurely, not at the end of our natural biological cycle, we may contemplate that in this Duality Trapped realm death is the natural antithesis and therefore balancing complement to life. This extreme mode of engagement with it – obsession or rejection – must be chalked up as another example of the lopsided, misguided and sheer bizarre things we do.

Trouble is, it's hard to understand something of which you have no personal experience. We fear the unknown, and doing so constantly wounds us. Apart from our dear Messiah (contentious for a couple of thousand years), his experiment Lazarus (ditto) and a relative handful of people out of the whole body of our species who claim to have crossed over into the beyond and returned, there is a disheartening lack of empirically verifiable material on what it is like to be dead. We are thus left, for the most part, guessing. Or just fearing. Imagining. Denying. Accepting, if we're fortunate or brave, but even then, we cannot fully know what it is that we are accepting ahead of the fact. We cannot taste the cake without actually dying. Or can we?

At the end of Gurdjieff's magnum opus, *Beelzebub's Tales To His Grandson*, through the central protagonist of the title a.k.a Satan or The Devil, Gurdjieff gives his view of the only thing that will save humanity:

"The sole means now for the saving of the beings of the planet Earth would be to implant again into their presences a new organ...of such properties that every one of these unfortunates during the process of existence should constantly sense and be cognizant of the inevitability of his own death as well as of the death of everyone upon whom his eyes or attention rests.

"Only such a sensation and such a cognizance can now destroy the egoism completely crystallised in them that has swallowed up the whole of their Essence and also that tendency to hate others which flows from it..."

In other words, after nearly 1200 pages of some pretty dense and far-out musings, the conclusion is that only living with a constant awareness of death will save us from ourselves. To do so, however, would require implanting a "new organ" of some description. Any takers? In *Beelzebub's Tales*, the surgeons of consciousness tasked with performing implants into human beings are Archangels, specifically the Arch-Chemist-Physician of the Universe. We all know the old joke about the difference between God and a surgeon, don't we? God knows he isn't a surgeon. Is there any medical genius out there we could trust in lieu of an angel? Hmm, this pickle could make the case for eugenics look like a Woke mission statement...

Practicalities aside, Gurdjieff is not alone in transmitting the principle of this realisation. In the western world since his departure, more and more hitherto obscure or previously untraveled ways and religions have come into the cultural awareness, many of which place a correlative importance on learning to live with death, in life, in the here and now. In the 1990s a book entitled *The Tibetan Book of Living and Dying* made a great splash in the US bestseller lists, going on to sell more than 2 million copies. Similarly *The Upanishads,* from the ancient Vedic tradition of India, have become known among a widespread community of occidentals with a desire to further their self-knowledge and awareness, none less than the fabled *Katha Upanishad* in which the hero, the boy Nachiketa, searches out Death as his teacher. From as far back as the 19th Century, this canon has impressed western thinkers, with the philosopher Arthur Sschopenhauer calling it: "The production of the highest human wisdom." And of course artists and writers like Charles Dickens (is there anyone like Dickens?) were showcasing this technique in their work way ahead of the hippie revolutions and revelations of the 1960s. Hence it is only when faced with his own stark and unattended grave that Ebenezer Scrooge finally turns from his selfish path, pledging to the Ghost of Christmas Yet to Come once and for all to change his ways.

This "Dialogue with Death" has hit mainstream culture, too. In the movie *Fight Club*, based on the novel of the same name by Chuck Palahniuk, there is a memorable scene in which Tyler drags a convenience store clerk into the parking lot out back and threatens to shoot him. Pointing a gun at his head, Tyler checks the victim's wallet and discovers the terrified clerk is one Raymond K. Hessel. He tells him he is going to die, then notices from an expired ID card in the wallet that Raymond is a lapsed college student. Tyler asks what he wanted to be.

"A veterinarian!" Raymond sobs.

Tyler asks if he'd rather be dead than go back to school. He then takes Raymond's driver's license, telling him that if he isn't back in school and on his way to being a vet in six weeks, he *will* be dead. He lets Raymond go.

"What the fuck was the point of that?" the Narrator, who has witnessed the whole scene, asks in sickened disbelief.

"Imagine how he feels," says Tyler. "Tomorrow will be the most beautiful day of Raymond K. Hessel's life. His breakfast will taste better than any meal you and I have ever tasted."

Raymond has licked the sugar off the cake. Now: what would happen if you ate it?

Let's return, if only briefly, to the Land of Uz. I could write several books about Ustoz and his crew. I even started some. By 2010 I had spent over a year in total with the tribe. Ah, Kin. I wish you that experience. They were the best of times, they were – well, you guessed it. For every livid summit there's a sepulchral cave. Maybe you have had your own similar sojourn on your journey? It doesn't matter what way, or philosophy, which life or country embraced you. Which "brand" of death and resurrection you imbibed. Maybe you, too, have felt that grace. In which case, there is nothing really, for you, that needs to be written here. Except in that it help us now to remember.

Whatever your present station, it may at least be of interest and solace to be informed that, believe it or not, death is not the end. If it were, what would be the point? We might as well just spend our lives being C.U.N.Ts. Which, of course, is what some of us do. Believing that life is pointless and all. Bygones. Nothing is set. Letting the above contentious sentence hang for a while, if we are able to suspend our disbelief for a moment, let us now approach the cave which inevitably beckons on any fully formed hero's journey.

In traditional Christianity (including most of its subsequent dominant sub-brands) the concept of death and resurrection is at the core of the religion. The old-school mainstream interpretation is that if you believe in God and follow his son, then like Christ (though not your earthly body – divisive) you will be reborn into eternal blissful life. Which is great, except for the lack of proof, and the fact that the concept can be used to justify and excuse all kinds of dubious shenanigans while you're still here. Like being thrown out of the community or flayed alive or massacred by the million with all your Kin if you don't 100% agree with the few power-addled, self-elected old men in charge of terrestrial operations. It's fine, they're mostly running international corporations now anyway. The point is, so long as you're down here, you just have to wait it out. The reward – never verified – comes later. Just be good. Whatever the guidelines for that are this century. Keep suffering, it'll all be okay once you're dead. Trust in God. Or at least, trust the inevitably flawed humans who have assumed the role of His chief press agents. And all the historically carefully censored narratives of their predecessors. No longer in Latin exclusively? Oops, that might have been a marketing error...

Never mind. There are other options. Before we tread any further together, however, please be aware this is not another addition of expired best-before chocolate sauce being poured on the old flaming pudding of which way is wrong or right. It is not, for me at least, about being pro or anti Christian. Or Islamic or Buddhist or Hindu or any other faith. It is not even about being pro or anti religion. Or science. Psychiatry, therapy, medicine, mindfulness, ice bathing: nada. It is about discerning the essence of transformative processes behind their ever-morphing outward forms and finding a fit for oneself. I hope you may sense, with faculties that both integrate and transcend your rational mind, the intention behind these and indeed any words you encounter, more than simply spend all your time trying exclusively to divine their specific meaning. For one thing, that's impossible. Follow your nose. Disclaimer over.

There are many ways, traditions and cultures on Earth that integrate death into their living practice. Sit with it, explore it, imagine its aspects; take drugs to approach it synaesthetically, even. Perform rituals around it beyond just mourning, contemplate and meditate on it. Incorporate it into life, embrace it, in the here and now. No doubt, we each consider it at least on occasion, and have our own individual ideas and beliefs. Among Zen schools and Sufis, the adage "Die before you die" is a well-known phrase. Beyond being simply a metaphor for the destruction of the present ego, it provides a foundation for rigorous self-practice. Or, perhaps more accurately, selfless-practice. Basically, it's a straightforward concept: you practice losing all attachment to yourself – to your mind, your body, your identity, your thoughts and feelings; your imaginings, your memories, your expectations. The experience of your own separate existence.

How?

In the parlance of 12-step recovery programs, you take the first 3: be honest about our own powerlessness as individuals; have faith in a higher power; surrender to it. You may wonder what this has to do with you – after all, aren't 12-step programs designed to help those with addictions? Fair enough. Now contemplate the addiction that consciously or unconsciously afflicts us all: the addiction to being you. Alive. An individual. On this journey. Here and now.

We are each of us addicted, to varying degrees, to the story of our own life as we perceive it. We tell it to ourselves and others, with varying intensity of awareness, minute on minute, through weeks and months and years. We're so used to feeding it and feeding off it, we do not even appreciate its absolute hold on us anymore. We still believe we are free. If we saw in one hit the terror, as G puts it, of our situation, we would terminate ourselves almost without a thought. Indeed, some people do exactly that. At the time of writing, it is happening more and more. We needn't, however, nor should, give up hope.

With the 12-steps, that often controversial notion of a 'higher power' may be expressed as "God as you understand him". If "He" as an independent entity is hard to define – and let's face it, after a long track record of trying, it's still kind of tricky to reach any consensus on the matter – then perhaps it is enough for the purpose of the process of healing and recovery to take a leap and accept that this higher power is present within that process. You don't know how it works, but you can feel it working. Like a pill whose exact contents elude you, or a placebo. In something like AA, that presence is felt within the group. The effect that in gathering as broken individuals, some reunifying occurrence beyond immediate comprehension is taking place. It doesn't work for everyone. It doesn't work all the time. Not everybody makes it. So it is with any journey. For many, however, it is still far better than the alternative.

In the ways of Zen and Sufism, and others besides, there is a different and more tangible expression of God's nature on which to rest one's clear attention. At least to begin with, you don't attempt to locate or envisage this unquantifiable concept of God. You are not obliged to try and understand Him, or Her or It at all. You simply step into your powerlessness. You step into the state of faith. You step up to surrender.

Against what? In what? To whom? Where do I turn?

The Master.

As I said earlier, I could write books about my time with Ustoz. Innumerable stories about what I witnessed, how it changed me, what I learned, forgot again, saw afresh long after, made my life anew – again and again and again. But to do so, here, would be to fall into a familiar trap: believing my own story about me. That may appear paradoxical, given the tale that has brought us to this point. And so it is. For we cannot detach ourselves from nothing. Thus a story must first exist to enable us to take the crucial step of relinquishing it. The many times I began to tell of my experiences, in writing, to friends, to strangers, the narrative eventually petered out. The trouble was, and Kin, it's quite insane how many years it took to realise, it was still always about me. Despite what you may feel or think about our journey so far, that is not what this transmission is about. If that were my purpose here, all that would happen would be that I fuel another round of addiction to the same basic substance, differing each time only in its apparent constitution. My intention was never to come here with me. It is to come here with you. From the tower, to the cave, and then –

But wait. Patient Friend. We're nearly there. There's a bit of me still standing in the way. Will you help me to see you past?

As Ustoz had told me in our phone conversation, I was lucky. The test I'd been given – by nature, God, my unhealthy living or accident, does it matter? – really couldn't have been packaged better. For starters, here was a condition which, thanks to science, could be controlled indefinitely.

A hundred years ago, in 1921, a trio of men at the University of Toronto named Banting, Best and Macleod, isolated the hormone insulin for the first time. By January of the following year, with the input of biochemist James Collip who purified it, the pioneers injected insulin from the pancreas of a dog into a 14 year-old diabetic boy. Life expectancy for diabetics before then was rarely more than a year or two at most. (Sadly, even less for the dog, or the cows that followed. These days, bacteria have thankfully taken over production.) After suffering the symptoms outlined earlier, the victim would eventually fall into a hyperglycaemic coma and die. It was therefore almost without exception a fatal condition and, a century later, it still is without either regular daily shots or a computerised pump attached to the body to release calculated doses on demand. Despite the many experiments and advances of our age, there is currently no cure. While most Type 1 diabetics are able to lead an otherwise reasonably normal life thanks to the above, life expectancy is reduced and secondary complications usually arise. These include: kidney failure, heart disease, blood vessel damage, nerve damage, eye damage, skin and mouth conditions, impotency, problems with pregnancy, and amputations. If you're the worrying type, there's much to look forward to.

On the other hand, I felt fortunate. It wasn't cancer, that dreaded word against which so many ailments are still measured. Type 1 as with Type 2, which is different in genesis and treatment, can make you feel bad and sluggish and ratty but, as long as you watch your diet, exercise and keep taking the juice, you're rarely debilitated, in either body or mind. You will probably have some close calls – surprise midnight lows that see you crawling, semi-blacking out, to the fridge for juice and chocolate – but over time you learn your slightly compromised body and adapt. It is more acute for some people than others. It teaches you to appreciate sweet food and drinks. Having it may help you stop smoking. Moreover, it is rarely an immediate death sentence.

In 2005, having got myself more or less used to my modified physical avatar, Simon and I climbed into an ex-military Land Rover and drove from London to Uzbekistan. It took six weeks, seven thousand miles and produced a lifetime of memories. Pre-satnav or smartphone as we were, we got lost, broke down, ran into things, got held up by people with guns, met with beauty, consorted with scoundrels, and eventually rolled into Ustoz's domain at a quarter to June. On the way, the fridge in the mobile sweathouse had failed, boiling my 6-month supply of insulin in the middle of the

Kazakh desert, which was now 50 degrees centigrade during the day. We got stranded at the same point without oil for the motor and walked blind until we found a train line and an adjacent hut where some Russian engineers were playing poker. An hour and a half later, we parted happily with a bottle of vodka inside us and 20 litres of liquid gold. We still ask ourselves to this day if it wasn't a mirage. In Bukhara, we stayed with the Minaret Mafia and got some ropey local insulin which was unpredictable and reminded me what real needles look like. In Samarkand, staying with Ziza and Co., I caught a fever for three days, which the sisters said afterwards they thought was the end of me. I hallucinated a meeting with a long-dead Sufi saint, navigated an underworld that made *Blade* look like a rom-com, and was eventually guided back to the land of the living by my grandfather, who had died ten years before. As a warm up for the main event, overall the trip was right on target.

Skip forward seven months and I found myself in Frankfurt, Germany. My visa had been revoked and I had taken the first available flight to a European city with an Uzbek consulate in the hope of getting it renewed. I had to wait a week. It was Christmas, and I walked the city, with its lights and busy people and wondrous Christmas village, like a ghost. My body was on the verge of failing. I had lost over a third of my body weight and was in an extreme state of hyperglycaemia. By choice, and against Ustoz's wishes, I had not taken any insulin for over three months. I could feel the function of my internal organs waning. In my hotel room, my cave, I exercised, meditated, prayed, performed *zikr*. I remember one day attempting some push ups in a bid to encourage a sense of strength in my physical being. Back in my early twenties, I had once showed off to a girlfriend by repping out more than eighty in a row. On this day, with superlative effort, I managed four. Only now, as I looked afterwards in the mirror out of hollow eyes at my alien, shrink-wrapped skull, did I yield. This time, I knew that when I made it back to Ustoz, my surrender would be complete. If it was not, I would die.

The next day, I floated back to the consulate in a waking dream. After the obligatory bureaucratic limbo of an hour in the deserted waiting room, the suspicious desk clerk gave me the news: visa denied. No explanations given. I thanked him and went back to the hotel. If anyone noticed me on the street on my way home, they might have been puzzled by the apparition: an emaciated, pale man moving slowly, no faster than a sated beetle, in a Russian winter hat and heavy Uzbek coat, through the snow, an enormous smile on his face.

I have never felt so peaceful.

Two days after that, a good friend collected me from the airport near London and drove me home to my parents' house. Both shocked and relieved to see me, they contacted one of dad's colleagues at the hospital and rushed me in. When I told the endocrinologist the bones of the story, she looked at me with a mixture of disbelief and justified censure and injected me with what felt like a pint of finest fast-slow insulin cocktail.

'He shouldn't be alive,' she told my father in confidence after. 'Give him the shots yourself and watch him carefully for the next few days.'

So the experiment ended.

There is a song by Leonard Cohen, one of my favourites, called appropriately enough *Master Song*. The song, in Cohen's own words, is "about the Trinity – leave that for the scholars". One such scholar, the poet Judith Fitzgerald, suggests it is essentially about "the entangling triangle, the ins and outings so associated with the way in which masters become slaves and slaves become masters". There is one line in particular, scrawled in spidery handwriting in my notebook from the time, that encapsulates my mood and indeed physical state that year:

"He was starving in some deep mystery, like a man who is sure what is true"

Like love, surrender is not surrender unless it is unconditional. It does not need a qualifier. To place conditions on the state is to leave it. Ego – you are duly notified.

Aside from failing my chief test, as I started to consider it, I had enjoyed some spectacular experiences and personal insights during my time among the tribe. As the embodiment of a chain of transmission that is forever evolving, I was intrigued by the choice of emblem adopted by this relatively obscure branch of Sufism: the swallow. One day, as we watched them in their hundreds above the plains from a hilltop behind the centre, Ustoz enlightened me as to why:

'We meditate on the swallow for many reasons, Jason jan,' he told me softly. 'For their grace, their beauty, their agility. Their purity of design. Their endurance. Their fragility. There is something above all, though, we attempt to honour in our own endeavours and efforts, clumsy as they may be in comparison. When they are migrating, following the call homeward using their innate inner compass, they seek out the strongest currents to help them fly swiftly forward on their journey. They do not simply choose a fixed course and fight their way through. The wind is their friend, and they let it carry them. Sometimes, it may feel that they are being taken off course, and even with the best currents it is not always easy flying. But they persevere. They keep flying.' He smiled at me. 'The swallow can tell you far more than I ever can,' he laughed. 'When you're having trouble, you can always watch them.'

As my body continued to destroy itself on the inside, and our current humanity continues to destroy both itself and the world outside, I pray he may yet be right. There were many wise words and practices I learned at that time from Ustoz. As I was, however, and whatever I believed, I still didn't know how to eat them. Watching the birdies wasn't enough for this hungry young seeker. I was far from through with my mistakes.

Apart from myself, the chief addictions of my youth were women and cars. Certainly, I indulged in many other fascinations offered by this life, as I am sure you have yourself, Kin. Some, like music and physical activity and reading, can be positive and healthy. Others, like excessive drugs and alcohol and pornography, may be less so. In the case of women, what is there to fathom? Young, insecure, heterosexual male: was it the need to be wanted, the "thrill of the chase"; the lust for sex, the companionship? Was it the romantic, Ouspenskian fantasy – that if you find the "Right One" you will forever be complete and everything would be roses, roses? Maybe this, and so much more. Either way, an early infatuation became an obsession and the Grail was always: women.

And then cars. Not so much the form, though like most passionate auto fanciers I had aesthetic requirements. Not even for the power alone, as much as adrenaline and testosterone are ecstatic, if potentially incendiary bedfellows. The mechanical empathy and the joy of driving – aye, now that's closer to the mark. To engage G's carriage metaphor, I just loved the sensation of the team unleashed on the open road. Road trips. Buddies. Finding the perfect strip of asphalt nirvana, creating a destination, be it a chateau or a dubious diner at the top of a winding mountain pass. Getting on a mission. Improving, modifying, seeking motoring perfection, surmounting obstacles, getting wilfully lost and discovering new ways. Feeling the road rise up to meet tyres, finding the machine's limits, playing on the very edge of adhesion to this mortal coil. Yes, that's more like it.

Whatever the motives and facts of the matter, such were my inclinations. Then, one July night in 2007, on a rainy ring road in Paris, I gathered all three addictive components together. There, in the space of a heartbeat, I destroyed the lot.

It had been going so well. Since getting back on insulin and returning, once again, to the ordinary world, my life was ostensibly on a decent course. A great friend from early school days, another brother to whom I am forever grateful and indebted, had become a senior executive for a global tobacco company. He offered me a job producing their business to business magazine. Branding and marketing: my bête noire. Working as the mouthpiece for a billion dollar gang of cheroot vendors was not the ultimate desire for my soul, maybe, but I had learned something practical in my time with Ustoz.

'How can I kill my ego?' one of my companions at the centre, a professional sports star and fellow European, asked our master one day.

'You cannot,' Ustoz responded. 'This is the question I hear so much. You equate your ego with the Devil, and wanting to purify yourself begin a great battle with him. This is a fundamental error. Don't you realise that the Devil is much stronger than you? He knows all your tricks, your weaknesses and fatal flaws. This world of human society in which we spend most of our lives is his playground – you understand? It is his feeding ground, he is immensely strong here. You will waste all your energy in this battle, and have nothing left over with which to perform real work.'

'Then how do we defeat him?' my friend asked, mystified. 'Isn't that our purpose: to work against our false personality, our *nafs*?'

'Your *nafs* need not be always bad. Like everything, it is in transition. You consider the Devil to be nothing but evil in opposition to God, but nothing can oppose God, because God created everything in full awareness. The Devil is like everything in creation, ourselves included: he is just on his way.' Ustoz paused and allowed the notion to sink in. 'You cannot fight the Devil and win,' he summarised. 'If you want to win, you must first make friends with him, get to know him – and get him to do your work.'

So that's what I did. I went to work for the Devil. I put on the suit and blended in. Played the part, met the top brass, observed at close proximity the glowing upward siphon of ill-gotten gold. "Render unto Caesar..." My friend was a good man mired in the same life struggle as all of us, and in private we shared our true feelings about this system we now almost exclusively live under on this upside-down planet. The deal broke for him, too, eventually, an ill-fitted suit becomes too uncomfortable to bear in the end. But we did what was necessary at the time. Saw, and dined and drank with the wizards behind the nefarious machine. Watched and learned its running from the inside. Then got out before it crushed us. There is only so long you can be plugged back into the Matrix before it has you again. Ustoz was right: whatever your noble ambitions, become too close an acquaintance of Signor Satan and ultimately he is always too strong. Like Cypher in the

Matrix movie, you can try to cut a deal to forget there was ever anything else, but ultimately, you're expendable. Besides, once you've seen and experienced it for what it is, you can never forget.

I got flown around the planet, put up in luxury hotels, took part in seemingly infinite last dances at the Babel of Versailles. I could not fly back, with my yearning swallow's heart, to Uzbekistan. My long unofficial stay of before had, I was informed courtesy of Ustoz's extensive local network, landed me in the state book of undesirable visitors. Another test to further fashion some patience. To keep my spirit pointing true, I joined, along with Kin One, a Shaolin Temple in London. However it may seem, I am not a spiritual seeking junkie. It's fine to taste all the treats on offer at the enlightenment complimentary buffet, but at some point you have to choose or accept one road, or you never go anywhere. Zen and Sufism share many principles and concepts, and while the specific focus and practices may vary, one school can find plenty that is familiar in the other. I remember the first time Kin One and myself set foot inside the temple in North East London: we looked at each other at the same moment and smiled. It was like teleporting through the front door of the centre in Uzbekistan. The taste was the same.

Then, of course, there was the girlfriend. Girlfriends. We're all different when it comes to romantic partners, irrelevant of gender or sexual persuasion. There are the infamous "serial monogamists'" and the even more infamous "players". The one hit wonders, the commitment-shy, beautiful losers, Prince and Princess Charming, sexual psychopaths, swingers, open relationship advocates, faithfuls to the bitter end, twisted deviants, emotional bullies, monster control freaks, damaged goods, martyrs, predators, biological desperados, reluctantly harnessed servants and eternal singles. I'm sure I've missed some. In any case, in this constantly messy and morphing Venn Diagram of sensual and romantic love, we find ourselves at various points on the board at different stages. I was always on the lookout for "The One" – whilst keeping myself busy. After several typical boom and bust cycles, I found...another "One". An Olympian and US ski champion, she was also into shamanism and natural health. We met through my former literary agent, and despite our radically different personalities and backgrounds, we were soon convinced it was meant to be. I invited her on a road trip to Italy, where in addition to the day job I was about to embark on a family restoration project. I felt I was in the best condition – physically, emotionally and psychologically – of my life. I packed up the old road-rocket with camping gear, the carefully programmed iPod, martial arts clobber and a mountain bike. Before turning off my phone at the Chanel Tunnel, I spoke to my pal and Kin, Danny.

'So – this is it, then, Bro?' he asked.

'Feels like it.'

'Good on you, Jay. You take care of her, now. God speed.'

According to the internet, it was George Santayana who first said: "Those who cannot remember the past are condemned to repeat it." The aphorism evolved into the well-known meme: "Those who do not learn from history are doomed to repeat it." You can debate the details of the differently nuanced meanings of these statements all you want, the intention behind the transmissions is pretty unified: watch out, lest we forget our mistakes.

I had always been an "enthusiastic" driver. I was seven years-old when I first learned to drive. My equally machine-obsessed father taught me in a Mini, around a field next to our home. A week later, I stuck it through a hedge, thankfully with little damage to boy or vehicle.

Should have paid attention earlier.

In my twenties, during those days of rage against the machine of our modern world, I often channelled said rage in tandem with machines of a smaller, more individualistic scale. More than once I had close calls, some of which ended with cars in body shops for minor repairs from metal workers who raised their eyebrows and relieved me of my precious addiction purse. I rarely came to personal physical harm. My closest call was probably when I found myself skating along the wrong side of a high street on my arse one night at sixty miles an hour, watching in slo-mo as the overpowered motorcycle I had been sitting on seconds earlier ploughed into a nearby parked car. I limped for a week, but the memory file didn't linger on my desktop for long. Such is the addictive cycle.

Had I looked to history that night in 2007, I may have recalled a cautionary tale from only a decade before. A famous princess from the land of my birth had been killed, along with her partner and driver, in a high speed chase through the winding tunnels beneath the bridges and streets of the city. The tunnels are well-known as accident black spots. Often, the ramps that descend towards the mouths of the subterranean three- or four-lane carriageways are choked for hours with traffic. Diesel from waiting trucks and service vehicles can spill and trickle down onto the surface of the main motorway. Eventually, weather and the action of a million of tyres will disperse it. In the summer, however, when the skies are clear for up to weeks on end, it can sit for much longer. Waiting for the rain.

It was approaching midnight. Jill and I had been on the road for more than five hours since leaving my home in England. Having lived in Paris, I decided we'd break our journey and I would show her around for a day or two. It's the world capital of amour, after all. The car was running well. This is not always a given with cheaply bought old sports cars, not even German ones. Before leaving, I had had it comprehensively checked over, and a little extra muscle squeezed out of the previously rebuilt turbocharged engine. The tyres were fresh, brake pads new. For an old timer, she was feeling fit. Jill was laughing: we had Ray LaMontagne for company, a month together before she returned to the States for training – perfect. The rain had been heavy earlier, but now it had lightened to a fine drizzle. I wasn't pushing, we were just clipping along nicely. Now we were south of the river, there would surely be a charming and typically romantic auberge nearby. I figured we'd pull off at the next exit.

I don't remember the impact. Under a bridge – a slow-medium left hander – on-ramp joining at right – gallery lights ahead – wipers swish – down – tightening – unexpected twitch from the back end – opposite lock, more gas – nothing – nothing – wipers swish – slide – tunnel wall – Jill screams –

o

When I came to, I found myself at the still, bright epicentre of carnage. I couldn't move. I couldn't turn my head. The dials were in front of me – my vision was blurred, though I could see someone had splashed ketchup on them – and the steering wheel boss had gone. My right knee was under my chin, my thigh pressed awkwardly against my chest. There was aching pain everywhere, though I couldn't clearly locate its numerous sources. My only instinct was to reach out feebly with my right arm, the sole limb I could move, to the seat next to me.

It was empty.

There was noise, and people, all around me.

'*Où est mademoiselle?*' I tried to ask. No one heard. In rising panic, I attempted to pull myself clear of the cockpit. I was stuck fast. '*Mademoiselle!*' I shouted. Only an indecipherable groan and a gurgle came out. However, my attempts to thrash my way clear had alerted the fire crew working beside me. I heard rotary saws switch off and run down, followed by a couple of shouts at my shoulder.

'Bouge pas, bouge pas' – 'Don't move, don't move.' A mask was placed over my face. I couldn't feel it on my skin. I breathed deeply.

'Mademoiselle...'

I went into Lester Burnham time. The oxygen hit my ringing mental centre and body's shellshocked cells and I made myself relax. *Breathe...* Sufi – kung fu – Shifu – Ustoz......

Where was Jill?

I was helpless. I was being helped. There were sirens, and saws, and voices, and horns, and hands, and questions. I floated in and out, never wholly leaving my present situation. Had one of the firemen said she had gone in an ambulance? Did they say she was all right? If they had, were they just saying it to keep me calm? I still couldn't turn or see well enough to take in the wrecked cabin. The only thing outside that I could feel was the crumbs of broken glass against my fingertips on the seat beside.

After what seemed like hours, the saws again fell silent. A man next to me lit a cigarette and conferred in a low voice with his colleagues. Frustrated as *I* may have been, I felt for them: stuck out on a motorway in the middle of the night, struggling to remove an idiot Englishman from a crushed sardine tin of his own making. I was aware of rain falling on both me and the instrument binnacle ahead of me – strange, I remember thinking, knowing that my undoubtedly now lifeless toy had been a coupe. I overheard one, essential line from their conversation. It remains ineradicably on the files:

'Il faut lui couper les jambes' – 'We must cut off his legs.'

Well, Kin. I have to tell you that in spite of earlier instructions, I moved about a bit at that. In very brief moments, the poor fireman's cigarette break was over and he was bent close to me through the doorless aperture, doing his very best to decipher the numb sounds coming out of my oddly uncooperative mouth. Despite the language barrier, created not by my French but, as I would later discover, by the effects of the non-airbag wheel connecting with my face at somewhere between fifty and sixty miles an hour with the force of a cracked engine block behind it, he appeared to interpret my pleadings – my desperate last entreaty from dying Uryens to hopeless Perceval – correctly:

'Try again.'

So he did. With great skill and effort, this veritable hero squeezed himself like a contortionist through the limited opening they had already created behind the repositioned front wheel and, using a miniature circular saw of the type you might use to trim up a guitar inlay or a sticking door hinge, little by little cut the pedals from where they had been fused with my left foot and training shoe, attempting not to remove too much biological tissue as he went. Finally, he was done. He pulled himself clear of the debris and lit another cigarette. I will never judge anyone else who does the same. I felt the ambient mood lift slightly, and then with another, louder *zurrrrrr* from behind me, I felt the back of my chair being ripped away. Arms from above took a hold of me. The team counted "three". With a jolt and a blast of exquisite agony from every compromised zone of my body, I was lifted from the wreck. The extraction had taken four hours.

In the ambulance, another team went quickly to work. My clothes were cut, dripping with rain and blood, from my body. Sticky patches, attached to wires that ran from beeping monitors near my head, were positioned tactically about my form. A paramedic talked to me calmly and efficiently throughout. Having placed my neck in a brace, he produced a sharp implement, and moved it over my lower limbs.

'Do you feel that?' he asked in English.

'No.'

'That?'

'No.'

He tried again. 'Can you feel this?'

I tried to put my mind into my legs, as the siren wailed and the machine took off like thunder, but I didn't sense anything.

'No,' I said again. 'Nothing.'

'Okay.' He turned to confer with a fellow medic beside him, then came back, a hissing mask in his hand. 'Relax,' he assured me.

I nodded that I understood.

All the lights went out.

Thankfully, Jill survived. You have to be tough to be a world champion mogul skier, physically and mentally, and in the accident and its aftermath, she proved she was that and more. In the two months following that I spent in the Hôpital Bicêtre at the Porte d' Italie (life is nothing if not ironic), she was with me, in soul if not always in person, even though for the first six weeks of that reframed romantic summer holiday of a lifetime I was for the most part in a coma.

Jill had also been knocked out on impact. She had a scar on her forehead to remind her of our outing together, and probably still does to this day. She broke a couple of fingers, ribs and toes, but – miraculously, as even unbelievers are known to say – she was otherwise physically undamaged. Poetically, the same could not be said of me.

To spare the full dark and enlightening story; to get us, before we expire, into your cave, Kin, and to the much needed Second Howl, here is the rundown:

My right leg was shattered below the knee. When the car hit the wall, the engine came at speed through the scuttle and into my side of the passenger compartment. In an instant, it turned my tibia and fibula into crunchy fragments of porcelain and pushed my knee up under my chin. The motor missed my left leg, but as the metal in the footwell buckled and moved rearward, it popped my femur through the back of my pelvis and crushed my left foot in the mangled pedals. My left arm had gone through the driver's window, snapping my ulna in a classic nightstick fracture. Amazingly, bar the obligatory bruising to my ribs, my torso had been exempt any internal injuries. The star prize, however, went to my face.

"Pulverised" was the description, one surgeon to another, that the scientific miracle worker known as Docteur Fain gave my father on his arrival in Paris twenty-four hours later. My skull, he expanded for the ortho-carpenter's benefit, was not simply in pieces. 'It is as if,' he explained, 'an elephant has stood on it. And jumped. It is fine bone powder. You understand.'

My head was now the size of a basketball and, by all accounts (no one was permitted to take photographs), somewhat disturbing to behold. There was nothing to be done immediately, however. The doctors had noticed that my occipital bone, at the lower back of the skull, had also been fractured and was now pushing on my spinal column. I was losing cerebrospinal fluid (CSF) at an alarming rate, though from where exactly no one could fathom. There was nothing to do but wait. Either the leaking would stop of its own accord or – dot dot dot.

Three days later, it stopped. Doctor Fain asked my family and Jill, who was now walking wounded, if they could provide some photographs of me with which to work. Why, I berated them all later, didn't they just Google some images of Johnny Depp or George Clooney? Talk about missed opportunity. If you have seen the movie *Vanilla Sky*, then you're already familiar with the injury I sustained. It's called a Le Fort fracture, and it measures on a scale of 1-3 the severity of an impact to the front of the skull. "3" being the worst, I was glad not to be outdone by Tom Cruise by claiming the further award of "3++".

Over the next few weeks, as I embraced Morpheus and his pals and went on one hell of an alternative summer adventure, Fain painstakingly reconstructed his moveable biological canvass to resemble as close as was possible the pictures my family provided. Performing a tracheotomy, his team effectively sealed off my head from the neck up and, using then cutting-edge laparoscopic techniques of threading cameras through incisions in my eyebrows and through my nasal passages and mouth, installed a finely crafted titanium frame for the re-knitting bone matter to use as a template. In-between times, his orthopaedic colleagues had reinserted my left femur and patched up the socket as best they could, set a pin in my left forearm, put a few more in my ankles and stuck a complex metal Christmas tree a.k.a an external fixator into the mush of my right lower leg, drilling into my thigh to hold it in place. In all, that summer I spent twenty-seven hours under the knife.

I don't remember any of this, of course. While everyone else was busy working, and comforting and supporting one another on my behalf, I was somewhere else.

The Bridge

There is a land of the living and a land of the dead, and the bridge is love, the only survival, the only meaning.

- Thornton Wilder, The Bridge of San Luis Rey

Not long after I inadvertently modified myself in Paris, an American neurosurgeon went on a trip of his own. Struck down by bacterial meningitis, he entered into a coma and on his subsequent travels about the interior visited Heaven and had a parley with God. Once the infection had cleared, revisiting the experience quite freaked him. His colleagues had not expected him to survive, or at any rate return with anything near to normal brain function. Yet here he was, alive and whole. Better, in fact, than ever. As a man of science, having believed neither in any deity nor in an afterlife, the neurosurgeon began making inquiries. Unable to find a clean scientific explanation for his visions, and finding his post-meningitis life laced with unaccountable coincidences that supported his coma recollections, he contemplated that what he had witnessed was true: consciousness is not a product of brain activity but exists, albeit linked with it, independently; Heaven is real; God exists and, moreover, He truly loves us. He went on to write a bestselling book about it all, *Proof Of Heaven*. Which was when the trouble started.

I read Dr. Eben Alexander's book soon after it was published in 2012. I have followed its progress on and off, and that of its author, out of curiosity since. Having ostensibly turned onto a new life path following his experience (some might incitingly call it a Damascus moment) by publishing further material and books, giving interviews to scientific journals and religious journals and appearing on Oprah etc., Dr. Alexander has on the one hand gathered many fans and followers, whilst on the other attracted innumerable critics, from both scientific and religious communities and others besides. Among the former of the critical camps was Sam Harris, author, philosopher and neuroscientist, who called Alexander's investigation into his Near Death Experience "alarmingly unscientific". Of all the brains to find yourself up against on the subject of brains... In the latter: moderate to far-out Christians, well-meaning Baptists, and a whole load of crazies.

Poor Dr. Alexander. I feel for the man. As often goes in our present age of the last five or so millennia, perhaps it was the presentation rather than the substance of his transmission that flustered so many feathers. *Proof Of Heaven* is one punchy, no prisoners title. Reading it, you can also sense it has been carefully worked – watered down – for mass consumption. Any blame for the hostility towards the book should therefore perhaps be directed towards the marketing and publicity side of the publishing team. The author himself wasn't happy with the title, wanting to call it rather *An N of One*: a reference to medical trials in which there is only a single patient. I would agree: more humility, more humour, more scientific. Less provocative. But then look at it from a publisher's POV: which would you bet on to sell more copies?

In my infuriating Zen fashion, gathering my right hand in my left sleeve, my left hand in my right sleeve, I can smile and say in good faith I am not partisan to the book's assertions either way. Were they mental hallucinations or real experiences of the soul? Were they both? Was the patient technically "braindead" and unequivocally unconscious when the perceived events took place, or had the bacteria and/or drugs created the whole episode before his brain activity descended below a threshold where one could not reasonably expect to experience any cognitive perception? I dunno, Kin. I'm not a scientist, I don't know the man. I wasn't there. I wasn't him. But I do empathise. I wish him well. Reason being, I had a similar trip.

In my case, it wasn't a grand Dante-esque vision of the cosmic ladder, from the universe's lowest vibrations to the highest shining Absolute Light. Nor did I get to ride on a giant butterfly – although, after my recent skid control demonstration, that was probably a wise choice from the beings that run things in the next realm. What I got was the same *taste* that I picked up through even some of the clunky text in Alexander's book. To be fair to his editors, there is a marked problem here: there really are no words to describe it, for any audience. In the six weeks I was under, I myself lived lifetimes. Lifetimes, Kin, I swear it. As parallel me's, as other people, aging and dying, reincarnating. Meeting some fairly badass representatives of the so-called unproven other side of the veil. And Ustoz – of course. What would he be doing, not being there?

Hand in hand with the more euphoric moments, there naturally came the less joyful experiences the other realm – or realms – have to offer. Watching agonised spirits in an emergency room full of dying human meat bodies is not much fun. Neither meeting relatives and friends who for some reason haven't made it over safely. Then, there are the premonitions. Jacking into the bodies of people who may not yet even be born, only to witness some of the horrors they may have yet to endure in our planet's future (is it written? Can it change?) certainly puts a dent in the coming round celebrations.

The Future. What if you saw it, and could do nothing about it? Do you think that would make you insane?

I say "may" have to endure. The fact that "there" feels so much more real than "here" doesn't mean, of course, it is therefore true. I sincerely hope it is not. But depending on how you eat your info, some of the scenes I took part in might be considered alarming.

Which is why I don't talk about it. Never have, not *really*. Never mind that to do so would be to invite those Furies of our age: I can't, and in all truth I really don't want to. I don't want to roughly bind and encase those untethered joys and hard, core lessons in the stone of my ongoing story. To do so, I feel, to out such experiences, is both incredibly brave and wholeheartedly foolish. Does trauma, plus drugs, plus imagination, plus repeated analysis and retelling, plus others' observations and responses create and define these memories? Are NDEs a by-product of our momentarily failing mortality that can be explained in the terms of that mortal world to which their hosts are bound? Are they a view through a window – a stepping foot through a doorway? A precious and unrepeatable link for the few to the interwoven Akashic fabric of existence which cannot be separated from, yet nor sensed by, our earthly sensing apparatus? I don't know. I don't believe that any of us does. But I'll tell you my own take on this whole matter, on our intellectual seeking to peer into and explain this state: to define it is to destroy it.

I will say this: it was only later, when the surgery was done and beginning to heal, and my incredibly patient and talented and beautiful doctors and nurses and carers reduced the medication to slowly bring me back, again, for good to the ordinary world, that the trip went bad. You might think that it would be exciting, coming home. To see and once more communicate with fellow humans, and family, and friends and loved ones. To realise you weren't going to die; that contrary to all previous expectations, there was a good chance you would walk again; that your face, scarred and still swollen and alien as it felt, was going to be functional, all right, and thanks to the genius of science and the skill and determination of some exceptional practitioners, even look quite normal, if never quite full A-list Hollywood. You might expect that to be a joyful return. But it wasn't. I wasn't home. In contrast to the places I'd been, here and now felt coarse, and grainy, and dull. Like going from a virtual headset back to a black and white TV, with a dial and a coat hanger hanging ungainly out to one side. One repetitive, listless channel to watch. Take part in. Reprise your role in. That wasn't the home I now knew.

I'm not ungrateful. I just can't forget. After all, I had chosen.

Do you want the truth? Is that what we all truly desire? Here it is: we can't handle the truth. But I'm not going to completely cop out now. Not having dragged you down this far, Kin. Into my cave. One of so many. They're not made for that.

"There is my truth, there is your truth, and there is THE truth" – Tierno Bokar, Malian Sufi, as presented by the fabulous director and Kin, Peter Brook.

I'm going to tell you the first kind, Kin, the only one I can know. I like to think I'm not the type to dole out flat advice – if the opposite is coming through in this text, kindly blame my editor. To make an exception to my own loosely-defined rule, this is my piece, based on the above quotation:

Always beware of anyone – anyone – claiming to represent, attempting to convince you of, or trying to sell you version 3. Be very aware.

Now, here's my truth: all this otherworldly argument stuff over Near Death Experience can be quite interesting. To some, it may provide some solace. Less certain, perhaps, is whether any of it is actually useful. I mean, if we discover as we continue on ahead as a species, assuming we will, long enough to make some breakthrough scientific discoveries about death and what happens during and after, what are we going to do about it? How will it change our lives? Will it change them for the better, or for worse? Not being a scientist as I mentioned, nor an oracle, and feeling a bit jaded about the whole thing in any case, I sometimes feel I have little more to add to the conversation. If there's anything so far, though, Kin, that might prove useful from this journey, and that may be useful for your journeys to come, then maybe – just maybe – I have something for you here.

The thing is, I received something that Eben Alexander didn't. Some might see it as a trump card, but I think that view is myopic. I guess I frame it more as just a peculiar blessing, for my unrelenting rational mind as much as for anything.

Alexander got hit with bacteria; I got hit with a tunnel. In hospital, we were both put on a cocktail of strong pharmaceutical drugs. In these states, as far as we subjectively know, we had the experiences outlined above. We can never tell empirically what produced them. However, there was one additional feature on my timeline that I haven't mentioned until now: by the time they put me in the ambulance – by the time the emergency services arrived at the scene, in fact – I had already died.

The Sufis have several names for the Almighty – Allah, God, Jehovah, so very many names. Among themselves, they often refer to the supreme deity as "The Beloved" or as simply "The Friend".

One night, Ustoz and me were sitting by the fire in the mountains.

'Do you know why we say "The Friend", Jasur?' my master asked me. I shook my head. 'A friend is someone with whom we share secrets. This is the most beautiful relationship we can have with our Creator. Total truth. No fear of judgement. God knows everything in our hearts already, of course, but nevertheless He is always waiting for us to share with Him, to come unveiled to Him with what we do not usually show. Always remember, then, the following is also true: whenever you tell a friend a sincere secret from your heart, you are telling it to God.'

The moment the car hit the tunnel wall and the various parts of it went through my body, I was out. Out of there, at any rate. But not out of awareness.

In my memory, which returned only later, I clearly recall standing on the bridge that crossed over the carriageway on the approach to the tunnel's entrance. The traffic was starting to back up from the site of the accident, hazards flashing, brake lights glowing in the mist of the finely falling rain. I stood, and watched. After some time, I couldn't tell how long, I heard the sirens behind me. The fire crew and ambulance slowly pushed and sounded their way through the accumulating jam. Having made it through, small figures emerged and began to assess the scene. I couldn't see the car itself, there was too much movement and too many vehicles around it. Just the empty, brightly lit tunnel beyond. I was aware of not having a body – I saw no part of myself, felt no mass, no movement of muscles, even when I squinted to try and see more clearly. Yet I was present; standing, or even floating, maybe, my feet felt no pressure.

Then I suddenly knew I was not alone.

I will never know what or who was beside me. Not in this life. As I say, despite inevitable attempts at defining my companion's identity since, nothing has helped sharpen the memory. So I have let it go. It simply was, and they were there.

What do you want to do?

The words, if they were words, were not voiced. The question in any case was clear.

What's my choice? I replied.

You can come with me now. Or you can stay.

I didn't need to ask where. We watched together for a while. Then the doors of an ambulance closed, a siren howled and the machine drove away through the tunnel. Directed by the emergency workers, one by one the waiting cars began to trickle slowly past.

I was completely calm. I didn't think. I didn't even feel. Somehow, we both knew the decision had been made. We parted company.

o

I was not given any medication at the scene. Following protocol, and due to the scenario, I was fed only brief bursts of oxygen during the four hours I was trapped. The rationale was straightforward: if I had suffered a spinal injury, they needed to know as soon as possible, and would not be able to perform accurate reflex tests if I had drugs in my system. They had not figured on the extent of the perfect disharmony betwixt man and machine. The crew took off the roof, the door, the shattered windscreen and the wing behind the front wheel, but I hung on involuntarily by my left foot. My father later saw the wreck. Like everybody, he was amazed anyone – Jill or me – had made it out alive. He was even more perplexed at how my shoe was still stuck in the pedal box, entwined and held fast by the now cut and twisted metal, yet they had managed to free its contents. On the night, he discovered, after three hours of trying, the firemen began to give up hope of getting me out alive. Though conscious, brimming once more with sensations and thoughts and feelings, I was in quite a state. Hence the hard but logical decision to remove my legs and speed my exit. Lucky for me, the smoking fireman, whose identity I never managed to discover, agreed to play along.

There it is, Kin. A secret – a taste of my truth, I share with you. Death is not the end. It is not the beginning. It is both and neither. Yes of course. Hand in hand with birth, it is but one face of the bookmark between eternal chapters. The shining intro and the dwindling final chord of ever cycling octaves, creating and filling the voidless void with the activity, the life we call the universe. Not to be feared. No more than we should fear life. Not to be fixated on. To recognise, and accept, in every moment we breathe air, as life's companion, as we stand together on that bridge across eternity, and witness the scenes of our existence unfold.

You have to die. It's going to happen at some point, Kin. Might as well get it done already. Trust me, it's always a little better the next time around. First, though, please let us be clear with each other on these words' intentions, for it is important: I'm not talking about physical suicide. I pray you never go there. I've contemplated it myself, both before and since, but I don't believe that's your way, Kin, I truly don't. If you listen close enough, I suspect you'll hear for yourself that you know that to be true. I remember coming round in the hospital one time, when they brought me back up for tests. Strapped to a gurney, ship all banged up, dry-docked in ICU with a face full of metal and a hole in my neck. 'Well,' I told myself, 'either you're breathing, or you're not. If you are, everything's possible.' That includes loving life, Kin. However hard it can feel. Don't go there any more – you hear? Stick with me. Be with Kin. Whether you feel it or not right now, we're here with you.

Die to yourself **in this life**. It doesn't matter what it takes. You don't always choose. Through drugs (careful), through an illness, through trauma, through despair; through madness, through an NDE, through dreams, through the practice of your way – through surrender. You have to die. If you don't, you can never truly know anything.

I'm not asking you to believe me. Rational me still has his agenda – even now, I hear him wanting to kick in, saying "Whoa – this is getting pretty hard to swallow, JB. You might want to let me edit some of this once the rush is over." And that's fine. But even JB, whoever or whatever he might be, isn't really in charge of this part of the page. So all I consciously hope is that you will understand me. All I hope is that you can love me. To make as clear as I am able, not the meaning, but the intention of that so carelessly used, so misinterpreted word, in this context: all I hope is that you allow me to belong to you. That is all, and that is everything, Kin, this I promise, I hope I may also do for you.

There it is. I ate the cake. And still have it. Thank you, comedian and gloriously dressed to kill Kin, Eddie Izzard, for inspiring me to mess around with your meme. You, and so many of your colleagues, are some of the staunchest defenders against those raging Black Dog nights and days. What the hell would we do here without a sense of humour to save us?

"I do rather laugh in the face of fear. Tweak the nose of terror."

Needs must when the devil vomits into your kettle. Some friends, huh?

In fairness, it wasn't a whole slice that I ingested. More of a nibble. Like Alice with her mushroom, however, the effects were potent enough. It won't be the last time. Of that, at least, we can be certain.

o

Seeing as we are about to enter the last chapter of our hero's journey together, let's wrap this one up with a few notes from the people and the stories that have inspired us.

2005 brought us the film *V For Vendetta*. A dystopian near-future set drama, it is uncomfortably pertinent at the time of writing, as the backdrop features a civil war in America and a virus released in Europe bringing intolerance, xenophobia, racism and fascism back to the fore. Never mind that mask. At one point in the film, the titular protagonist, V, stages a mock incarceration and death sentence on Evey, the young woman he initially rescued from the authoritarian state's secret police. Believing fully it is the ruthless Fingermen that have captured her, Evey is locked in an underground cell, humiliated, threatened and tortured. She is told she will be executed unless she gives up the identity and whereabouts of the "terrorist" known as V. Deprived of everything else, Evey finds a note, stashed secretly in the wall of her cell. It describes the last days of a former inmate, also arrested and tortured by the same captors. The tale gives her courage, until at last the moment comes for her final decision: give up V, or die. Evey chooses death.

"Then you have no fear anymore," says her jailor. "You're completely free." Leaving the cell door open, he walks away.

Evey is stupefied. Uncomprehending, she makes her way out of the dungeon – her cave – and up into the world above. She finds herself in V's apartment. He is waiting for her.

"You did this to me," she whispers in disbelief. "Why?"

"You said you wanted to live without fear," V replies. "I wish there'd been an easier way."

There are no easy ways, Kin. Keep flying. Keep flying.

Tyler Durden again, our friend and mentor from *Fight Club*: "First, you have to know that someday, you are going to die. Until you know that, you will be useless."

Do you want to be happy here, Kin? Or do you want to be useful? Here's a tip: you might find some of the former state through the latter, but if happiness is your goal, you'll never be either. Die before you die, and maybe – maybe – you can die happy.

Jacob's Ladder. Spoiler alert: it has a lot to do with dying. There's one beautiful scene, not the only one, where Jacob is being treated by a chiropractor, Louis, for a chronically slipped disc.

"I was in Hell," Jacob tells him. "I don't want to die, Louis. It's all pain."

Louis listens as he works. He then quotes Meister Eckhart: "The only thing that burns in Hell is the part of you that won't let go of your life. But they're not punishing you – they're freeing your soul... The way he sees it," continues Louis, whom we suspect by now may be more than a straightforward bone-cracker and healer figure: "if you're frightened of dying, and you're holding on, you'll see devils tearing your life away. But if you've made your peace, then the devils are really angels, freeing you from the Earth."

Last words, and the microphone, back to Jim Morrison, de facto patron of the 27 Club. We've looked at numerous movies from other people; let's thank them for their company and inspiration, and go and make our own. If you're still here only with your curious intellect – in which case, congratulations, Kin, I can't believe you've lasted this long – then let's appeal to that ego to get this wagon train in motion. Maybe we can tempt our friend into action through vanity – play the Devil with its own trick, so to speak. Over to you, Jim, and your final question:

"Did you have a good world when you died – enough to base a movie on?"

No Road Back

Wake up, grow up, clean up, show up – and fuck up.

- Doshin Nelson Roshi

'This life is a bus stop,' said Ustoz.

Okay. So what do we do while we're waiting?

When you've already died, and realised none of this matters, and that everything somehow matters, the extra life you get is both a magical bonus game and a frustrating extra detention you're obliged to serve before being allowed home from school. It's wonderful to be in the car with Luc Besson's *Lucy* and be able to empathise when she tells us "We never really die". The more pertinent question to self in the aftermath is: while we're stuck down here, how should we really live?

As hard as we try to resist or beat or fight it, the ordinary world keeps pulling us back. We came out of it, it produced us, informed us, tailored us to survive in its environment. There are bits of it we fear and despise – mostly those aspects produced by our relatively recent history as the dominant species in our supposedly shared biosphere. Those same bits also addict us: money, power, status, comfort, stuff. Apparent security from the one thing we have no security against: our own demise. And another thing, so everyday to most of us that we tend to take it for granted: people.

You can live alone in your cave forever, but then why be here at all? If you happen to be an enlightened guru open to visitors, like our 12th Century influencer Khodja Yassaviy, fair enough. Even a moderate non-spiritual, anti-woo-woo materialist might accede that retreat is a valuable station on our journey. Teaching the burned-out, the disillusioned, the wounded, the depressed and the uninitiated how to better be with self and by extension fellow humans fulfils some form of community service. The cave is but a station, however, not a destination. If we're unwilling to get involved and risk getting messy with the great foaming Petri dish of present humanity, of what value are our deeds? What purpose our struggles? What will we have learned? Moreover: would our Mother be proud?

Ah, Mother. Do you think they'll drop the bomb?

Before we do, however, let's be of use. Whatever the perceived ills and limited capitalist goals installed by my early social education, one thing at least, as I saw it, contained merit: to be of service.

'We do not have rights,' my wise grandfather used to say, 'only duties.'

Let's not go down that rabbit hole just now. It'll be bloody.

In any case, such was my programme. The only question: who to serve? With a receding limp and not too many glances in the mirror, six months after the accident, I got back to work.

Let's compress this story. What is the art of writing but folding time? If words cannot shorten the distance between shared experiences then really, what business have they? I feel a howl coming on.

As the circle on this tale – though not our shared journey, Kin – inevitably closes, we find ourselves back with our friend and inspiration, Michel de Montaigne: "The soul which has no fixed purpose in life is lost," said he; "to be everywhere is to be nowhere."

There are so many directions we can walk in – so many cups from which to drink. Especially in our current society. As with any community in which balance is lost, for many of us now the extreme number of options, the myriad diverse ways to inform ourselves, paradoxically ends up throwing the whole system. Essentially, we come to a standstill, and eat until we burst. We are not spoiled for choice – we are ruined by it. After my extended time out, I wanted to reset everything.

Jill and I didn't make it. Not together, at any rate. The why is irrelevant now. The river flows on. Wherever you are, with all my heart I wish you well. I thank you, and I'm sorry for any hurt or harm I caused you.

I say the same, right now, to all and any whose paths have crossed my own: family, lovers, strangers, friends. Kin. Some of you may see this as an atonement too late. I can only raise my hands. For the current journey, you may consider it as coming in ahead of time. Steps 8 and 9 within the temple of recovery. Well, knowing the way back, and the fact that this time will be different, I'm going to bend the rules a little. It's taken me all this story, these years and these words, to realise my true destination here, Kin. It's taken this journey with you. There may not be another chance.

Don't worry, Kin, we're not leaving the planet – not just yet. Your destination, as ever, is up to you. If you feel there is someone you may wish to ask for forgiveness, however, or anything to atone for from your previous journeys, now is always the best time.

Come on, Kin: we can take a minute. Who would you call? I'd like to share this moment with you.

OOO

I got busy. I started a publishing company. It was called Guerilla Books. Its goal, its "mission statement" if you believed the hype, was to print beautiful books full of stories with soul. I didn't want to take on the mainstream – "You lack a knight's humility!" – I just wanted to put something charmed back in the river. For any Kin who might be fishing. Looking for that taste within the melee of transmissions that come thundering at us 24/7, dressed up and made up and packaged to perfection to entice us to eat them and swallow them and come back begging for more. Better to light a candle than rage against the dying of the light – etc. So I did. The books were critically well-received. The second title, *The Restorer*, won an international award. The authors I was looking for began to find us first. I borrowed money off friends so we could expand.

At the same time, I was still working for the world's second largest tobacco empire and renovating a ruined monastery in Tuscany. The latter would balance the former by becoming a centre for artists and seekers and anyone needing time out from the Matrix. I spent a month in New York City co-writing a film script and started to make a documentary on Uzbek Sufism. Meanwhile, Ustoz spoke to a friend, who called an acquaintance, who owed someone a favour, who knew of Ustoz, and hey, presto: I was granted a new entry visa. We went up to the mountains for a month, picking herbs in minefields, bathing in rivers, eating stew made with lethal snakes caught by the murids, and generally thanking our stars. Much as I loved it, and could often fantasise a future there, I knew that culturally, at any rate, theirs was not my way.

'Are you a Sufi?' I was asked by one of Ustoz's acquaintances.

'Yes,' I replied.

The man was puzzled. 'Are you a Muslim?' he asked.

'He is a Christian Sufi,' my master responded on my behalf, one eye on me. Afterwards, when we were alone, Uztoz told me: 'Among ourselves, we can forget labels. They are there only to avoid outside suspicion. In the group, we rarely use the term Sufi anymore. The way must evolve. You remember what I told you? That time?'

I did remember. Ustoz had said: 'We must appear to choose sides. The world is entering another phase of polarization. Anyone without an identity will be persecuted by the extreme warring factions. We are seen as the changelings – in their sight, without definition, uncommitted, refusing to wear colours, and therefore dangerous, not to be trusted. We must hide once more in plain sight. The chain must survive.'

It was uncanny to be reminded just at that moment. Accustomed as I was to surprises from the master, I was impressed that Ustoz remembered. Though I did indeed recall these words and more, with perfect clarity, from when he first spoke them, at the time I had been over six thousand miles away, lying in a Parisian hospital, in the depths of a coma.

o

I got married. Hoo-hah!

'Why did you marry me?' I ask my wife at lunch, nearly ten years after the fact.

'Because you saw through me. Because it wasn't just romance. It was the opposite, really. All that fuzzy love just keeps the old cycle going. Once you've been seen – well, that's it, really. I wouldn't have said so then. I didn't know. A lot of the time, I didn't like it. It made me uncomfortable. You were high risk. You didn't seem to be that interested in me. But when you've been known, all the games and the nonsense disappear.' She smiles. 'What about you?'

Because you are patient. Because you are brave enough to be known. Because you see through the bullshit, and understand it without letting yourself be taken in. Because you see beyond my stupidity, my selfishness, my flaws. Because you tolerate my whims and foolish desires, yet not so much as to allow them to erode your integrity. Because you don't care for the baubles of this world, but recognise quality at once in people, in nature, in ideas, in craft, in things. Because you wish to learn, and never stand still, unless to surrender to a moment. Because you wished to be a mother, and you love to work. Because you know this is not about "I" and "you" and "us", yet all three must still be served. Because I knew you'd love our children. Because you understand the essential nature of play. Because you can fight and yield, and for the greater part know which to do when. Because you call yourself back. Because you don't let your story define you. Because every day you choose. Because you allow me to belong to you a little more with each passing year. Because you are modest, and have resolve, and feel the music, and submit to life's teachers, and embrace the arduous path, and in all of this, I knew then, knowing nothing, you would become as you are now: more beautiful every day.

Because I talk too much. And you are content with silence.

Because, because, because......

Some see marriage as a book. For others, it's a sentence. Like everything, I guess it depends on how you cat it. Well, honey, overly sentimental as I sometimes am, allow me to leave the last words to a more qualified song writer:

"The book of life is brief
And once a page is read
All but love is dead

That is my belief"

- Don McLean

No trip is perfect. That's what makes them so. Just as you'd expect, starting our voyage under clear skies, it wasn't long before the storm clouds came.

I had spread myself too thin. There were too many plates spinning. Being a diehard idealist, the first to be dropped was the corporate tobacco gig. Why trade precious time in return for Caesar's dirty coin? We could make the rest work. The publishing was receiving positive press, I had even made the Independent on Sunday "Happy List" of people who make Britain a "better balanced, happier country". I was being invited to give talks. We would have to take a hit, but we could ride it. Shouldn't we embrace the struggle?

Struggle was what we got. The books didn't sell, not enough. I loved creating them – editing, designing, discovering authors, writing, launching. I couldn't sell them. Self-promotion wasn't my skill. All my energy and resources went into preparing the feast, but I was coming up short on all the things big industry and its chiefs know are the keys to generate a feeding frenzy: presentation, marketing, exposure, product placement, networking, advertising, promotion. The books were beautiful – of course they were: it's where I put all the money. Other people's money. By the time I found myself, alongside one of my authors, selling his debut rebel masterpiece out of a vintage pram in Covent

Garden, I knew this battle was over. The Guerillas would have to retreat, and regroup.

Then the bank called in the loan on the Tuscan retreat centre. The Italian Job had gone sour. Did anyone have any ideas? As ever, my father did, but as he had initially guaranteed the loan and recently lost his own lucrative career, we had to accept that for now, at least, the dream was over. Hadn't we watched *Excalibur* enough times? Camelot doesn't last forever. I remember laughing ruefully with him one time, during the collapse, when his cards were declined at the local petrol station and he didn't have enough cash for the drive home. A man who months before, on paper, had been worth several million pounds.

A powerful deceiver, Kin, these pages we read on parchment and screen. Lest we forget what we believe we are truly worth.

We took in lodgers and went out to work. Anything. My wife qualified as a masseuse and a cousin set her up at her company in The City, rubbing away the stress and hangovers from the capital's prized worker bees. I called on the mercy of friends who had become successful entrepreneurs. I worked as a gardener, as a waiter, a carpenter, a driver, removal man, labourer. For six months, with a great pal and brother who had his own IT consultancy firm, I pulled cables through the ceilings, walls and floors of a government building site in Westminster. An ant for the Matrix. "Real work" – "honest toil" – "How most people live". Yeah, yeah, bring on the "taste of real life humility" lecture. What hurt wasn't the work itself, bar the obligatory aches and pains. It wasn't so much that I had a young family, was nearing forty, and believed I had no career and few prospects, though that steady negative drip would take its toll. You know the score, don't you Kin? No, what needled most was who and what I was ultimately doing all this for: a culture I didn't believe in.

I wrestled with some demons, they were middle class and tame...

Well, if Saint Leonard had to go back on tour in his seventies to pay the bills on account of a thieving, unscrupulous manager, hell: I'm in.

So that's what you tell yourself. Again and again and again. I'm in. Like it or not, this is how we live now on this unfortunate planet. Get your head down. Be humble. Compare your lot: you're not starving. You have a roof. It's as good as it gets. Then, one day, you pause and you know: the words you're telling yourself are hollow. You know it – don't you, Kin? That feeling? Something triggers it, and you realise you're there, yet again: the story you're telling yourself to stay afloat doesn't have any air. You've been putting off accepting it, but the water around and above you, if you listen to the muted roar, if you truly try to fill your lungs, is all you need to know: you're sinking. You can thrash and kick and shout all you want. You're not coming up again. The Matrix has you.

What is my purpose here? What are we *for*? Do you know, Kin? Why are we doing what we do? I felt I used to know. It's amazing what we keep, and what we send to trash, in this fickle companion of ours, this "memory". Personal – and collective.

As Merlin so presciently reminds us: "It is the doom of men that they forget."

One of our daughter's first books was called *A Bit Lost*. She loved it and it's still one of our favourites. Simple in concept and execution, a baby owl falls from its nest and becomes separated from its mummy. The owl's fellow woodland creatures, after a few cases of mistaken identity, eventually succeed in reuniting them. They all go up to the nest for some biscuits. The baby owl dozes off and wobbles again. "Uh-oh!"

At the end of our well-worn edition, there is a quotation from Defoe's *Robinson Crusoe*: "Thus we never see the true State of our Condition, till it is illustrated to us by its Contraries; nor know how to value what we enjoy, but by the want of it." The author, Chris Haughton, dedicates the book to Mum and Dad.

To be found. To be home. In yourself – in the world. When you feel so fucking far from it. What does that take? Do we really need to add anything to ourselves? Money, status, control, luxury, adoration, career, dreams? What if we just gave it up? Maybe we can't change the outcome of the Duality Trap, it's what defines our here and now. But what if we stopped buying in?

I love that little book, not least in relation to so many of its own "Contraries". It's not even the daily deluge of average pulp that gets produced and absorbed that rankles, we see it everywhere: in books, media, on

TV, the internet, radio – in restaurants, supermarkets, clothing stores, car showrooms, DIY depots, political rallies and hair salons. It's how we support it by merely considering it. The comments. The adulation. The unfounded apotheosis.

"Genius" is one that gets slapped on the cover of many a middling book these days. "Masterpiece" is another. One typically bandwagon children's book came to us with the promotional admonition emblazoned upon it that "If you haven't read this book, you haven't lived".

Really? I guess I won't. Not like that.

What sounds like a bag of grapefruits from a failed publisher and author is, of course, partly just that. However, this corruption of perception and devaluation of language points to a deeper, more sinister malaise in our everyday, and in truth anything but ordinary world: we have become so conditioned into believing the hype, that it becomes the default standard by which we trade our life experiences.

Wake up, grow up, clean up... – again, again, again......

An old school friend got married in Sicily. He'd made a fortune in the Californian technology industry, one of the good guys. Indeed, it's good to recall that Kin are everywhere. His integrity would bite him later financially, but we cope when we know that's an essential part of the journey.

The wedding was a fairytale. The night before, there was a party at what was basically the Modern Earth version of Rivendell. During the ceremony, my wife, daughter and I sat behind an A-list Hollywood star. There was a dinner table outside under the trees the length of a runway. I couldn't bring myself to sit at it. On that perfect evening, my own story overpowered me. Sadness. Disappointment. Shame. I sat beneath the trees in a quiet corner of the vast garden, watching myself disinterestedly yet still unable to do anything about it. My wife and daughter came to find me, and we took a bus back down to our campsite on the beach. The next day, as other guests left their villas and jetted back to L.A. and Istanbul and Miami to continue their socially prestigious lives, we took a cheap flight and an airport bus back to our rented shelter in North London. My wife and daughter held my hand.

'We're flying the wrong way,' I said.

'EasyJet?' said my wife, smiling.

Soon after, there came a balmy way-stop in the wasteland of my previous vision and convictions. A comedian turned activist and seeker was giving a talk on the importance of reading for The Reading Agency, a society engaged in boosting exposure to books for young people. I'd missed much of his ascent to fame and controversial celebrity status, initially writing him off in the way we do when we fail to make the effort to slip our own judgment and try to understand other people. At first, I'd chalked him down as a gobby Messianic handbag of a man. Recently, I'd grown curious. His name was Russell Brand.

The gathering was on a cold Tuesday evening in winter in a theatre in Central London. Dressed in my regulation site gear of cement-plastered boots, heavy trousers and dust-choked hoodie, I watched, and listened, and laughed with the rest of the audience as the transmission working through the actor known as Brand filled the hall. Afterwards, he didn't leave. The eager fans and sceptics alike pushed forward to the stage where he engaged with people, individually and in groups, for over half an hour. Eventually, one of the organisers asked his minders if they could get their man moving off. They'd a dinner reservation waiting.

'You'll just have to wait,' one of Brand's people replied. 'This is what he does. I've been doing this job for years and I've never seen anything like it.'

Observing at the front near the exit, I figured that having received my unexpected glinting nugget from the coal mine, a pebble of absurd good hope, I'd seen enough and should be getting back to my hutch. Brand, too, appeared finally ready to move on. As he walked back towards the wings, he caught my eye.

'Are you all right, mate?' he asked.

I didn't stop to think. Looking, and probably smelling, like a nocturnal trash compactor operator, I walked up onto the stage and looked him straight in the eye:

'Russell,' I said, 'I love you.'

'I love you too, mate,' he replied. To the bewilderment of the audience and bystanders still present, we then hugged each other for a good half minute.

'You keep going,' he said as we separated.

'You too,' said I.

When I got home some time later, my wife was waiting.

'Well?' she asked.

'He's real,' I reported. 'We had a hug. Don't be jealous.'

She smiled. 'I knew you'd see each other,' she said. 'You had to. I don't really fancy him,' she added. 'He's a bit too pretty. So: do I get a hug?'

Fragments, Kin. These fragments. Keep them safe.

A few months later, we were back in Florence. My old Balkan bar-owning buddy had by now become a big player restaurateur in the tourist-clogged historic centre of the Tuscan capital.

'Come and manage my new restaurant,' Dimi offered. 'The work isn't glamorous and it's long hours, but you are workers and I'll look after you guys. If you wanted to stay, you could take it over. Franchise it off me. I know it's not what you dreamed of, but the money is good.'

We packed our little survival unit into the car and started again. It may not have been the ultimate grail, but our friend's generosity literally got us out of jail.

By the end of the summer season, I could feel I was losing myself. Where once I had played, I was now a desensitized cog in the tourist industry machine. Pasta, pizza, cappuccino – I dreamt in unit prices and table numbers. Florence has traded on visitors since she first rose to prominence almost a millennium ago. Even in the fifteen years since I had last enjoyed her streets and humming squares, the tipping point had been breached. Where there were once artisans and carpenters and framers in small medieval doorways, now there was nothing but sandwich shops and juice bars. We rarely served Italians, let alone local Florentines. The city had become a full-blown historic theme park. Waves of tour ship day-trippers inundated the ancient cobbled streets, stumbling over their selfie sticks and stilettos into the piazza kill zones, where touts at the restaurant entrances efficiently and ruthlessly picked them off in scores. Nothing murders success like success. The money was pouring in, but the old matriarch's spirit was little more than a lurking spectre – a phantom of mothballed grandeur to unpack and print onto every awning and museum banner and cheap T-shirt and trinket in town.

'I don't know how you stay sane,' I said to my friend one night as I handed him the regular fistful of cash from the till.

'Really I'm not,' Dimi replied. 'But you are spoiled English. Compared to where I come from, this is still heaven. And besides – ' He indicated a group of pretty American students at a nearby table.

'That just makes it worse.'

He chuckled. 'Your problem is loving your wife too much. How is she? Do you need anything?'

She was pregnant, which he knew. 'Thanks, Dimi. We're fine.'

'Ah JZ...' He sighed. 'When I was young, all I wanted to do was play music. And the obvious, of course. Now I have money, and no time. When I do have the time, all I have is worries. Something else is always waiting to break my balls. Whatever success I have here, I am still always just that little Balkan foreigner. But it's okay. Here – cheers.' There was a cry and a chorus of laughter from the students.

I turned back. 'You remember that Bukowski poem?'

'The girls we once followed home are now the bag ladies,' he recited. We laughed. 'My friend, I don't know about all your Sufi stuff. You know, I hope to God that He is real, even though I don't think He will be very pleased with how I lived my life. In the end, you know what I think will be on my gravestone? "It was not that great." But at least I have enjoyed my mistakes. I take care of my family, maybe I helped somebody, I don't know. I really don't think I should regret one stupid thing I have done.'

No regrets. Easy to say. How do you shake them? If we do, do we make ourselves unaccountable for our former actions and, by extension, those we've not yet committed? Ah, the marked cards our egos deal us. I walked the night route home, alone under the street lights save for my ever-shifting shadow. What would Ustoz say? I knew what G would say: how are you considering? Dumbass dog.

It was after one in the morning but my brain wouldn't quit. To change the tuning, I found something trending on YouTube about a guy who had unintentionally started an outlaw Porsche cult from a deserted L.A. warehouse. My own Porsche was probably paperclips by now, but I could still get my kicks vicariously. I settled in.

His name was Magnus Walker, a Brit who'd followed his dream of moving to the States and started a clothing line, customizing second-hand jeans. As a boy in dreary '70s Britain, inspired by their latest 911 he had seen at a show, he had written to Porsche and asked for a job. To their credit, the firm replied to the star-struck young fan. Thanks for writing, get through school and come back to us, the missive basically said. Now, four decades later, Porsche US had approached him to be one of their brand ambassadors. Here was Magnus, tinkering away in his sprawling converted warehouse, bought for pennies before the gentrification boom, and living the dream. Dude.

I checked what else he had up online. There was a TedX talk, entitled: "Go With Your Gut."

An idea started to percolate and condense.

"Your body already knows the answers to most of the questions your mind is frantically asking." Paraphrase Ustoz.

"I must create a system, or be enslaved by another man's. I will not reason and compare: my business is to create." William Blake.

"I cannot help you unless you ask me what you want here. That is how it works. Unless you ask, nothing can be given." G.I. Gurdjieff.

Elena...

You will not find the last quotation through a Google search. The memory was passed on to me firsthand.

Do you remember how I said that by the time I was questioning the validity of The Fourth Way's global legacy I was fairly sure all of Gurdjieff's former students would be dead, or at least so old as to make little difference? They weren't. As ever, that uncanny device of seeker and sought mutually calling to one another through the veils of perception, and generally labelled by us in everyday life as "coincidence", brought me into contact with a rare jewel. Already in her nineties when we met, Elena was still lucid and shining. Her granddaughter was at university with one of my biological brothers. One afternoon in the pub, that epicentre of meaningful student activity, my brother casually mentioned my trips to Central Asia and interest in esoteric matters. His companion perked up at the mention of Gurdjieff.

'My granny studied with Gurdjieff for two years when she was younger. In Paris. Just before he died. Your brother should go and see her.'

It was like meeting the oracle. No – she *was* the oracle. Of Ukrainian origin, having escaped the revolution as a girl and come, as so many did, to France, she had later married an Englishman and moved to London, where she lived still. She had first studied under Ouspensky, then G, and later others, including the ever controversial Shah brothers. Little bigger than Yoda in stature, and just as well hidden, in her discreet Georgian-fronted townhouse with its protective family guardians and cave of wonders within, to be granted access and pass into her presence was to cheat time and slip through the cracks of reality into another dimension.

'I really don't know why they keep me here,' she would say, to herself and whatever else may have been present in the quiet temple of her front living room, as much as to her visitor. She would regard you, for minutes sometimes, in silence. Then: 'Ah yes. Of course. There is one further introduction we must make.'

Whenever I was in London, I visited her. Alone, or in the full and festive company of her family and other remarkable people, the moments shared within those unassuming walls remain among my most treasured fragments of memory.

Now, sitting on a sweaty sofa before my laptop in our cramped Florentine apartment, it came back to me.

'He was terrifying.' I heard Elena's frail but determined voice in my mind. 'He saw you exactly as you were. You could hide nothing. "Are you a parasite?" he demanded. "Ask! Or there is nothing for you here."'

○

And now we're here, Kin. Nearing midnight, sitting in my tower. Where I write to you. And you, evidently, despite all my ramblings and the twists and challenges of our journey together, are still listening. I thank you again for your patience. Now I have a question to ask – the one I asked myself that night, and so many times both before and since:

How do you wish to be?

Don't answer straight away. Not in words. Such secrets take time, years, even, to unearth, let alone share. All being relative, I'm sure we'll know soon enough.

It's now more than five years since I had that eureka moment. Watching YouTube in the dark after the usual fourteen-hour shift, while my daughter and pregnant wife slept soundly nearby in our little urban cavern. What providence brought me here?

I did something I have always been particularly bad at doing: I asked for help. Not so much from a higher power. From my in-laws.

My wife's father was born in London to Polish immigrants. After the war, as with so many of their Kin who survived the hell of that manmade catastrophe, they sought refuge in the country they had fought alongside with the aim of starting again. My father-in-law's parents, he a former Colonel who fought with Clark at Monte Cassino, and his wife who had escaped from Stalin's camps, set up in Acton in North London. They bought a modest but relatively spacious townhouse which they filled with fellow refugees and lodgers, and worked out the rest of their days as a doorman and laundry maid respectively in one of the capital's most prestigious hotels. When *Babcia* died, the house went to her son. By the end of the Noughties, still crammed full with tenants, it was run down and faded.

My wife and daughter and I lived there during our two years in London. Over that time, we cleaned and fixed it up and took in lodgers of our own to help cover the rent. Once we returned to Italy, the house went into limbo. My wife's parents weren't overly keen to live there, and while the rental value was reasonable, it would require considerable investment to maintain or bring it up to match modern expectations of comfort and aesthetics.

Thankfully, the Devil was doing our work.

When a developer first made an offer for the well-constructed but otherwise unexceptional 4-bedroom building, with its postage stamp garden at rear, my habitually reserved father-in-law's eyes fairly shot out of his skull. In what felt like a matter of months, gentrification had oozed its slimy golden fingers over the previously unappealing postcode.

'I just can't believe it,' he told his daughter over the phone. 'I'm glad *Babcia's* not alive to see this. She'd have a heart attack.'

Being a Leo, my wife told him to refuse the offer and hold firm.

The street around it turned into a building site. Prices attached to the sudden flurry of surrounding billboards were scrolling up like figures on a petrol pump. With extra zeros. What should he do?

That was when I had my idea.

Fast forward a year and for the value of the living room, kitchen, front room and downstairs toilet in West 14, we had purchased a crumbling medieval ensemble in the South of France. With terrain and outbuildings galore offering endless "potential for conversion", our tribe had found Our Land. My mother-in-law was the first to find it, her husband the last through the door.

'This'll do me fine when I'm past it,' he nodded approvingly, looking around the former piggery. He winked and patted my shoulder. 'Just get me a decent-sized flat screen, someone to empty my bag regularly, and we're all square.'

The work is never done, of course, but then, that's how it is down here, isn't it, Kin? If you really think you're finished, it's probably time to move on. There are drains to dig out, leaking roofs to fix, barns to shore up, windows to repair, abandoned spaces to reclaim and gauche '70s decor to tolerate as we focus on other things. Oscar Wilde wouldn't stick around long. Then of course, there's the garden.

The main house was first constructed in the 11th Century, as a fortified tower surrounded by a courtyard. The top of the tower is no longer, a victim to changes during the 1700s, but the walls that were saved to form the basis of the present farmhouse are still there. The small window behind me in my attic study, where I now sit tapping at the escritoire, from outside is a tiny rectangle in a tall, long-bricked up doorway. Only the shades of the former lords and ladies may pass. They have been quite welcoming to the scions of their old Anglican adversaries. From here, across the treetops and the small valley and the meadows, I can see, and occasionally hear and even smell our neighbours. Ah, the sweet spreading of the cowshit! When it's not winter and chill and wuthering, I watch the swallows, and the birds of prey, and hear the bees and the bugs and hornets, it takes all sorts to keep this symphony in harmonious progress. I see the vegetable patch and the orchard, my wife's essence labour and her joy. Looking beyond, I can make out where the land dips down, and then rises once more to the manmade hill that was raised up by workers in the 7th Century, atop which once stood a fort, witnessed only by the ruins of an old stone chapel that still stand beside it. Where this medieval watchtower once dominated, there are now only trees. Below it, the old chemin is still accessible, along which over a thousand years ago our ancestors and their horses and mules daily trod.

And there is a cave.

'Man, you're crazy.' Dimi poured me another as we stood behind the bar, the metal shutter pulled halfway down after closing. 'You will get so bored. What are you going to do there? Are there even any people near? What will you do for money?'

'I don't know,' I said. 'We'll find our way. It's got a well, woods, meadows, vegetable garden. You're welcome to come and stay when the Apocalypse comes.'

'Hah-hah. Well, good for you, my friend. Maybe one day I'll come and make music there.'

As I write, Dimi is in the process of selling up in Florence, rendered a ghost town by the current pandemic, and of buying an old hotel and restaurant with some land, ten minutes down the road from us.

> There is a place in the heart that will never be filled and we will wait and wait in that space.

- Charles Bukowski

I still struggled to work out my purpose, naturally. With whatever the world gives you, it throws in some demons whose job is to never rest. Such is our Duality Deal. There are worse out there. If you want to learn from history, type in the word "Brexit".

I had my treasures. My wife and our clan. My own parents came to live nearby. Then a brother. With my modest carpentry skills, I fixed up the atelier and we started running courses as we had done in Italy. It attracted fellow artisans and artists, as well as people just needing a break. We livened up the gîte and began giving English classes to French holiday makers, and vice versa. We had more children, *sacré bleu*..! A fertile corner, this.

The summer before COVID 19 hit the planet, we received a visit from some American friends. An older traveller and comrade, Marc arrived with his beautiful young companion, Kelsey, and we took time out to explore the region together. One highlight was a visit to the Chateau de Montaigne: the authentically preserved tower and castle estate of our mutual hero, Michel. Our elder children came with us, and we took in the tour and for a moment occupied the same space in which Michel had downloaded and transmitted his message to the world. Afterwards, we enjoyed a glass of wine from the still active estate vineyard.

'Are you writing anything, Master J?' Marc asked me later over dinner.

I told him I had undertaken a commission for a centenary book from my old school in England.

'Well, that's terrific,' he enthused. 'But tell me: are you writing anything of your own? Something more Guerilla?'

I had all but given up on the books. They continued to sell in dribbles online, but nothing new was in the offing. Save for a few hastily scrawled and equally hastily forgotten intros to my definitive tome on the Uzbek Sufis, I'd written nothing in years.

'You know,' he said, a glint in his eye, 'now that you're blessed with this place and your wonderful family, I have a feeling the best is yet to come. Have you ever heard about automatic writing? It happens when your everyday conscious attention is directed elsewhere. Or at least, turned down a notch. Writing from the heart. Know what I mean?'

I said that I did, but of course I truly didn't. To know, and not to do, is to know nothing. If you don't like this story, or feel it has wasted your time in any way, please submit your complaint for the wise attention of architect, author, my editor and incomparable essence Kin, Marc G. Montry.

It was around that time the crying started. Like the hero Kenneth Toomey in Anthony Burgess' incomparable novel, *Earthly Powers*, the mention or mere consideration of the notion of "home" began to make me well up behind the eyes. The kids' Disney/Pixar/Ghibli screenings started to become a disconcerting ordeal.

'Papa – what's wrong?' Followed by hugs from the all-knowing child.

Having an inoperable lacerated tear duct from the car crash, I had a handy excuse ready if I found myself losing it in public. Internally, there was no running away.

The damn finally broke, in time- and cliché-honoured fashion, after another wedding. It was my old friend and brother, H – he who had all but carried me back up the field before my diabetes revelation. Somewhat of a late starter, he had finally found his companion, a naturally wise and free French mademoiselle, and to the joy and relief of the rest of our Kin circle, they got hitched. After the speeches and the dancing, I found myself outside by a fire pit with another gorgeous couple, near-lifelong friends. To balance the mood around us, we talked openly and honestly about depression, and our respective struggles with it.

'You know what?' said Mick at length in his airy Canadian brogue: 'For me the breakthrough came when I just stopped fighting it all the time. I gave up. Stopped struggling, stopped analysing. It was like "Okay – so you won, Black Dog. Now let's sit down together. Tell me what you want."'

These dots of light by which we may plot our course.

I was halfway home the next day, in the middle of France in a thunderstorm, when the deluge broke. I couldn't stop. I had to pull off the motorway. Huge, bodily, breaking sobs shook my form. I sat there, in my little Suzuki jeep beside the forecourt of the service station, the elements pelting against the glass, and rained out my sadness. *Lacrimae mundi*. Tinged with unbearable sweetness.

Such eternal, graceful sweetness.

o

I now visit my cave regularly. I don't always cry. Oftentimes I simply sit. Sometimes, I light a fire in the small earthen grate, and lie down, and watch the flames. On occasion, I sleep there at night. I keep some matches and a candle there, which I always light, just as I used to do in my windswept tent on the mountainside, as a younger me, all those years ago.

No one knows how old it is. It may have been dug by the builders of the original mound, to serve the fort in some way. Some opine it is much older, like the many caves and grottos that can be found about the surrounding region, inhabited by our ancestors as long as twenty thousand years ago. Whatever the truth of it, I always remember to thank them. What they created is timeless. What can be found within is timelessness itself.

It was there that the Howl found me, Kin. In the Cave. In her sepulchral, patient stillness. In the backwards way of the world, the Second Howl – the one we are about to share – approached me first. Later, it introduced me to its buddies, and another trinity was born in me.

For many years, I'd always felt this *Something* inside that was nagging. This splinter, this restlessness, dis-ease – name it what you will. Be careful what you attach to the name. All my so-called adult life. I know you feel it, too, Kin. If you didn't, you wouldn't still be here. Would you? Are you sure? Be still, Kin. Sit. Keep sitting.

Then I realised: it wasn't nagging. It wasn't an illness or defect. What a painted lens, this language through which the so-called rational mind inexorably perceives our universe. That was merely how I had interpreted it. Because in attempting to bury that softly probing, insistent presence beneath my own limited view of myself, it only made the so-called rational me feel more uncomfortable, unconnected, misplaced. A bit lost. So I suppressed and tried to punish it.

What if this Something wasn't trying to gain my attention in order to make my life less easy; less as I had envisaged it, less planned or less perfect, after all? What if it were calling? And what if, instead of continually pushing it back, or trying to extract it, I were to let go, and breathe, and allow it to rise? To belong?

What if I answered?

The Second Howl

Go into your Cave. It can be your basement, your bathroom, your shed, your closet under the stairs, your wardrobe – any enclosed space of your own invention. If you have to, take a blanket or a duvet and hang them over the kitchen table. Don't worry about making it perfect – everything you need is already inside you.

Light a candle if you have one. Close your eyes and imagine one if you don't. Place it before you. Sit with it, keeping your eyes on the flame. Notice how the flame consists of three parts: the hot outer blue or non-luminous zone with its veil; the bright orange luminous zone in the middle; and the dark innermost area around the wick. Focus on it, letting your eyes and attention move around the zones. Have you ever put your attention there before? Start to breathe slowly, consciously, feeling the air pass through your mouth and nasal passages, into your chest cavity, and then allow your belly to expand at the naval.

Your belly. Focus on it. Feel it. This is the area we are feeding and freeing. This is the seat of our two primary emotions, from which all the others are composed: positive and negative; creator and destroyer; love and fear. In life we require both, they are not in themselves "right" or "wrong". They are the source of our feelings, the raw materials for the evolution of our heart. If there is unbalance, disharmony, conflict in their domain, it will be expressed in the rest of our world. We must release any tension we have put there, knowingly or unknowingly; thoughts and experiences we have suppressed or repressed. Pain, shame, disappointment, anger, bitterness: whatever you **feel** that unbalances you – it's time to let it go.

It's time to howl it out.

Direct your eyes or your mind's eye to the dark zone at the base of the candle flame. This is the dark zone in you. In your belly. Draw it in to you. Feel it there, inside you. Take time.

Look at the orange, luminous zone and feel that inside you also. Your heart.

Now, see the flame's penumbra: the high temperature, thin encasement in which the remaining impurities from the wax, along with oxygen, are burned off. Your mind.

Feel the wax as your biological body feeding the flame. Breathe in and out deeply, slowly, in through the nose, out through the mouth, feeling the upward movement of energy and the air on exhalation. Feel the wick as the base of your spine, supporting the flame. Feel everything, pay no heed to thoughts in your head or even to sensations in your chest. This is the deep howl, the chthonic, earthly howl: primeval, before language, before history, before gardens and cities and towers. When we first tore away from raw animal state to begin the voyage to something new, unimagined, unknown, merely scented. As the link to unremembered human being was being forged. Let it begin as a groan, if it wishes. An anguished moan to be released from its womb of wax and earth and blood. Let it repeat, unlocking all your forgotten woes, your sadness, your grief, your loss:

Howwwww.....
Howwwwwww........
Howwwwwwwwwww..........

No filters, no hesitation, no gates: let it build, let it crescendo, let it surge up from deep within you; softly at first, barely aspirated, only the breath; then more insistent, filling your belly to full capacity, rhythmic waves pounding, the sound begins to flow:

Howwwwww.....
HOWWWWWW.........
HOWWWWWWWWW...........

Remember all those who have loved you. Remember all those times that have hurt you. Remember these moments which bear us, and kill us, time and time and time and time again. Let them go. Let it all go. What you see as yourself, your past and future, here and now – your Story: let it die. Surrender all of it. ALL. You will be reborn. In a moment, you will live anew.

HOWWWWWWWWWWWWW!
HOWWWWWWWWWOWOWOWOWOWWWWW
WWL!
HOWWWWWWWWWWWWWWOWOWOWOWO
WOWOWOOOOOOOL!

When you're done – rest. Curl up in the foetal state, like a newborn. Cuddle what Tolle calls "the pain body" if your belly and your heart tell you it is calling.

Rest.

Sleep.

Rest in the arms of the Dragon...

Sleep. Dream. She will nurture you. She will heal you. She composes you.

Your Cave.

Our Mother.

She is always waiting. In the stillness.

Waiting...

For us to return.

THE GARDEN

As long as you are alive, the Book of Love will not be fulfilled.

- Khodja Ahmad Yassaviy

This is where we arose; this is where we are heading; this is where we belong.

Hello, Kin. How are we doing? Still here? That's great. It's all possible now.

It's late in my tower. You'd be forgiven for thinking I'm a night owl. In fact, much of what has come before was laid down during daylight hours. Sometimes, digging into the memory banks for intimate files doesn't always sit well with the second bleary morning coffee and a small child screaming down the hallway below for her bum to be wiped, but you know what they say: discipline will set you free. It's good not to get too alone sometimes, besides.

Michel and Thomas Stearns are still here, of course. The most exquisite, most humble and unrepeatable, St Leonard of Cohen, is performing as usual. Along with a host of others from our journey to here, Kin: voices and echoes, ghosts and mirrors all. They are always most welcome. But if there's one aspect I love about this midnight writing gig, while the cows and goats and donkeys stand and steam outside in the dark, fox and badger and boar scour the woods beyond the old rampart, treasures sleep deeply in their cushioned night-time chests, it's that the veil feels lifted between myself and another in particular.

You.

How are you, Kin, I wonder, where your heart is now beating? Has our journey been worthwhile? Has sharing this story with you been of any interest, any solace, any use? Has it brought us together at all?

It will soon be spring here. All around, the pandemic is still raging. The planetary climate imbalance is still raging. People are still raging.

Je m'en fous de ce bordel!

Only I'm not: I'm not done with this mess. As long as I'm here, I can't be. I can't give up hope. Can you, Kin? What if it's all we've got?

The Hero's Journey can be a useful template. Our own lives and experiences do not always fit to it as though 3D printed, granted – we have to be flexible, for it rarely proceeds in one graceful, perfectly fired linear arc between womb and tomb. It can be a good guide and road map, though. For telling stories, there are worse ways to navigate. It's part of our purpose here. I hope you've enjoyed it.

But there's a problem: what happens in the Cave can be terminal. Be it literal or mythic or symbolic, thereafter there is sometimes simply no road back. Not to the ordinary world. Not for everyone. It's taken me years to realise it. Now, I know it's true.

In most tellings, once the hero has been resurrected after their ordeal, they are transformed. They atone for their old ways, receive the elixir, then leave the special realm and return to the ordinary world in order to share it with their brethren. In doing so, the hero becomes "Master of Two Worlds". Belonging fully to neither one nor the other, they nonetheless succeed in walking both with a nonchalant air of knowingness and wisdom about the whole show for, of course, ordinary mortals who have not made the journey themselves cannot see behind the illusion. Their attention is fixed solely on the two-dimensional screen that is presented to them at any given moment.

Apt, huh?

The hero thus appears relatively smart and experienced: worth noting, listening to, admiring and even wondering at. If they're not careful, they can even come across as ever so slightly self-important. Smug, sometimes. Such heroes are two-a-penny in Hollywood and all kinds of fiction. And that's fine and human. We all have egos and, so long as they're hooked up and live, they are receptive to all the forces, both out there and in here, that have it in their interest to help them grow.

But those heroes are stuck. Worse, now, than ever. Stuck in the Duality Trap. Masters of it – and slaves to it. "Two Worlds" – one special; one ordinary. Each with its own rules, and players, and levels. Each distinct; each separate. Apparently irreconcilable, navigated only by maintaining one foot in each, or requiring a different identity in each, or through becoming a changeling, practised in the art of expressing or transforming different parts of oneself to suit the immediate environment.

We don't need to look to the movies or books to know it. Look at our own lives. The face we show at work versus the one we wear during leisure hours, for example. The face we present our client against that we take home to our spouse or partner. The way we treat the attractive bar tender against the way we behave towards the homeless person who asks us for money later on our way home. Our image on social media compared to the one we see in the bathroom mirror.

We all fly through special and ordinary worlds every day. The hero's cycle begins when we awake in the morning and concludes when we close our eyes at night. Little stories within bigger stories, within bigger stories, pushed off course by yet more enormous stories, or maybe even by the suggestion of a tiny little episode that a part of us believes could just tickle us right that day. Worlds within worlds within worlds. Masters and slaves of all and none.

What are we to do with this information? Are we to believe that even if we succeed – even if we triumph against adversity and our shadows and everything life throws at us, we're still destined to be forever split in two? Forever not whole?

I really like the Batman story. Especially *The Dark Knight Trilogy*, and its ending. (Spoiler alert...) Here we witness the ultimate dual world issue in real time: Bruce Wayne and Batman living in one another's suits day and night for years. Bruce has the mansion – his Tower – as his stronghold, while Batman has – what else could it be? –

his Cave. Here in each, respectively, they can function reasonably well as individuals, whilst always being aware that the other character may require them at a moment's notice. In Gotham City, however...

Gotham is the stage on which Bruce-Batman is ultimately torn apart. Sure, one moment he plays billionaire director playboy Wayne, the next he is in Kevlar and boot polish heaving gorilla-sized hoodlums about the place. He appears to master both roles. But he can't. Despite his wealth, and his skills, and his strong-mindedness, life throws him too many irreconcilable choices. He cannot preserve both. Nor can he preserve all those he loves, nor the values and truths for which he stands.

In *The Dark Knight Rises* (the clue, as often, is in the name) he finds the solution. After decades, and many changes of actor, which have led to his ultimate crisis, the hero pulls the ultimate stunt: he dies. At least, he appears to die. Bruce Wayne disappears and leaves his mansion to Gotham City as an orphanage and his remaining estate to Alfred, the butler. Batman, too, is presumed dead, following his last heroic act, destroyed by the blast of the bomb he selflessly carried out to sea. The city mourns, whilst covertly, the grail and talisman – the Cave and its secret – are handed on to the next, now-initiated hero who might make use of them. Meanwhile, where is Bruce the Bat?

In Florence, of course. That's Florence, Italy: having lunch with his new girlfriend Selina Kyle/ Catwoman – who apparently has dealt with some personality struggles of her own – in the "flowering" city. No doubt, by now he is wishing he hadn't bequeathed Alfred *all* of his money. His latest challenge is working out how to pay the extortionate tab at Dimi's restaurant. In spite of this, life appears rosy.

Bruce and Batman are dead. There was no road back. He has passed over and gone into the Garden – the One World in which all worlds are comprised. He is now who he is.

We never get his name.

Affirming – denying – reconciling; affirming – denying – reconciling...

Let us return, finally, to our hero from the outset of this Quest: our poor, frozen Swallow. Remember the question? "Why – why did she turn?" Why did she abandon her natural inner programme and head north, into the snowy wasteland, and to her own untimely demise? The answer is both simple and a trick of our imagining:

She didn't.

The story is not true. It's obvious, now, isn't it? Her tale, imbued with moral teachings and with amusing reference to our wayward human nature, is a ruse. This is what we do as humans. We take our own doubts, and failings and fears and desires and separateness, and distance ourselves from them by projecting them onto other characters, even species, whom we then ask to bear and play out our own flaws. To keep us protected from them. Sure, they're just stories. They have a function: to release the pressures exerted by our own fractured being; allow us to laugh, and cry; reflect us at a safe distance from our immediate perceived reality. Make us feel less foolish, less erroneous. Less alone. And it works. For a while.

That Swallow would not fly north alone. That's just the thought-dream of a fragile human mind. She would never leave her Kin. The reason for this is also simple, perhaps terrifyingly so. And it's this:

Her Kin are all flying in the right direction. As a group, and as individuals, they are following the call.

We hear a lot in this day and age about "emotional intelligence". Usually, in true duality-focused fashion, it is put up and measured against its perceived opposite or balancer, "intellectual" or "cognitive intelligence". EQ vs IQ. Modern psychology is having some banter over the matter. Some of it is undoubtedly of interest. It appears to be a debate which is for the most part centred around a control study of a sole species – an N of One creature: us.

What sort of intelligence does the Swallow use? What does all life use, if we take intelligence to mean that quality that is revealed through behaviour as purposeful, systematic, structured and functional in its outcome? Curious, and playful, too, in its engagement. Is it perhaps "natural" intelligence? Is that not available to us humans, also? Are we exempt? Can we not belong here in this shared habitat among our fellow life-bearing chemical-biological organisms, dwindling in variety as they may be, and harmoniously coexist with them, and among ourselves, while together we ride evolution's mysterious and sometimes choppy wave?

Is that a dream, now? Merlin – what say you?

"A dream, to some; a nightmare to others!"

Hmm. Guessed as much.

Once again, we fall. The old DT. What *is* our nature? What is it that makes us human, apart from simply naming us so?

Some maintain we are "clever apes". There are a few anomalous wrinkles yet to iron out – some of our steps on the way to here seem even now a little freaky – but in essence, we're terrestrially formed and anchored primates who are the recipients of an accidental genetic learning spree. Others say we are something other. As the Jesuit priest, philosopher and much lambasted (pseudo?) scientist Pierre Teilhard de Chardin famously wrote: "We are not human beings having a spiritual experience. We are spiritual beings having a human experience." Now there's a minefield of a bunny warren.

What are you, Kin? What is your nature? Can you define it? Can you rationalise it? Do you feel it? Do you think, feel or believe or intuit that you express it? Is it really yours? Does it belong to you, do you possess it?

Or do you merely transmit it?

Dukkha... Samudaya...

The nature of our nature. So many questions, Kin. I told you at the start: I don't have the answers. Not for you. I don't see a valid way. Not for all of us together. Not right now. I'm not a defeatist. But maybe – maybe – we should stop fighting so hard, stop shouting so loud, to make one. If we stop and listen, maybe the Garden is way enough.

o

Pain is a fierce driver. When you're riding in its wagon, suffering, thrown this way and that, on a trajectory that is beyond your control, one thing is sure: it wakes you up. Everything that was important and so pressing before all at once becomes second tier on your previously critical list of "things you have to do". Instinctively, your principal wish is to make it stop, or lessen its progress at least. Yet the state of wakefulness, you fear, may also depart with it. You're now in a conundrum. You can have heightened awareness, but must continue on the ride with pain; or you get the comfort and respite you desperately desire, but lose that quality of altered consciousness with it. It's no wonder that depression, among many other afflictions, can be so dangerously addictive, despite its inevitable complications.

There's an easy way to produce pain: when a force acts upon you, resist it. At the time of writing, as with so many times before and still to come, we humans are in crisis. Despite the myriad ways and cultures and ethnic and social groups into which our several billion-celled body of humanity can be divided and defined, our home planet if nothing else shows us that the path we have been treading as a unit of late cannot continue. Nonetheless, there are still those who would see that it does. Whatever definition you personally hold with of how this catastrophe is unfolding, whether it is due to a nefarious and corrupt elite – the "one million evil men" of *Shantaram* – who run the world, or because of our collectively godless ways, or because aliens have infiltrated our leaders, or simply because in the spiralling process of inexorable evolution our present phase has had its day, what is undeniable is that within our numbers there is resistance to that apparently unflinching momentum. There is conflict wherever the polarised forces meet. From it arises suffering and pain.

"The crisis" says Antonio Gramsci and, if we can transcend our petty personal politics for a moment, I feel he has a point, "consists precisely in the fact that the old is dying and the new cannot be born."

Birth and death. Resistance to both. Equals crisis.

One could argue that those events inherently contain a considerable quota of pain even on a good day. This indeed appears true. However, to live in a realm that is already created – by accident or design – as a dualistic dance of seemingly opposing forces was never our choice. How we cope with and respond to it, on the other, certainly is.

In World War Two, and later in *Star Wars*, if we can still have faith in any of our precious stories, The Resistance was a small group of fighters who took on a towering, evil empire. They made up a relatively tiny yet resolute and noble positive force against a monstrous behemoth of darkness intent on destroying universal balance and snuffing out the light once and for all. No doubt, as it must have felt to the protagonists involved, against all the odds.

Fate, it seems, is not without a sense of irony...

As ever, stories are told from their narrator's relative standpoint. What is labelled as "The Resistance" in the above scenarios – and we are witnessing today the roots and shoots of a new Resistance to our lumpy, lumbering, bludgeoning collective way that poses as the vainglorious, attention-loving, ball-hogging star player in this "Team Earth" biosphere match – is not, objectively, the resisting force at all. The real resisting party, when viewed from a wider, cosmic perspective, is The Empire itself.

It is the mainstream that is resisting. The mass cultural story, which we have inherited and believe and continue to build on, haphazardly, irresponsibly, unethically – vertically. The story that puts us as the "Top Dog" – top or not, we shall die like... As the number one species, the most important, the apparently majority shareholder yet in truth minority stake amidst our biological planetary corporate endeavour. It was the Nazis who were resisting. Emperor Palpatine and his Sith Order vassals and Stormtroopers. The Corporate Hegemony. Our individual and amplified collective selfish desires.

Resisting what?

Conscious evolution. The evolution of consciousness. Swing it either way. Like a two-pin plug in an AC socket, the results are the same.

A.k.a: the road to The Garden. The way home.

Some call it transcendence. Others go with complexity. Mystics call it union. Choose your illusion. We work with what we're given.

Now imagine another story: visualise a flight of swallows. Hundreds, thousands of individual birds. Hatched in precarious nests on a cliff, in a cave or a barn, far from the equator in America, or Asia or Europe. Their parents feed them, watch them fledge, show them how to fly, catch food and drink on the wing. In three months, they must be ready for a voyage of several thousand miles. As the Autumn sun wanes, they gather in vast numbers. Many have never ventured beyond the fields and the meadows that surround the geographical needle point of their arising. Preparing, they call to one another, and ready their twenty gram forms for the journey. As the wind calls, they take flight and set off towards their unseen destination. Gathering as one, they merge, a single body of thousands, and head...

...north.

To disaster. To unbearable cold. To cunning predators, extreme conditions, an apparently limitless wasteland. To scattering, to isolation. To premature and painful death.

This, Kin, is how humanity is flying.

What if we answered a different call?

What if we were to stop resisting? What if we checked our inner compass, and turned?

Tawba... Inaba... Awaba...

How?

Well, that's a good question, Kin. Let's begin with our teachers outside.

When I was living in London, suffering the seemingly relentless and visceral ride atop the thorny back of the ever-roaring mood-dragon, I attended a workshop with a warm and luminous, juice-loving Kin. His name is Jamie Catto. A songwriter, filmmaker and former band member of a famous electronic group, his way has taken him, accompanied by music, on many Hero's Journeys of his own. Jamie, I would say, does not follow any particular or definable way. He makes his own. On it, he shares and gives back. Things of interest, solace and use he has found.

During the two-day workshop, we practised and shared in various exercises. Taken together, they serve the umbrella mission of "transforming shadows into rocket fuel". One of the many phrases that resonated with me and others there was the idea of becoming "walking permission slips" for ourselves and other people. Through allowing ourselves to recognise, sit with and accept the hidden and gnarly parts of ourselves, we encourage the sometimes scary, often faltering yet inexorably sweet and beautiful journey out of the shadows of our being to begin and unfold. By the end of it, I felt that the fragile embers of buried hope and trust and love we all carry within us had been breathed on. They were glowing again. The effect was amplified and reciprocated by the proximity of and lowering of typical social barriers among fellow human beings. And yes, in glorious pre-COVID fashion, there were hugs aplenty.

We are, every one of us, like a wise guru in charge of a mental patient.

– Jamie Catto

Permission. Letting go. We need only permit ourselves. To step away from ourselves, let go of any critical appraisal, and to invite all the shadows to reveal themselves in the wings; to appear onstage beneath the light of our attention, our forgiveness – our love. Once we know and accept the whole cast, for all the wild and wicked roles they may play, something shifts. The drama recedes. We can move off the stage together and sit in the auditorium for a while, drink tea together, unmasked, and chat together about how the production is going. Where it might go. The understanding director – our wise guru – may then share some notes and observations. Who knows: maybe the next performance will follow a different script?

Here is the good news: there are teachers and Kin everywhere. Peppered, these resilient, sweet dog roses, across the whole apparent dung heap of human action.

Tell me what you want...

I have been fortunate in my life – so very, very blessed. We say that when the student is ready, the teacher appears: well, Kin, I don't know about you but I don't always feel ready. Sometimes, I feel ready only to die. Yet here they come. Out of movies, from books, appearing in songs; in meetings with apparent strangers, in lovers, in friends. Relentless. Calling...

'Don't give up, Jason.' Dearest, ecstatically inebriated, ever heart-full Alex: 'You've got to make it – do you understand? For all of us. Keep going. You must keep going. I love you so very much. You're my best friend. My greatest friend.'

'She wants to heal you. Listen.' Mario... 'If you allow her, she will heal you.' Seeker, photographer and filmmaker, working together in his humid Manhattan studio and eating sushi. Summer 2006.

'You don't have to try so hard.' Reeyaz – Sheikh of the Ansari Sufi group. London. 'He is patient. You don't need to worry about not doing zikr, practice – you have a family. You are busy working in life. Just look at what He is giving you.' Saviours of my heart.

Split a piece of wood and you will find me; lift up a stone, and I am there...

Alec, Fourth Way Teacher: 'What if you don't need to fill the balloon? What if you already have all the gas you need? Sometimes, perhaps you just need to throw out the baggage. The balloon rises by itself.'

Talking with Philippa, author of the epic poem, *Involution – Reconciling Science To God*, on the train home.

Carpentry with my Grandfather.

Listening to Al Maranca's *Survived* after the day on the building site from hell, and remembering our Kin are with us.

Finding, being joined with, marrying my true companion; crying, like a newborn, in the church.

Harry Harris on the stereo, singing *Simple Things,* as I drive the truck through an interminable foggy night, dear old Tommy asleep beside me.

Saying goodbye, for the last time, to my dear essence Kin, Joe, after he drowned in the ocean, aged nineteen.

...heard, half-heard, in the stillness
Between two waves of the sea...

Reading Kidal's writing, probably never to be published, and knowing, without envy, I would never write anything so raw, so honest or so pure, myself.

Being there to witness the arrival of our treasures, and experiencing immediate, unfathomable entanglement.

Sitting with Ustoz in his garden. Watching him cut and share an apple. "Olma," he smiles. The *Zadik*'s laces are tied.

Polly Paulusma's *Mea Culpa* and *All Is Well*. Two of my mother's favourite songs. Listening to them again, on the day that she died.

Quick now, here, now, always...

Always calling.

Fragments...

In these, and in those most graceful events of all: in the mishaps, accidents, and colossal errors and failings. In death, and loss, and disease. They come, often quiet, ever shining, to illuminate the teacher and Kin we bear inside.

Such precious grace. Ah, my Kin – my Beloved. All *is* well. Truly, you are everywhere.

Tanha... Nirodha...

The only permission we need give ourselves, and others, is the permission to let go. Permission to detach ourselves from the hurtling, crazy, wrong-way one-way flight. To turn, and re-turn, and return and turn again.

The American architect, designer, theorist and visionary Buckminster Fuller once said: "You never change things by fighting the existing reality. To change something, build a new model that makes the existing model obsolete."

If we wish to change our current model, both as a global society and as individuals, we need first to detach ourselves from the old. If we carry the same tools and desires to the next job, it's likely we will end up with the same result. That way, madness lies.

And what of the materials at our disposal? As ever, whatever its inherent substance, it comes to us in the same package: information. Information is what we use – to fashion our knowledge, and plot our onward course. Beware that we expect the raw materials contained therein to magically accomplish our task on our behalf. We can be given gold, yet turn it unwittingly into dust. Fortunately, down here, as it is, the opposite is also true.

Given that our egos know the greatest tricks with which to constantly trump us, how should we approach the world outside? The everyday world in which we live, the one that supplies us with all our readily perceptible information? With caution and with discernment, for sure. Accepting that there is little new under the sun, and that be it from a hunter-gatherer's gesticulations, or a tribal gathering, or from a pulpit, or a leaflet or a book or a television set or the Internet, information will surely flow to us, how do we filter it to achieve our noble aims?

Be aware of what we eat.

Kin, it heartens me to inform you that I feel closer to you now than when we first began our journey. I hope the same may be true for you. Though it matters little, for hearts in sync transcend and play with time, I still don't know where or when you are. Are you stuck somewhere in lockdown, waiting for the virus to end? Are you on the road and free, with a spring in your step and not much more than the shirt on your back? Have you dug this manuscript out of a mysterious old cave, protected in its casket from centuries of natural decay, in a wild part of a land that was once called France? Wherever you are getting your information about your presence on this planet that you came out of, remember: try to divine if you can the information's intentions for you before you swallow it whole.

In our current age, the only one in which I can presently write, most of the information that is accessed daily by our fellow beings is held by and transmitted through a global computer network called the Internet. You may well have found the book you're now reading on it. As things have turned out, it's amazing to think that only a quarter of a century ago, we all managed to have fun and fuck up quite well without it. Such is progress. Today, it acts as our almost constant compass. Figuratively, and indeed literally – can anyone under twenty even read a paper map anymore? If they've been forest schooled, apparently. But enough middle-aged griping.

As we touched on earlier, as with any system, the Internet has inherent merits and vices. Those qualities in themselves are for the most part neither good nor bad but generally inert. Until, that is, they are transmitted. Into whom? Into the host, or "user".

Many of our Kin have already pointed out the possibly perturbing connotations that can be aligned with that last term in particular. It is the term we apply to those people who have fallen into the abyss of addiction. Drink, drugs, sex, money, power, self, food, cults, TV, news, shopping, you frame it. To this list we can add the Internet. Only, this is a potentially hazardous fix like never before. Why? Because alongside its own intrinsically hypnotic abilities, it also acts as a portal, a gateway, to all the others.

We are what we eat. Never was a pat truism so ominously applicable. Having reached The Garden at last with you, dear Kin, I do not wish to miss its splendour and beauty on account of sounding off on the potential perils of our digital age. You know them as well or even better than I. But not doing is not knowing. If we let ourselves become saturated, become soaked with this phenomenal and potentially wondrous device, if we do not turn from it, at least by some degrees, well: you know the story about The Matrix, don't you? It doesn't go well for The Garden – nor for her children.

Maybe we can take inspiration from Fuller. I'm not suggesting we try to render the Internet obsolete. I'm sure something even faster, ever cleverer and even more addictive will be along any minute now. Virtual reality, anyone? AI? But again, some things never change. The delivery systems may evolve, but our response to the messenger – that's always up to us. So this is what we do:

We use the Devil's own tricks against him. We don't take on the whole of Hell in one "Afghanistanstyle" campaign. Don't we know our Wikipedia? We practice our own will, that weak and little-tested psychological muscle group, on a sole aspect to start with. I would suggest we begin with social media. We don't just get off it. That's an abnegation of responsibility. We go one step further: we make it seriously uncool.

As Gurdjieff proclaimed in *Beelzebub's Tales* (whatever he was or wasn't, he must have had the sight, because he saw social media coming from half a century off) on the subject of fashion: "This custom, so maleficent for them, consists in periodically changing the external form of what is called the 'covering of their nullity.'"

What dear old Lucy was referring to at the time was, of course, the literal sense of fashion as 'cool clothing'. If you look at the essence of the thing, however, is it not evident how apt the description is? What do we do when we refresh our feeds and post up our selfies and dreamlike doctored lifestyle images and quotations for all to see? Is it anything but the periodic, no doubt frequent, changing of our external form? What do our social media presentations attempt so vainly to actually cover?

Let's make it uncool. Then bit by bit, post at a time, we can let it go.

"I need it for business!" "It's about being connected!" "I really don't look at it that much!" "I follow only educational and non-profit profiles!"

Okay, okay: I'm not suggesting we simply kill it. I'm not saying it's all bad. We're too enlightened to make that judgment – right? Hah! Let's just watch what we eat. Besides, as any teen knows, being ignored can be kind of empowering. Bless the stars, there are few who can cope with lacking in cool quotient. Although...isn't "uncool" the new cool?

Ah, dear Kin. I know, I know. Foot stuck in yet another rabbit hole. Every natural garden has them. Even now. Let's drop this, too, wander on and admire the view. There is one tree in particular under which I wish to share some moments with you before we part.

o

Fana...

Teachers. So many teachers. It was dear Ustoz, unsurprisingly, as close to me even now as my own breathing, who got me thinking about the whole Internet phenomenon.

"If you want to talk with God, now is a good time. Everyone is busy looking down – looking at their phones. He has very little to do. You don't need an appointment or an agent. Just check in with Him, pay him a visit. You can go to Him yourself. He is available all the time."

It was Ustoz who gave me permission. First, to belong to him, and him to me. Then, to belong with him. Finally, permission to give myself permission: permission to set myself free.

It has been a long road. In truth, it never ends.

"Be in your space" – another of his perfect, exquisitely-cut tiny gems. That took a few years to feel.

"If you are afraid," he once said, sharing another secret, "you might as well go and dig yourself a grave. You *will* be protected. And you are always alone."

This from a visitation he received in a dream. Transmitted to me – and now to you.

We never lose the love we share with our true teachers. Like the quantum entanglement theory of our current physics, the "spooky action at a distance" never seems to ebb in spite of the most avid efforts from classical time and space. We remain forever tied. All the same, what he told me rings true.

We are always alone.

Aren't we, Kin? However much we may share. Feel it now. Is there any other way?

Yet however much the concept may daunt or terrify us, I believe that we need not despair. The solution, as so often, is right here before us. It is the greatest, yet most obvious, secret of all. Hiding in plain sight.

Alone – All One.

Dear old entangled language.

For that is indeed what we always are. Wrapped up compassionately in a Duality Trap-transcending paradox.

So how do we unpack it?

Al Haraka Baraka...

God may not play dice, but that doesn't mean He sits still.

The Andalusian poet, scholar and mystic Ibn 'Arabi wrote many things. If you read them all, you might go insane. I certainly haven't – I speak of reading, not of sanity – but two of his works in particular are never far. One of them is sitting on the desk behind my computer, keeping company with Kidal's Extra Joker, as I write. In English, it is called: *"Journey To The Lord Of Power – A Sufi Manual On Retreat."*

There's nothing I can say about it here at this hour, Kin, that would either make any sense of it or honour it. If you've read it yourself, you'll undoubtedly know why. So I shan't. It is, however, a most constant companion. I've been reading and re-reading it for years. Most of the time it still gives me the heebie-jeebies. In a positive way. It's one of "those" friends. You know what happens when you let them into your life, but you also know your life will be a lot duller and less meaningful without them. So you keep in the loop. Maybe just not every night. If you want to take the trip, it's badder than Ram Dass on acid. Go brother, go sister.

There is one phrase, however, that I cannot, would not, shake. It repeats throughout the text, which given the title is no surprise. In fact, it makes a pretty good mantram. It is simply:

"And if you do not stop with this..."

Obvious, isn't it? In its repetition, it scribes the fundamental essence of The Journey. If we stop – it's over. It's so simple. Yet it's what we all do.

We stop. We achieve a station or state. We think to ourselves: "This will do. This is really it, now. This me is good enough. These views and opinions are fairly robust. These feelings are under control. This knowledge is as much as I need. I'm satisfied. I think I'll stick." Except that we don't. There is no sticking. Everything, from the tiniest particle to the biggest galaxy, is in constant motion. When we stop, we resist the onward dance. What happens when we stop during the dance? I'm sure you've seen it at weddings. We mess up the happy revelling for a moment, and then we either join in again or we fall out. Sit it out until the end. Only in this universe, there is no end. The dance never stops. One way or another, on the way or in it, we're in that jiving, reeling divine disco tent for good.

There is only movement. In movement, there is blessing. In movement, we are all one.

How do we move?

We don't. That's simply the fabled illusion of separateness. If we're all one, we cannot be individuals. Ask a quantum physicist (the right one, obviously): one moves – all moves.

It moves through us.

Want to call "it" – God?
Happier calling "it" – consciousness?
Rather put "it" down as – energy?
Getting funky and calling "it" – isness?

I believe "it" doesn't mind what we call it. Just as long as we are calling. Because "it" is calling us.

Movement happens through transmission. When we permit our calling to move through us, when we extricate the self-generated, resisting perceptions of "me" and "I" and "you" and "them" from the progress, from the dance, "it" flows. We are "in our space" – everywhere, and nowhere. We un-fix ourselves. From space and time. In this state of complete self-annihilation, the final state before everything dissolves, before "it" renews again, we arrive in The Garden.

How do we get there?

By doing what we have just done. We make the journey, Kin. Again – and again – and again. Along our way, whichever of the billions we choose or have been given, we may either resist, or accept and make use of the grace that comes to us in its many forms. In the form of teachers, of companions, of friends. Of information, knowledge and wisdom. Of the mythical tools of the Hero on their Quest: the talisman, the grail and the elixir.

Breathe...

It's time to share our last story. For now.

In 1998 there was a movie released called *The Red Violin*. About three months ago, after I had already started upon this meandering trail with you, my brethren, I watched it for the first time. A kindly and thoughtful new neighbour of ours, being on his own way and having shared some secrets together, suggested we check it out. So we did.

Lacrimae mundi, Kin – now that was a trip. If there is still electricity and digital access where you are, hook it up.

In brief: the story follows the journey of an old handmade violin. Told through the device of a Tarot card reading that predicts the voyage, the instrument is the finest, and final, work of an Italian maestro violin maker at the end of the 17th Century. A gift for his unborn son, the master's wife and child die in childbirth. The violin is then passed through many keepers and guardians through the centuries until it is discovered and put up for auction in the present day.

"The most beautiful thing we can experience," said our wise and glowing Kin, "is the mysterious".

For once, I won't spoil it for you. Needless to say, each of us will receive and interpret the film in our own subjective way. You may see it as the story of an artefact that goes on an interesting but accidental adventure. It could be interpreted as a treatise on the power of music, or the bearing out of an unjust curse through the ages. An investigation into different cultures across geography and time, and how there is no set definition of what is valuable or of worth, save viewed through the specific lens of the moment. A morality tale full of warning as to the power of obsession, of greed, mass hysteria and brainwashing, of making plans and our fragile mortality. As we see it, so it becomes.

If you watch the film, I wish only that you would also meditate on this: for me, it is one of the clearest lessons in how we, the hero of our own story, create and evolve our relationship with an instrument of grace. The red violin of the title is both the talisman and the grail. The music it produces through the action of the successive heroes is the elixir – the potion, the mysterious and otherworldly essence manifesting as substance here and now, that takes us into an altered state, into union with another realm. Being created as it was through a kind of alchemy, a bonding of the living and the dead, of masculine and feminine, creative and destructive forces both, the violin exists on Earth in a state of precarious fragility. It has a purpose here, but it is not of this world. As a talisman, it can be broken. As the grail, it can be lost. In times of crisis, it must be used wisely, or remain hidden. It is stardust to those who recognise it for its true identity – but its allure can also destroy them. A child is too pure to wield its purity. The seducer is himself seduced by it. With the best intentions, the lost soul cannot hold on to it. The greedy and the vain are tricked by it. And the righteous?

Samuel L Jackson plays the part of Charles Morritz, a modern-day expert of elite classical instruments. Out of his usual comfort zone of scary yet loveable, curse-declaiming anti-heroes, he is outstanding. There is one scene, the only clip we need share here, that had me through the heart. It is the moment that Morritz is showing a selection of extremely rare and precious violins to a collector, himself a famous but pompous master violinist, before the auction takes place. The collector, Ruselsky, notices the tired-looking red violin and asks to try it. Morritz, intuitively protective, tries to put him off, but the other insists and picks it up. He starts to play.

Look at Morritz's face. Just look at it. I'm not sure what the director told Jackson before the shot was taken. Perhaps: "Okay, Sam – so we want to see that your character's soul is being transfigured by the grace of God through divine music channelled from another realm, and while you listen you know that you have dissolved completely, self-annihilated, disappeared, and there is only left the unquenchable longing for permanent union with the Beloved, to make this moment last for eternity, with the awareness that afterwards your life will never be the same, it is complete, and at the same time, over, for you can never repeat tasting that incomparable beauty for the first time ever again as long as you live. Think you can manage that? One take if you can, we're on a budget."

The film hardly made back its investment at the box office. It won a few awards, including an Oscar for Best Musical Score. To the mainstream, it then sank from view. Hidden, obscured, abiding in the deeper currents beneath the racing cultural torrent above. Waiting to be found, by those fisher Kin who are searching in the wasteland for a balm. After more than twenty years, it found its way here, just now. To us.

Once you have tasted, once you know, it's over. How does one describe that taste? We can't. Not in language. If we're lucky, we can witness it. If we are graced, we experience it. There is nothing anybody can tell you. Once you know, and are known, you know.

O

Wield the talisman; find the grail; share the elixir...

Kin: this Journey is over. If you are reading these words, it means we have made it. Together. I thank you, with all my being, for coming with me so far. We stand now in The Garden, and The Tree is waiting. Let us discover what it wishes to share.

In the Sufi tradition of the way there is a law: until you have given back, you cannot receive more. As a constant apprentice of service to the inner master – your innate teacher, that wise guru we bear inside – you must return something of what is given to those who come with you and follow behind. If you do not, you can go no further.

I thought I had given back. Poor, ignorant, foolish little me. After my experiences, and all those strange and wonderful, terrifying journeys, I believed I had shared. Through writing some books. By starting a resistance-style publishing enterprise. Gathering together fellow Kin who, I told myself, shared in my ideals.

Hogwash. My intentions, perhaps, were not entirely without integrity. But they were always tempered in my mind. The mind that wishes incessantly to define itself, against its fear of nothingness, as something of consequence. Something to be recognised: to be understood; at times, even, adored.

Thank God for all my failures. Without them, we wouldn't have met. Not at the start, and not like this at the end.

There is no end...

So after many illusory beginnings and snares, I now realise my mistake: I desired to share a way. I thought I had discovered something, in the presence of my teachers, which might serve as a path for others to tread. But a way is not transmitted. It appears beneath the sole of each descending foot and disappears the moment the foot rises. For that instant, we may meet there, and share. But the way is ever ours, and ours alone.

Another teacher and, as tends to happen here, controversially received traveller, Osho, once answered a question about purpose. How do we know our purpose in this life, a student asked? What are we here for? In typical disarming style, Osho took the egotistical fizz out of the conundrum and responded simply:

"The purpose of life, is life."

Can we extrapolate the notion? If the purpose of life is life, can it then be divined that the purpose of being, is being? If we hold this as our truth, and detach from our selfish desires, we suddenly find ourselves in a blissful scenario: wherever, and whenever, we return to the state of simply being, our purpose is inherently fulfilled.

Transmission is itself its own purpose. As my foot descends, as my fingers press and release on the keyboard, this transmission is calling you.

There is my truth; there is your truth...

What is yours is mine. What is mine is yours. Ain't that the truth?

The transmission now calling, Kin, is The Howl. The third, the final, the omnipresent and reconciling Howl. It is the Talisman I share. It is calling you.

I am Lazarus, come from the dead...

My heart, your heart – our heart – is the Grail.

I didn't know how empty was my soul, until it was filled...

The Elixir is Love.

Let's be clear on the intention of that word. Once again, from Ustoz: 'When people talk of love, they often think of romance. Romantic love can be real, yes, but it cannot last down here. When we experience it, it is the taste of another realm. But it can only be a taste. It cannot endure in this world. This is why it arrives, and departs, so quickly.' He smiles. 'It is the advertisement for what is to come.'

Let us know now, Kin, let us remember, the feeling so hard to express in words. It is not the desire, the longing. It is the belonging. Not to you, nor to Him, or to me. Just: belong.

o

THE SILENT KIN HOWL

I write, and as I do, I know these words are entering your mind. Think about it. This is no symbolic gesture or breezy metaphor. This is physical, it's happening here. In your head. The thoughts from the mind of a person you've never met, quite possibly long dead – crossing over into you. In real time. Now. What was inside of me, is now inside of you. Transmitted. As long as you keep reading, there is more.

We have already visited on the subject of words. We know they can be useful and fickle in equal measure. There is meaning, and there is intention. The two are never perfectly aligned. You have your processor – I have mine. While they may use the same code, they cannot ever quite match in understanding. We see the finger pointing, but the Moon looks a shade different to each of us. This can be frustrating, but it helps keep creation colourful and diverse.

If we wish to join in union, we must transcend the frequency of words. Once the mind gets in on the game, it's finished. Words stick like spilt wine on the cosmic dance floor. Let's prepare to abandon them.

The First Howl shook our Tower. It breaks the rigid patterns of our mind, constructed as it is by words.

The Second Howl reconnected us to our Cave. In here, in our belly, our primeval and subconscious existence is rooted. Our howling resets the balance, clears us of trauma, and reconnects us to our Earthly home.

The Third Howl reconciles the two. Do not attempt to grasp its nature with your logic. If you find your mind wrestling, return to your belly and then centre again. In your Heart.

Your Heart, Kin. The cup that holds eternal life. The Silent Kin Howl arises, and dies, in your heart.

With every heartbeat. With every pulse, and every lull, of your Heart.

Do you feel it?

Your heartbeat.

Be still. Feel it. Turn from thought, back to primal emotion, and return to your heart again.

There are no words, here. There is no contract, no treaty you need make. It is happening. Since before you were born. Before you first tasted air. To your very last, your final yielding, dying breath. Trust in it.

Nirvana... Ephphatha...

Every beat is a rebirth; every silence is a death. Surrender to it. This is how the frequency of our lives is composed. Moment on moment. Minute on minute. Years on years on years. Like the particles that inform us.

Like the stars from whose light we arise, and into whose extinguishing we fade.

Surrender. The Howl is our being. It is the call that first shattered us. It is the call that is guiding us home.

It is calling to itself. Be still – listen. Be infused with the ceaseless still motion. It is kind, Kin. Let it become you. Let it dance you. Let it belong.

OOO

When we return, as in this life inevitably we must, we may find ourselves seated beneath The Tree.

Ibn 'Arabi's *Journey To The Lord Of Power* has an equally disruptive sibling. Its name is *The Tree Of Being*. In it, the magus describes the whole of existence in the terms of a cosmic tree. The tree grew out of a seed when God pronounced the Word that initiated all creation. Its lower branches are the material world, its upper reaches are the heavens, and within it we all find our level, moving up and down and side to side according to His will.

Frankly, Kin, and especially given all that we've been through, it's quite a lot at this point to take in. Whether the universe began with a word, or a bang or (this is my bet) with a howl, perhaps we should just kiss the joy as it flies and bask in the moment here. Want to fart around?

Head-fryingly potent as it may be, I get a warm resonance from Ibn 'Arabi's glorious and often apparently impenetrable work. We don't need to be a saint or a mystic to know the symbol of The Tree as something meaningful, for we can simply enjoy the thing itself. In this day and age, given our propensity to destroy so many of them, just contemplating trees can give us a sense of security and belonging, allied to the anxiety of what would happen if they disappeared from the face of the planet. Indeed, Mother would not be pleased.

I was juggling some of these notions over coffee as you do, when a realisation came to me: what if it never was a splinter in my mind at all? What if I'd bought into Hollywood too much and fooled myself all along? What if all that restlessness and frustration and anger and suffering was caused not by some invasive and uncomfortable needle wriggling into the bubble of my awareness? Could it be that instead it was the tip of a shoot from a branch – attached to a limb to the trunk of the great cosmic tree itself? That my resistance to it was causing all the pain? And that it was simply budding and growing within me? Pushing gently through my conditioned mind, down into my chest, and into the cavity of my heart, where it waited patiently to bloom.

All I know is that as long as there are trees, let us meet under them. Let us not confine ourselves to watching each other and raising our voices to one another from our towers. Towers, like everything, have their purpose. In them we may work, and in rough times find safety, and certainly entertain a wider view. But we need not inhabit them permanently. We need not hide in them, or throw rocks and missiles at other towers that we perceive as different or threatening. We need not keep building them so high and so fast that they prevent the sunlight from reaching the garden all around us. Remember that they do not endure. Above all, we must remind ourselves that if we stand over everything, we will understand nothing. Whatever is transmitted through them, so high above the ground, must also find its way to the earth if we are to forge a connection; to make the bridge, hook up a live circuit, an energy transmitting system, where we can exist in constant flow. There is much our empirical observations, our science, can help us with.

However, the knowledge we have learned in our heads we must gradually move into our hearts. So the mystics say. This is what it is to transform knowledge into wisdom. What is wisdom, if not knowledge, lovingly applied? In constant motion. No one else, no teaching or Instagram profile or Google search will do it for us. We will make mistakes, and fail, and fall, time and again. We must not give up. We will put many tomatoes in many fruit salads before we feel confident enough to share. Yet we are patient. We are resilient, we have resolve. We are heroes, after all. However small our theatre or dilapidated the stage, we have a part here. It is our purpose. If we should falter, and there is nothing else to do, we can always light the candle in our cave.

Lord/Lady Heart of Truth and Grace, belong with me, that I may serve.

There was so much more to say, Kin. There is always more. Dear Thomas Stearns would agree. Thanks to you, however, to your presence through these many pages, I sense the imminent arrival of the bliss that comes with silence. The Muse calls – not to take up the talisman again, but to be still. These words, in any case, are not our own.

"Isn't it wonderful," said the achingly tender songwriter Nick Cave, "when people just shut the fuck up?"

Thus like the conference of birds, arriving at the abode of the fabled *Simorgh* and realising after their many trying journeys that all we ever truly see is our own self, if only reflected in the sunlight as though in a mirror, I see you, Kin. ***I see you,*** and I love you. I hope most fervently, with the howl in my heart, that we may belong. I know we shall meet again.

I will speak no more, I shall abide until
I am spoken for – if it be your will

It is time to transmit this story, and to bury it. Deliver it to the Africa-sized picnic park of information we call the Web, somewhere among the 17.5 and more quadrillion pages of other juicy and not-so juicy victuals. And another copy, somewhere more earthy and closer to home. May it sleep safely there.

Remember: alone as we are, we are always among Kin. Find them, and be found by them, and keep in touch. The world may yet need us. When the time is right, a talisman will rise. You will recognise each other by the call. Listen for the howling, in whatever form it appears. From the towers in the cities, from the caves in the forest; most of all, from the garden, beneath the tree. The Silent Kin Howl of your heart.

Don't worry too much about the C.U.N.Ts of this world. They are just on their way. Remember we are one: another's apparent C.U.N.Tishness is but a reflection of our own. It's a sliding scale we all constantly play. If in doubt, listen to the music your own instrument is producing before you try to redirect the orchestra. All we can do is keep it noble. Right, K.I.N? Be a little more Kin, a little less – you know. Every day.

I know you know. If I squint just a little, and feel myself floating, I can see you. We're not far, now. We're so close. Just keep flying. Follow the compass. If you lose your direction, check with your heart. Ask any swallow. It knows its way.

Through the crack in my tower, I see my wife in the garden. I think I'll come down now. Breathe again for the first time, begin once more. The Howl is silent now, thank you. It never leaves me. I will go and light the candle in the cave. Then return to the garden. I know the way well, for as my wise companion says: 'You know the best way to make a path, don't you?' 'No?' I say. My wife smiles. 'Keep walking it.'

And so I shall, my Beloved, my Friend. So I shall.

I will put my arm around her, and maybe we'll imagine the swallows that I am sure will soon arrive.

I lean over. As gently as I possibly can, I whisper in her ear. What do I say?

What all lovers say best, of course.
I whisper...sweet............

A swallow is flying...

...a swallow is flying;

...a swallow is flying;

...a swallow is

END TRANSMISSION

BEGIN MISSION...

Acknowledgments

The author and the publishers wish to express their thanks and appreciation to all those fellow artists behind the various excerpts used, explicitly and allusively, throughout the text. We hope, in all consciousness, to honour and amplify the transmissions of those who endeavoured to pass on their insights. If any responsible still living feel either aggrieved or neglected, please contact:

Editor@GuerrillaBooks.com

If, by the time of reading, all the above are dead: *bon courage*, Kin - can we pretend it doesn't matter?

About the Author

Jason Beacon

?

Si tu pouvais lire dans mon coeur, tu verrais la place où je t'ai mise.

- Flaubert

Printed in Great Britain
by Amazon